Cultural Influences on IT Use

Cultural Influences on IT Use

A UK–Japanese Comparison

Norio Kambayashi

Foreword by Harry Scarbrough

palgrave
macmillan

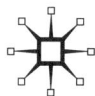

First published 2003 by
PALGRAVE MACMILLAN
Houndmills, Basingstoke, Hampshire RG21 6XS and
175 Fifth Avenue, New York, N.Y. 10010
Companies and representatives throughout the world

PALGRAVE MACMILLAN is the global academic imprint of the Palgrave
Macmillan division of St. Martin's Press, LLC and of Palgrave Macmillan Ltd.
Macmillan® is a registered trademark in the United States, United Kingdom
and other countries. Palgrave is a registered trademark in the European
Union and other countries.

ISBN 1–4039–0140–6

This book is printed on paper suitable for recycling and made from fully
managed and sustained forest sources.

A catalogue record for this book is available from the British Library.

Library of Congress Cataloging-in-Publication Data
Cultural influences on IT use
    p. cm.
  ISBN 1–4039–0140–6 (cloth)
  1. Information technology—Social aspects—Great Britain.
  2. Information technology—Social aspects—Japan.
  HM851 .C848 2002
  303.48'33'0941—dc21   2002072080

10   9   8   7   6   5   4   3   2   1
12 11 10 09 08 07 06 05 04 03

Printed and bound in Great Britain by
Antony Rowe Ltd, Chippenham and Eastbourne

To Asako and Aoi with love

Contents

List of Figures

List of Tables

List of Abbreviations

ANOVA	Analysis of variance
BPR	Business process reengineering
CAD	Computer-aided design
CAE	Computer-assisted engineering
CAM	Computer-aided manufacturing
CIM	Computer-integrated manufacturing
CIU	Control-oriented information technology use
CNC	Computerised numerical control
DNC	Direct numerical control
DSS	Decision support systems
EIS	Executive information system
FMS	Flexible manufacturing system
GDSS	Group decision support system
GPT	Group technology
IIU	Individual-oriented information technology use
JFB	Japanese factories located in Britain
JIT	Just-in-time
LAN	Local-area networks
MER	Market-oriented employment relation
MC	Machining centre
MIS	Management information systems
MRP	Materials requirements planning
MRP2	Manufacture resource planning
NC	Numerical control
OER	Organisation-oriented employment relation
SIS	Strategic information system
VAN	Value-added networks
WAN	Wide-area networks

Foreword

Few would doubt that Information Technology (IT) and national culture both exert an enormous influence on the way people behave at the workplace. IT, we know, has helped to bring about major shifts in the way work is organised and the skills required of the employees who conduct it. National culture, meanwhile, is seen as subtly influencing behaviour through the largely implicit effect of underlying norms and values. But, while we may even-handedly acknowledge the important influence of these different forces, our tendency is to bracket them as opposite poles of the environment shaping organisational life. IT is often viewed as an external force, the product of science, which shapes and re-shapes organisation structures and practices from the outside. Technology is equated with progress and is seen as determining change in the way people work. In contrast, national culture is seen as having a much more diffuse and indeterminate effect – its implications for the way we work are subliminal rather than tangible.

This opposition of technology and culture, however, is arguably more reflective of our own polarised thinking than it is of the actual influences these forces exert on managerial and employee behaviour. Maybe the influence of IT is actually indirect rather than deterministic. And maybe national culture does at times operate in a more constraining way than we sometimes recognise. These permutations, however, have been relatively unexplored till now because our analytical (and disciplinary) separation of technology and culture has discouraged studies which addressed their effects and interplay.

We are fortunate, therefore, in benefitting from the work of Norio Kambayashi on this topic. Norio's empirical study, on which this book is based, sought to make good this lack in the existing literature. As he notes, a number of studies have investigated relationships between IT and organisations, and some studies have conducted international comparisons on the theme. Few studies, however, have sought to address the role which national culture plays in shaping the interplay between IT and the organisations.

In addressing this role, the study outlined here benefits from Norio Kambayashi's skill in working across national cultural boundaries and in developing a comparative framework which systematically linked his research in Japan to the research undertaken at Warwick Business

School in the UK. Importantly, this study benefits from a carefully developed analytical framework which avoids the casual reductions seen in other work. Thus, the account developed here highlights the 'emergent' nature of the interaction between IT and organisational practices at both the managerial and employee levels. It does not subscribe to simple, linear assumptions about the effects of IT. At the same time, national culture is carefully differentiated from other possible influences on IT use, including sectoral and institutional factors. The tendency to reduce cultural effects to a question of stereotypical 'mindsets' or predispositions is carefully avoided.

In applying this framework to empirical research, Dr Kambayashi's approach has both strengths and weaknesses which he freely acknowledges. Survey methods make it more difficult to obtain a sense of the processual interplay between cultural and technological factors. On the other hand, such methods do enable a more objectively discriminating account of the relative influence of different factors. And when applied to relatively large samples as presented here, such methods are capable of some subtlety in their inferences. In particular, as outlined here, such methods allow us to identify at both broad and detailed levels the particular mechanisms through which national cultural factors influence IT use. By developing a comparative study which links two very different national cultural contexts, Dr Kambayashi is able to explore the mechanisms of cultural influence in a way which differentiates them from other external influences. In particular, two patterns of organisational IT use are conceptualised: control-oriented IT use (CIU) and individual-oriented IT use (IIU), both of which are shown to display national cultural influences.

This account allows us to identify with some precision the influence of national culture as both managerial and employee use of IT is considered through samples drawn from Britain, Japan and Japanese firms in Britain. This leads to the important finding that cultural influences do indeed exert an influence on the use of IT through the cultural modalities defined by control-oriented and individual-oriented IT use. In this way, Norio Kambayashi's study makes an important contribution to overcoming the polarities in the current debate and in seeing cultural and technological influences not as opposing forces or paradigms, but rather as intensively intertwined and interdependent.

Warwick Business School, University of Warwick   HARRY SCARBROUGH

Preface

Although a number of studies have investigated relationships between information technology (IT) and organisations, relatively few studies have conducted international comparisons on the theme, and even fewer have focused on national culture in their analytical framework. This research clarifies the role national culture plays in shaping the 'emergent' relationship between IT and organisations. I develop a view that technological/organisational determinism approaches have drawbacks in the IT era, and that the emergent perspective is relevant in understanding the use of IT in organisations. I use the perspective to indicate some of the mechanisms through which national culture may influence IT use. I look for some empirical evidence about the possibility of cultural influences and their possible implications, and evidence about how such influences operate in reality.

Considering the research topic, the survey approach was adopted. The data were sampled from three types of manufacturing companies: British factories, Japanese factories, and Japanese factories located in Britain (JFB). Considering that national culture is a diffuse and contextual phenomenon, the aim was to collect a broad and large sample and to take a comparative approach. Two patterns of organisational IT use are conceptualised: control-oriented IT use (CIU) and individual-oriented IT use (IIU), both of which are shown to display national cultural influences.

The most important finding from the study is that national culture is actually playing an important role in the emergent process shaping organisational IT use. Also, it is identified that the influence of national culture is more likely to be displayed in the dimension of CIU than in that of IIU. CIU in Japanese factories is found to be higher than that in British factories due to the difference of national culture between the two countries. National culture has been less fully examined in studies on technology and organisation, but my data suggest the necessity of a detailed examination of the concept in a cross-national comparison.

This book, which is derived from my PhD thesis submitted to the University of Warwick in 1999, would not have been possible without the willing cooperation of numerous people and organisations. I would like to acknowledge those who have directly and indirectly helped me with my research and this book. In the first place, I owe a great debt to the employees of the companies which participated in the survey project for this research. More than 1400 manufacturing companies, British and Japanese, have cooperated in the survey questionnaire which included questions that needed detailed, time-consuming replies. Their cooperation and patience helped this research become a reality.

I would like to express my sincere thanks and appreciation to Professor Harry Scarbrough of the University of Warwick, who supervised my PhD thesis. He kept me on schedule and close to the subject. Even before my becoming a doctoral course student, he showed me a challenging research subject and helped me to develop the theoretical framework in this thesis. His comments and recommendations have always been penetrating and full of suggestions in theoretical terms in particular, and always helped motivate me in the hard work required for a PhD. Other important suggestions came from my second supervisor Professor Jacky Swan. Her comments and recommendations, especially in terms of the collection and analysis of empirical data, really helped to develop how I analysed and presented the data that I collected. Professor Bob Galliers, the internal examiner, and Dr Anthony Wensley, the external examiner from the University of Toronto, gave me many useful comments and advice in the viva to improve the work. Professor Harukiyo Hasegawa, University of Sheffield, kindly read the whole manuscript and recommended me to publish this work.

Many thanks to all those at Warwick Business School, academics and administrative staff, whose encouragement was much appreciated. I would particularly like to mention: Ms Sue Watts, the secretary of Warwick Business School Research Bureau, who often had to cope with my demanding requirements on the collection of the survey questionnaire in Britain. It was very difficult for a foreign student like myself to gain access to companies in Britain. Without her help, I could not have acquired any data on British companies. Also, special thanks to academic and administrative staff at Kobe University in Japan, particularly to Professor Koji Okubayashi, Professor Masayuki Munakata, Professor Tadao Kagono, Professor Akinobu Sakashita and Professor Toshihiro Kanai. They provided me with an excellent study environment in the shape of a long sabbatical (two years!). Part of the research in Japan was funded by the Japanese Education Ministry whom I also want to acknowledge.

Finally, but not least, I pay tribute to my family: my wife Asako and daughter Aoi, who permitted me to conduct this long-lasting research and supported me in many ways. Without their smiles and encouragement, I would have given up continuing the research project a long time ago.

Kobe, Japan   NORIO KAMBAYASHI

1
Introduction

Research objectives: use of IT under the influence of national culture

The recent development of information technology (IT) since the 1980s has brought about a huge interest amongst academics and business practitioners. According to Davis (1992), for example, the following topics have been investigated by academics: organisation and management of the information system (IS) function in an organisation; specifications for and requirements of classes of systems common to organisations, for example decision support systems (DSS); IS application requirements; IS development, implementation and maintenance; impact/interaction of IT/IS and effects on individual users in various settings. Furthermore, Watson and Brancheau's (1992) study reports the major concerns of IS executives are: improving IS strategic planning; aligning IS and corporate goals; educating senior management with regard to IS's potential and role; using IS for competitive advantage; developing an information architecture, and so on. Many pieces of research for each topic area have been conducted.

As I will review in Chapter 2, such huge interest in IT/IS has led some researchers to international comparisons of these IT issues in organisational settings. Despite the relative boom of theoretical insights and many predictions for the future which can be seen in, for example, Drucker (1989), relatively few studies have shown empirical evidence on the effects of IT-based systems in an international context, and still fewer have focused attention on the relationship between IT and national culture in particular. This research is based on empirical research on IT use in a factory setting in different national cultural contexts, through the international comparison between British and Japanese manufacturing firms.

The overall objective of the research is to explore the influence of national culture on the use of IT in factories in different national cultural settings. While the importance of contextual factors has been intensively debated in relation to industry (Scott Morton, 1991) and organisational effects (Orlikowski, 1992), national culture has long been less fully examined in management studies. Based on crude technological determinism, a convergent 'culture-free' thesis has been popular in organisation theory, especially the contingency school (Elger and Smith, 1994). The convergence debate was inaugurated by Kerr and his colleagues (1960), where industrialism is argued to be a worldwide phenomenon based on science and technology speaking a universal language. In their view, technology diffuses globally so that the world is apparently divided into nations which are industrialised and those in the process of industrialisation irrespective of their cultural traditions. The idea of convergence was subsequently developed by Hickson *et al.* (1974) who studied whether relationships between structure (specialisation, formalisation and centralisation) and context (organisational size, operating technology and dependence on other organisations) were consistent in 14 countries; they found that the relationships were similar whilst there were variations in scores between countries. The results of their study suggest that whatever the nation and culture, larger organisations are more specialised and formalised in structure (see also Clark, 1996).

Despite the popularity of 'culture-free' theory in the development of organisation theory, some recent studies have indicated problems from cross-national studies. For example, Rose's (1985) study has revealed persistent differences between societies and sectors sharing the same political economy and technological basis. Clark (1987) suggests that one finds a variety of patterns in societies rather than a single one. Sorge (1991) maintains that, in interpreting cross-national comparisons of technology, organisation and human resources through previous studies, societal specificity continues to be reproduced despite the sharing and borrowing of similar institutional arrangements between societies. These studies suggest that due to the specificity of each country's historical and cultural tradition and development, each society is relatively unique and has certain unchanging aspects.

There is a similar convergence/divergence debate in discussions on the relationship between IT and organisation structure. As I will outline in Chapter 2, a review of previous studies on the technology–organisation relationship will show that both technological and organisational determinism have drawbacks in themselves, and a third perspective, called the 'emergent perspective', is useful in explaining the organisational use of technology in the IT era in particular. Instead of arguing about convergence or divergence, the emergent view attempts to focus on reciprocal interactions between IT and organisation structure over time, thereby denying that either technology or culture 'determines' IT use. Thus the present research aims to identify whether cultural influences are an important/unimportant element in the emergent processes shaping IT use. I am employing the emergent perspective to indicate some of the organisational mechanisms through which national culture may influence organisational IT use. Outlining the ways in which cultural factors feed into IT use will help to establish the possibility of national cultural influences and their possible implications for IT use in a factory. The view also helps to indicate that if cultural influences operate, they are likely to do so through a complex interactive process, and are not merely a question of linear causality.

To my knowledge, no studies to date have provided empirical evidence on IT use in British and Japanese manufacturing firms from the viewpoint developed above. In spite of the success of Japanese firms in the world economy in the 1980s and the subsequent increase of interest in 'Japanisation' and the so-called Japanese management system among British academics, few studies have tackled the issue of IT use in either British or Japanese factories with empirical evidence. As we will see in a later section of the chapter, Dore's (1973) influential study of an international comparison between British and Japanese factories is suggestive, but too much attention has been paid to institutional arrangements to discuss national cultural traditions and developments in both societies. Much of the 'Japanisation' discussion in Britain has neglected, or at least has made light of, cultural aspects.

In short, this study is trying to clarify the role national culture plays in shaping the 'emergent' relationship between IT and the organisation: whether or not IT use in organisations in Japan is different from that in Britain due to the different national cultures. In other words, I am developing an analytical and empirical approach to explore national cultural influence and specific organisational mechanisms for that influence on IT use in Britain and Japan. It is therefore appropriate to clarify here what 'IT use' and 'national culture' refer to in this research.

Definition of terms

IT use in organisations

IT is used in many situations in an organisation. My colleagues and I (Okubayashi *et al.*, 1994; Kambayashi, 1998) conducted a pilot survey of

Japanese manufacturing firms in 1994 on IT use on the shop-floor in Japanese factories located in Japan. The survey found that shop-floor workers in fact used IT-based systems in 162 out of the 183 respondent factories (88.5 per cent), and of these 37.6 per cent replied that IT was useful for the improvement of product quality; 35.8 per cent that IT could reduce processing time of manufacturing goods; and 20.7 per cent that IT increased production capabilities of similar products. We found that most of the machines installed on the shop-floor were equipped with IT, thus the operating need of these machines was one of the most demanding abilities required by shop-floor workers. In Kavrakoğlu's (1992) similar survey of management's use of IT in the Turkish Glass Corporation, overall production-related managers were reported to use IT more (36.6 per cent) than other managers, such as general managers (13.3 per cent), accounting and personnel managers (23.3 per cent) and marketing and sales managers (22.2 per cent). The survey also indicated that 56 per cent of these managers used IT a few times a day, followed by 'a few times a week' (18.0 per cent) and 'a few times a month' (11.0 per cent). The objectives of IT use involve 'looking at certain data, such as sales, profit/loss, production and so forth' (91.0 per cent), which is followed by 'engineering and other calculations' (9.0 per cent).

These surveys from different national settings suggest that various IT-equipped machines are widely used both at the shop-floor and management level in factories. At the shop-floor level, previous studies (such as Okubayashi *et al.*, 1994) suggest that IT/IS refers to automated production systems employing electronically automated control devices (that is, microcomputers, electronic circuits, and so on): industrial robots; numerical control (NC); computerised numerical control (CNC); machining centres (MC); direct numerical control (DNC); flexible manufacturing systems (FMS – production systems using NC, MC, robots or automated transportation devices that are linked to and controlled by a computer); cellular manufacturing systems; group technology (GPT); computer-aided design (CAD); computer-aided manufacturing (CAM); CAD/CAM systems; computer-assisted engineering (CAE); computer-integrated manufacturing (CIM); materials requirements planning (MRP); manufacture resource planning (MRP2); just-in-time (JIT) or *kanban* production systems, and so on. At the management level, the usual definition of IT/IS refers to management information systems (MIS) employing computers and/or other information and telecommunications technology: mainframe computers; terminals connected to a mainframe system; personal computers (PC); local-area networks (LAN); value-added networks (VAN);

wide-area networks (WAN); decision support systems (DSS); group decision support systems (GDSS); executive information systems (EIS); strategic information systems (SIS), and so on (Ciborra, 1996; Shimada, 1991).

In this book, all of these machines equipped with IT are collectively called 'IT-based systems', with no specific focus on a single technology. The main reason for the attention to the whole 'IT-based system' is that I would like to investigate the whole systematic effects of IT instead of the effects of some specific technologies. IT, which is sometimes called 'new technology', is distinguished from previous technologies in being based on information, rather than mechanical models and apparatus (Sproull and Goodman, 1990). My analysis tries to clarify the influence of the whole technological system of IT that can be distinguished from older machine technologies.[1] Secondly, as Badham (1994) suggests, when an international comparison on IT use is conducted, it is necessary to take into consideration the different trajectories of technology. Even when taking an identical technology to make a comparison, it is likely that the technological trajectory has been developed in a variety of ways which reflect national demands and requirements. For example, in comparing the diffusion and effects of 'CIM' technology in two different nations, we are limited in our ability to generalise about the national context because the definition of CIM, and the development and configuration within the specific system architecture, may differ between the two nations.

National culture

Mead (1998) suggests that many external environmental factors are involved in organisational decision-making: the national and the international economy; decisions made by competitors; decisions made by suppliers and/or customers; trade unions; national laws and regulations; industry; technology; the political context, and so on. National culture is maintained to be one of these factors, and it naturally appears to relate to organisational decision-making on IT use.

As Nath (1988) suggests, culture can be briefly summarised as the beliefs, value system, norms, mores, myths and structural elements of a given organisation, tribe or society. Thus culture is considered to exist at the national, regional and organisational levels (Watson, Ho and Raman, 1994). Most previous research in the discipline of IT and organisation studies, however, has discussed *organisational* culture, for instance the inertial impact of organisational culture on IT implementation and uses (Cooper, 1994). Relatively few researchers have tackled issues of *national* culture, although national culture is considered to have a substantial influence on organisational decision-making (Raman and Watson, 1994). This appears to be partly because of the difficulty in defining what national culture is.

National culture is defined by Hofstede (1980) as 'the collective programming of the mind which distinguishes the members of one human group from another' (p. 25) and identifies its four dimensions: power distance, uncertainty avoidance, individualism/collectivism and masculinity/femininity. As we will see in later chapters, it is shown that most previous studies on national culture, empirical ones in particular, have used the dimensional approach developed by Hofstede. In this research project, I develop and extend the discussion by using this definition of national culture, as it makes it possible to measure and analyse the concept and operationalise it for organisational IT use.

What I mean by this definition of national culture is that the concept is distinguished from the key social institutions of a nation, such as the state, the financial system, or the educational and training system (Maurice, Sorge and Warner, 1980). Although national culture and institutional context cannot be seen as perfectly independent, and thus it is difficult to specify the order of causality or precedence between the two (Giddens, 1979; Sorge, 1995), it is important to distinguish culture from institutions (Guerrieri and Tylecote, 1998). An institution is an established rule, custom and practice while culture is more concerned with softer aspects of people, such as values, norms and preferences. As I will review in Chapter 2, Whittaker (1990) claimed that some institutional aspects of a nation, such as market-oriented employment relations (MER) and organisation-oriented employment relations (OER), have a significant effect on IT use, based on the investigation of a comparison of CNC uses in British factories and Japanese factories. However, Dore (1973) suggested that it is even possible for people in two countries which are based on the same social institutions to behave quite differently as a result of their different cultural systems. For example, in Sri Lanka, where social institutions such as a lifetime employment system, a seniority wage system and in-company labour unions are very similar to those in Japan, the attitudes and behaviours of the employees are quite different to those of Japanese firms. The so-called typical Japanese features such as diligence and a cooperative relationship between the management and workers cannot be identified in firms in Sri Lanka even on the same social institutional basis.[2] As Rowlinson (1997) claims, even though based on the same social institutions, it is difficult for nation states to emulate each other: Western industrial economies such as Britain could not have copied Japan's success, because of the difficulty in identifying and changing the informal constraints that make up national cultures (Hamilton and Biggart, 1988). Also, any social constitution has been shaped and chosen by something cultural in historical terms (Clark, 1987). Of course, there is an argument that national differences mainly reflect institutional business systems rather than culture, as much cultural influence has been communicated through more proximate institutions (Whitley, 1992). However, taking Dore's illustration into consideration, and also taking into account the fact that Asian countries share more or less homogeneous cultural values on which Whitley's argument is based, it is both possible and important to clarify in this study what are the British and Japanese cultures broadly defined in the sense that they are differentiated from institutions, and how these 'national cultures', as we can label them, can affect organisational IT use.

Outline of the book

This study looks specifically at IT use in factories located in different national cultural contexts, in order to attempt to examine whether national culture is an important/unimportant element for organisational IT use. To cover the research aims, the book consists of eight chapters. In the next chapter, I will try to establish the theoretical contexts for empirical research through reviews of previous studies, both theoretical and empirical, at three levels: first the examination of the relationship between technology and organisational structure; secondly national cultural influences on IT use; and thirdly specific British/Japanese cultural influences on IT use. The 'emergent perspective' on the relationship between technology and organisational structure, instead of technological/organisational determinism, will be indicated to be particularly useful for the analysis in the IT era, as will reviewing previous studies on national cultural influences upon IT use on the basis of this perspective. Through this examination, my analysis tries to clarify how and to what degree previous studies have illuminated the theme, and what aspects remain to be discussed and analysed further.

In Chapter 3, the research methodology and the analytical framework will be presented in detail. The relevance of the survey approach for the study will be explained: two major approaches to the IT research discipline, the survey and case study approaches, will be compared with each other in terms of their advantages and disadvantages, and the relevance of the survey approach to the theme of this study will be demonstrated.

The analytical level of organisational IT use will be discussed in the next section to indicate that IT use will be measured both at the shop-floor level and at the management level of a factory. Both managerial preference for, and actual practices of, IT use will be measured in order to isolate cultural effects from other factors. Then the operationalisation of the concept of national culture will be examined in reviewing previous studies on national culture to indicate and specify the patterns of IT use that are sensitive to cultural influences. Two patterns of IT use, control-oriented IT use (CIU) and individual-oriented IT use (IIU), will be conceptualised as those which are most open to cultural influences. The whole picture of the analytical model for the study and hypothesis to be tested will be shown in the following section. In some subsequent sections, methodological details of the design and the process of the empirical research will be depicted. The preliminary work for the field research and details of the structure of the survey such as sampling procedures and the structure of the collected samples will be illustrated. Explanations will be given particularly with regard to the reasoning behind the survey and to show how the theoretical categories involved, such as managerial preferences and actual practices in IT use, reflect the conceptual issues described in the previous sections of the chapter.

In Chapter 4, I will analyse data on the wider context. Some contextual factors to be controlled for will be examined in order to isolate cultural effects from other effects on organisational IT use. They include factors such as kinds of technology/systems, industries, and those regarding individual organisations, for example size of organisations, batch size, unionisation and organisational sub-cultures. Through the analysis of the collected sample, it will be shown that industries and the size of organisations in particular should be controlled for in the present study.

In the following three chapters, findings of the questionnaire survey will be clarified in detail, and this will constitute the heart of this study. In Chapter 5, some evidence for national cultural influences on organisational IT use will be elucidated by using the empirical data collected. The data will be presented in terms of the two patterns of IT use respectively – CIU and IIU. The general feature of managerial preferences for IT use in British factories and Japanese factories will be clarified, and some differences and similarities between the two groups of factories on the preferences will also be identified. It will then be shown how the Japanese factories in Britain (JFB) can be situated with regard to CIU and IIU.

Chapters 6 and 7 will examine the actual practices of IT use, providing evidence on how cultural influences operate in reality. Chapter 6 will be on those at the shop-floor level of the factories and Chapter 7 will be on those at the management level. The empirical data will be presented in a similar way to the preceding chapter, that is, in terms of CIU and IIU respectively. In the last section of Chapters 6 and 7 some implications of the findings will be discussed. Through examination of the data it will be clarified empirically whether or not national culture is an important factor in shaping organisational IT use in the emergent process of interaction between IT and organisations.

Finally, in Chapter 8, the findings of this research will be integrated and the lessons and the implications learned from the research will be summarised. Needs for further research will be suggested, and the research's key contribution to knowledge will also be summarised briefly.

2
Concepts of IT and National Culture

Introduction

This chapter examines how the two main concepts of the study, IT and national culture, have been discussed in an organisational context in previous studies. The review will be developed at three levels. Firstly, the relationship between IT and organisations in general, which involves three perspectives – 'technology-determined', 'organisation-determined' and the newly-developed 'emergent' perspective. Secondly, previous studies on national cultural influences on IT use will be reviewed, as this study attempts to focus on IT use in different national cultures. An examination of how previous studies have tackled the issue will be given by focusing on their analytical framework on the international comparison. Finally, specific British/Japanese cultural influences on IT use will be examined to illustrate how and to what extent previous studies have clarified that British/Japanese culture relates to IT use in organisations. These reviews will outline what previous studies have shed light on and what implications they have concerning the theme of this study.

The relationships between IT and organisations

IT has been a central focus in organisation studies since the 1980s. Its discussion has been varied depending on what specific topic has been discussed and on whether it is discussed from the standpoint of labour or from the view of capital (Beirne and Ramsay, 1992). Indeed, research exploring the relationship between technology and organisational structure – not only IT but also previous mechanical technologies – has been a fundamental question for the past 35 years (Sampler, 1996).

Although the topic and viewpoint has been very diversified (Fry, 1982), it is possible to classify these different IT–organisation relationships in terms of how IT is dealt with in each analytical framework. Conventional debates about the relationships between technology and organisations have suggested the following three perspectives: technological determinism, organisational choice, and the 'emergent' paradigm (Markus and Robey, 1988). The first and second perspectives, although they expect results in an opposite direction, share a common ground in the sense that both suggest that one variable, either technology or organisational requirements, determines the other. This is a decisively different point from the third perspective. This section presents a review of literature on these three paradigms in order to indicate which perspective is the most relevant for the theme of this study.

Technological/organisational determinism

Technological determinism

Under the perspective of technological determinism, technology is regarded as the main factor in forming the structure of organisations and 'organisations have little choice but adapt their skills and work organisation to the requirements of technology' (Scarbrough and Corbett, 1992, p. 4). According to Winner (1986), this perspective suggests that 'the adoption of a given technical system . . . requires the creation and maintenance of a particular set of social conditions as the operating environment of that system' (p. 32). In other words, in its crudest sense, this perspective presents any major social changes as inevitable reflexes of the 'fixed' technological development, exerting a neutral 'impact' upon work organisation and experience (Beirne and Ramsay, 1992). As Bloomfield, Coombs and Owen (1994) suggest, some writers argue that technology determines even the pattern of management control as well as organisational structure. In this view, therefore, system standards and measures would take precedence over nation-state diversity, and economics dominates politics; countries would become more or less the same as they adopt the same efficiency imperatives based on the technology (Elger and Smith, 1994).

From Marx's (1847) provocative claim that different types of social relation were necessary for a steam-mill as compared to a hand-mill, this kind of deterministic view predates the IT era. For instance, Blauner (1964) suggests that technological development might well promote automation of unskilled jobs, which can prevent deskilling of workers. Woodward (1965) asserts that 'technology, although not the only variable affecting organisation, was one that could be isolated for study without too much difficulty' and 'there are prescribed and functional relationships between structure and technical demands' (p. 51). Bell (1973) also claims that 'technology has been one of the chief forces in the diremption [*sic*] of social time . . . [thus] technology has transformed social relationships and our way of looking at the world' (p. 188) and discusses the possibility of the realisation of 'post-industrial' society. The deterministic perspective suggests, as Ellul (1974) argues, that people's behaviour cannot help being subordinated to the rationality of science and its enframement of technology.

Even during the IT era, the deterministic perspective was being maintained at least at its earlier stage, that is, up to the early 1980s. For example, Leavitt and Whisler (1958) predicted that IT would cause centralisation of decision-making in an organisation as IT would help to decrease the number of middle managers, which would enable top management to assume more creative roles in the organisation since they could obtain large amounts of real-time information. Other studies also suggest that IT would tend to strengthen management control as senior management could obtain more accurate information from computers (Hoos, 1960; Whisler, 1970). Leifer and McDonough (1985) examined empirically the specific impact of IT on organisations to find that work groups which used IT more extensively were more centralised than those which used IT less extensively. On the other hand, some studies indicate quite the opposite conclusions: Klatsky (1970) argued that IT would take over routine work at the lower and middle levels so that managers at these levels could be engaged in less routine work which could empower them; Pfeffer and Leblebici (1977) examined how IT affected manufacturing firms controlled for other institutional and environmental factors, and found that IT had a tendency to cause decentralisation of the decision-making authority structure. What is important here, therefore, is not whether IT causes centralisation or decentralisation, but that IT is viewed as an independent variable affecting organisational structure (Sampler, 1996). Thus the framework of analysis of these studies should be classified in the deterministic perspective.[1]

Organisational determinism

An alternative viewpoint to technological determinism is one in which organisational characteristics, such as information processing needs, determine how technology will be used. Sometimes this organisational determinism is also referred to as the 'culturally determined' perspective, as culture can be seen as an expression of social and organisational reality (Kono and Clegg, 2001; Kimble and McLoughlin, 1994). Under this perspective, technology is understood as the factor which organisations have a chance to choose and design at their will according to their requirements; complex and various kinds of social relations are involved in the process, such as authority and power, which are needed for the analysis of relationships between technology and organisations. The central argument of the perspective is that, according to Kimble and McLoughlin (1994), 'technology does not emerge unsullied from some objective notion of scientific progress but that social values are inevitably "built into" a technology with the intention of bringing about a certain outcome' (p. 160). Such ideas as 'culturally-determined' or 'organisational choice' date back to Trist *et al.* (1963) – the origin of socio-technical systems theory.

Whilst technological determinists usually take older technology as their model, for instance a belt conveyer system as mass production technology, advocates of organisational determinism are likely to take newer technology including IT as the standard of technology (Scarbrough and Corbett, 1992). Also, in contrast with technological determinism, the organisational determinism approach has become dominant since the 1980s, after which IT innovation began in earnest, although the prototype of the idea was formed in a much earlier era.

For instance, Wilkinson (1983) investigates the relationship between new technology, organisations and skills of employees and concludes that

> technology is not autonomous and therefore does not have impacts regardless of the social context, and that . . . the technical and social organisation of work . . . is a negotiable phenomenon, determined by social and political processes whose outcomes are never certain.
>
> (p. 94)

Therefore, this perspective indicates that 'strategic choice' (Child, 1972) plays a key role in determining how to use technology and it can be stated that 'technology . . . has limited impact on people or performance in an organisation independent of purposes of those who would use it and the responses of those who have to work with it' (Buchanan and Huczynski, 1991, p. 277). In other words, technological change is regarded as a factor which can enlarge the matrix of the strategic choice for firms and which makes 'the coupling between central areas of choice, such as product strategy, technology and work organisation, less determinate and richer of functional alternatives and equivalents' (Sorge and Streeck, 1988, p. 41).

Some empirical studies have shown support for the organisational determinism perspective: for instance, Daft and Macintosh (1981) clarified that, based on the 'information processing model' suggested by Galbraith (1973), task characteristics affected the choice of type of IT appropriate for dealing with the information associated with the task. However, the pursuit of explanatory models for the relationship between IT and organisational structure continues as empirical support for these arguments has been relatively limited (Sampler, 1996).

The emergent perspective

In recent years, a new perspective for the IT–organisation relationship has developed in which 'the uses and consequences of IT emerge unpredictably from complex social interactions' (Markus and Robey, 1988, p. 588). This perspective originally corresponds to Pfeffer's (1982) 'emergent' view of action in organisations:

> because participation in organisational decisions is both segmented and discontinuous, because preferences develop and change over time, and because the interpretation of the results of actions – the meaning of history – is often problematic; behaviour cannot be predicted *a priori* either by the intention of individual actors or by the conditions of the environment.   (p. 9)

Under the emergent view, technology is seen as a process rather than as aggregations of machines and systems, and the mutuality of technology and organisation is analysed (Scarbrough and Corbett, 1992), instead of if being considered that one 'determines' the other. Proponents of this perspective claim that the perception (and hence the use) of IT is subjective and that the meanings associated with IT are socially constructed (Sampler, 1996). In other words, technology and organisations are neither independent nor dependent variables in a true sense; IT can be an independent variable affecting organisational structure at one stage, but it can be a dependent variable as well at the next stage; IT and organisations develop each other dynamically over time. IT is not thought to be a factor which either reinforces or aids in shifting the organisation to a new structure, for instance from centralised to decentralised. Rather, IT and organisations have an ongoing interaction and simultaneously constrain and change each other (Orlikowski and Robey, 1991).

Barley (1986) demonstrated that, having studied the introduction of computerised tomography (CT) scanners in a radiology department in a hospital, the new IT could alter the organisational and occupational structure of radiological work. However, the identical technologies can occasion similar dynamics and yet lead to different structural outcomes in different settings. According to Barley, the organisation changed not because of its inherent characteristics, as technological determinism would hold, but because the new CT scanners 'became social objects whose meanings were defined by the context of their use' (p. 106):

> Through this interplay, called the process of structuring, institutional practices shape human actions, which, in turn, reaffirm or modify the institutional structure. The technology presented an *occasion* for structural change, but did not *determine* which alternatives actually emerged from the process of structuring. Thus, the study of structuring involves investigating how the institutional realm and the realm of action configure each other. (p. 80)

Orlikowski and Robey (1991) assert that IT assumes a dual role in organisations: first, IT possesses an objective set of rules and resources that both enhances and constrains the roles of workers within organisations. IT also possesses a unique culturally-specific component at the same time, because it alters the roles and the social fabric of work. Therefore a complex interaction between these dual roles for IT would determine how IT is perceived and used within an organisation. Weick (1990) also admits that causality between technology and organisation should be viewed as loosely structured, with reciprocal effects evolving over time. Technological changes follow changes in social structure, that is organisational structure, as agents in groups or organisations develop social constructions of the technology, which in turn change the technology. This evolution is difficult to predict *a priori*, as it is loosely structured and disorganised. Under the emergent perspective, technology is regarded both as an independent variable at one time and as a dependent variable at another time, and interactions between IT and organisational structure are evolving dynamically over time: Shimada (1991) calls it the 'spiral model'.

Because of the complex interaction between technology and organisations, it has become more difficult to distinguish technology *per se* from organisations; the idea that IT and organisational structures are separate entities, which is the basic assumption of much of the previous research, is becoming invalid as IT itself is becoming the organisational structure because it is increasingly the principal source of information transmission (Sampler, 1996). New arrangements in the IT era, 'fleet of foot' organisations such as networked organisations and virtual corporations, are allowed to exist by IT, in which it is impossible to tell the new organisational arrangements from IT itself.

This emergent perspective particularly holds good for the IT era; in fact, this view began to be claimed in the late 1980s, which saw a major diffusion of IT-based systems. Weick (1990) explains that the emergent perspective fits especially for analysing IT, as technologies become more fluid and more difficult to comprehend, with less transparent effects on shifting organisational structures. Thus he calls the disposition of IT, 'technology as equivoque'. Therefore, it is asserted that making predictions about the relationships between technology and organisations is not achieved until we understand, taking the complex interaction into consideration, both the proposed uses and features of technology and the evolving organisational processes around the use and implementation of the technology (Sampler, 1996). According to Sampler (1996), the rejection of the 'deterministic' point of view, whether it be technological determinism or organisational determinism, is a dominant theme in the emergent perspective. Causality is viewed as loosely structured, with reciprocal effects evolving over time. As Sproull and Goodman (1990) maintain, technology and social actors (individuals, groups) represent the initial causal agents in this view. 'Changes in technology lead to changes in social structure, as agents in groups or organisations develop constructions of the technology and social structure . . . this evolution is loosely structured, disorganised, and difficult to predict' (p. 258).

The reasons for the unpredictable relationships between IT and organisational structure in the emergent perspective can be explained in several ways. Scott (1990) explains why IT has variable effects on organisation structure by employing Zuboff's (1985) distinction between 'automate' and 'informate' functions of IT. Zuboff notes that IT

can be applied in order to automate operations. For example, a numerically controlled machine tool will operate by computerised instructions without the physical intervention of an operator . . . In its second function, the technology creates information . . . [It has the] capacity to *informate* the production process. That is, the intelligence of the microprocessor that resides at the base of virtually every application not only applies instructions to equipment but can convert the current state of product or process into information. (p. 105)

Sproull and Goodman (1990) explained why variable relationships can be observed using Weick's (1990) concept of a 'technical system', defined to be a specific combination of machines and methods employed to produce a desired outcome. Providing an argument on multi-way causality between IT and organisational structure, 'the machines found in a particular technical system are not irreducible givens but rather are themselves shaped by the results of social processes' (Sproull and Goodman, 1990, p. 255). There is an underlying dimension of IT that is qualitatively different from that of previous technologies: the dimension of programmability. According to Sproull and Goodman (1990),

> precisely because programmability is new, people and organisations have few methods for managing and understanding it. Therefore, they create technical systems with machines that are programmable and methods that are mechanical. Thus, the technology may be fundamentally new, but the technical systems are not. (p. 257)

Given such dispositions of IT as involving stochastic and continuous processing (Weick, 1990), and taking into account the systemic view such as the 'technical system' or the 'IT-based system' rather than each technology *per se*, it is important to acknowledge that the relationship between technology and organisations is an interactive one, not a question of linear causality which technological/organisational determinism would hold.

The emergent perspective is useful in indicating some of the mechanisms through which national culture may influence IT use and possible implications for IT use. Outlining the ways in which cultural factors feed into technology use helps to establish that, if cultural influences operate, they are likely to do so through a complex interactive process – it is not a question of either technology or culture 'determining' IT use. Therefore, the objective of my research is to identify empirically whether the effects of national culture are an important/unimportant element in the emergent processes shaping organisational IT use.[2] In the next section I review how previous studies have focused on the way cultural influences on IT use would operate in an emergent way.

National cultural influences on IT use

National culture has been a hitherto less fully examined concept in studies on IT, as most researchers have focused more on *corporate* or *organisational*

culture in the use of IT (Tidd, Bessant and Pavitt, 1997; Cooper, 1994).
Also, although a considerable number of previous studies have focused
on the relationship between IT and organisations, as reviewed in the
last section, relatively few have examined the cross-national comparisons
on the relationship between the two. In this section, I will attempt to
illustrate how previous studies have approached international issues,
the effects of national culture on IT use in particular.[3] Based particularly
on the studies utilising 'emergent perspective', I will show how cultural
influences on IT use would operate in an emergent way.

Relatively few studies in the IT/IS area have conducted international
comparisons in their empirical analysis of the relationship between IT
and organisations, and even fewer have considered cultural influences
on IT use in an organisational setting. Some theorists in the camp of the
labour-process approach (Knights and Willmott, 1988; Beirne and Ramsay,
1992) have attempted to examine the realisation of organisational
democracy in each country under the influence of IT. Germany, Sweden
and Japan are the most often cited examples in this context. For example,
it has been claimed that recent flexible and enskilling responses to automation and computerisation have led to a more effective realisation or
humanised form of work organisation in these countries, whereas
Britain is not as enthusiastic as these countries about the use of IT in
a humanised form (Beirne and Ramsay, 1992). Some evidence has shown
that Britain is at least lagging in skill formation regardless of training
(Senker, 1989; Hyman, 1988). One of the characteristics of the labour-
process approach is that they have referred to and tried to evaluate the
representative influence, whether through unions, works councils or other
bodies, the process of introduction of IT-based systems in their cross-
national comparisons on IT use. These representative influences should
be controlled for in the study if we are to examine genuine cultural
influences on IT use – I will return to this issue in Chapter 4. Therefore,
it can be judged that the concept of culture has been neglected in these
particular studies as having no significant role in organisational IT use.

Badham (1994) has indicated that there are three main international
perspectives on recent computer integrated manufacturing (CIM) experiences: societal effects and industrial culture perspectives; anti-Taylorist
or anti-technocratic CIM design approaches; and national systems
approaches to innovation. These three perspectives are claimed to share
common criticisms towards the traditional concept of the 'automatic'
and/or 'unmanned' factory, as they have commonly recognised the
importance of the human factor in successful innovation. In the ensuing
debate over the effects of new CIM technologies, the first approach has

made an assumption that socio-technical events are 'strategically influenced by tentative, piecemeal experimentation and innovation, under a focus that brings technical, organisational and labour considerations to bear on each other' (Sorge *et al.*, 1983, p. 9). Also Hildebrandt (1989), a proponent of the industrial culture approach, has emphasised the central role of the social constitution of firms in determining the use of CIM systems. According to Hildebrandt, social constitutions are defined as the overall ensemble of the most important norms and rules permitted or effective in the plant that influence the employee's attitude toward work and behaviour at work.

The anti-Taylorist or anti-technocratic CIM design approach takes the view that 'a design ideal is upheld that is committed to the creation of human–machine systems that subordinate the hardware and software of machine systems to the control of human operators' (Badham, 1994, p. 316). The national systems approach to innovation, on the other hand, has recognised the importance of the national institutional frameworks. The Swedish national system of innovation is an example of this approach. Although some works in the first approach have dealt with international comparisons, most in the latter two perspectives have limited their attention to a localised area, and there have been no references to the concept of national culture.

Fewer studies have focused on cultural effects on IT use in an organisation, as it has been believed that, although cultural systems have been important influences on business systems, much of these influences have been exercised through more proximate social institutions (Whitley, 1992). Yet the work of Sorge *et al.* (1983), classified in the first category above, is noteworthy for the study here, as they grasped national culture as a reasonably distinct concept from societal institution, and took such cultural influences into consideration in the analytical framework on an international comparison of computerised numerical control (CNC) use between Britain and West Germany. Sorge and his colleagues investigated the influence of national socio-economic conditions on the development and use of CNC, in which they made a comparison of comparable engineering firms between the two countries. The research showed that, in the face of similar developments of CNC technologies, the reactions of firms differ in different national contexts. The factors discovered to have a key influence were size of company and plant, batch size, type of machinery, national institutions, management and training, and socio-economic conditions.[4] The results of the analysis showed the manner in which the West German national systems of education and training influenced the development of organisational structures and processes which, in turn, influenced the development and use of CNC technologies.

However, as Badham (1994) notes of this study, their analysis gave an insight into key variations in the organisational components of IT-based systems rather than the real effects of societal and organisational variables on uses of technologies, as they lacked an analysis of how the incremental modification and development of CNC technologies was influenced by and combined with organisational conditions to form significantly different socio-technical trajectories. Also, their term 'societal traits' was not very clear, as they presumed that

> differences between societies are so pervasive as to be immediately and consistently noticeable in every unit...societal traits show strongly in every enterprise, so that a small number of selected units can well yield representative results about national differences.
>
> (Sorge *et al.*, 1983, p. 54)

The ambiguous definition of societal traits might have led to the lack of clear-cut *effects* of societal characteristics on use of technologies.

Yet the concept of cultural effects has been developed into a more sophisticated one in Sorge and Warner (1986). In their study, they made comments criticising previous cultural investigations to claim that 'the unexplained residual was...ascribed to the influence of cultural differences...' (p. 39). Thus cultural and societal differences were reduced to a residual role in such a way that, where method was concerned, 'they figured as that part of the variance of international comparisons which could not be explained by well-known variables' and in substance, 'they were only adduced to explain social-organisational variation to the extent that other known variables proved insufficient' (p. 39). They then selected a small number of factories for investigation in different countries, which were alike as far as possible along the dimensions of such variables as size, technology and the task environment, as they hypothesised if there were no sizeable influences of national culture on organisation structure, then it follows that organisational features of factories in different countries would not vary if they are under the same constraints regarding these variables. In fact, they selected matched case studies to make an international comparison. However, as they admit, suspicions still remain on the representation of national culture in the selected factories: they admit that 'the unrepresentative and non-random character of a sample, together with its small size, make it hard to isolate explanatory variables and weigh them one against the other, by means of the accepted correlation and regression techniques' (p. 50), since the selection of explanatory variables are suspected of being arbitrary.

Taking consideration into results of his and his colleagues' previous empirical works (Sorge *et al.*, 1983; Sorge and Warner, 1986), Sorge (1995) summarised the theoretical features and central tenets of the societal-effect approach. According to him, the following four dimensions are of particular importance: organisation of work and of the enterprise; human resources, education, training and socialisation; industrial and sectoral structures, and relations between such industries and sectors; and labour markets as the sum total of events and arrangements which constitute the exchange of labour power for an equivalent such as intrinsic satisfaction, social affiliation or money. In this approach, it is believed that characteristics of any of the four dimensions are related to specific and parallel characteristics of every other dimension: this is the first tenet of the approach. Secondly, therefore, actors reproduce characteristics of any dimension of society and the interrelations between such dimensions. He claims that

> this happens because structural properties and rules of the game, that is, the 'system' properties, tend to load the individual 'choices' that actors make in a specific way ... [and] also happens because the actors learn to see particular 'choices' as generally favourable, and develop a specific 'programming of the mind'. ... The emphasis is on the interactive relationship between systems characteristics and mental programming. (p. 116)

This leads to the third tenet, that is, the reproduction of characteristics on every dimension above, and their interrelations, are defined as non-identical.

This approach provides the basis for the view that true *convergence* between countries hardly ever takes place, since any change tends to consist of such non-identical reproduction. All results in empirical studies as shown in Sorge *et al.* (1983) and Sorge and Warner (1986) are interpreted as the reiteration of the point that organisational outcomes differ quantitatively and qualitatively from one society to another. Therefore, what kinds of outcomes firms achieve, and how successful they are in which market segment or activity, can 'be explained by the society in which they are embedded' (Sorge, 1995, p. 122). These characteristics and tenets of the societal effect approach are suggestive, in the sense that they indicate an analytical framework in which organisational outcomes, say IT use in a factory, are not quite the same in every society, and in which the different outcomes between countries are due to their society's specific effects. There still seems to remain the question, however, of what kind of attributes a national culture refers to and its possible implications for organisational IT use.

Clark and Staunton's (1989) study was another suggestive study of an international comparison of innovation in technology and organisations. They examined the process of technological innovation between different societies which are located in different cultures, such as the USA, Japan and Britain. According to them, an innovation refers to something that is perceived as new by an individual and which is communicated from one individual to another in a social system over time (Clark and Staunton, 1989). The case of teamwork and its different meanings in American and British cultures has been used to illustrate the international transfer of technological innovation. Clark (1987) explained the significance of cross-cultural studies as a possibility of the examination of 'what happens when the same innovation crosses national boundaries' (p. 7). As far as national cultural patterns of an innovation are concerned, it was argued that national patterns of innovation did exist so that 'a typical variety' was able to be identified. However, there still appears to remain the problem of what kind of attributes a national culture specifically refers to and what the effects of national culture really mean.

National culture has been described as an elusive concept, that is 'a fuzzy, difficult-to-define construct' (Triandis *et al.*, 1986), and thus the effect of national culture has been hard to specify and underdeveloped. Also, many cross-cultural studies treated culture as a residual factor, 'which is presumed to account for national variations that have neither been postulated before the research nor explained after its completion' (Child, 1981, p. 306). In this context, the studies by Hofstede (1980) are full of suggestions, as he articulates what a culture is and defines it as 'the collective programming of the mind which distinguishes the members of one human group from another' (p. 25), and identifies four main dimensions of national culture to operationalise: power distance, uncertainty avoidance, individualism/collectivism, and masculinity/ femininity.[5] However, Hofstede failed to discuss technology in any detail with only fleeting references such as

technological modernisation is an important force towards change which lead to partly similar developments in different societies.

However, it does not wipe out differences among societies and may even enlarge them; as on the basis of pre-existing value systems societies cope with technological modernisation in different ways.

(Hofstede, 1984, pp. 233–4)

Hofstede's work is relevant in the sense that it can disentangle the concept of national culture from other possible influences on IT use and can identify the main dimensions to operationalise. However, the work itself was not an investigation on the specific influences of national culture on *IT use*. Recent developments in Management Information System (MIS) and Group Decision Support System (GDSS) technologies in particular, in international practice, have made some suggestions which relate to this theme. According to Briggs, Nunamaker and Sprague (1998), one of the key issues on cross-national development of GDSS is whether or not it can provide a new common ground for interaction among several national cultures, and how members of one culture can adapt to better interact with members of another culture on the basis of GDSS technologies. In these studies, it is believed that information is not data; there is a process of transformation involved which is subject to a cultural milieu (Tricker, 1988).

The highly influential framework to analyse national culture suggested by Hofstede (1980) has been used most frequently for empirical investigations on the relationship between culture and use of MIS/GDSS. For example, Griffith (1996) suggests that, focusing on GDSS technologies in Bulgaria, cultural differences contribute to differences in satisfaction at the implementation of the technologies, with high 'power-distance' cultures showing more resistance to change. Also, using Hofstede's dimensions of national culture, Straub (1994) studied the effects of national culture on IT diffusion in Japan and the USA, to show that high 'uncertainty avoidance' in Japan and structural features of the Japanese written language could explain Japanese perceptions about new work technologies such as email and fax. Generally speaking, cultural effects have been shown to play an important role in the predisposition towards and selection of electronic communications media, that is, predisposition of Japanese knowledge workers against email but in favour of fax.

Mejias *et al.* (1997) discussed the influence of national culture along the same lines. They investigated the effects of national culture (US and Mexican) on group consensus levels and perceptions of participation and satisfaction within GDSS environments and manual, or non-GDSS, environments. According to the study, while US group participants showed no significant differences in satisfaction among experimental treatments, Mexican participants showed higher satisfaction levels using GDSS-supported environments. In a similar pattern, US participants reported no differences in perceived participation among treatments, whilst Mexican GDSS participants reported higher perceived participation than Mexican manual participants. A cross-cultural comparison found that Mexican participants across all treatments perceived higher levels of satisfaction and participation than US participants with the main effects due to national culture that Hofstede (1980) named as 'uncertainty avoidance', 'power distance' and 'individualism/collectivism'.

Also, Watson, Ho and Raman (1994) have suggested that differences in cross-cultural use of GDSS technologies occur primarily in convergent activities. For instance, it has been clarified that groups from countries with a high 'power distance' – that is, those with highly stratified and differentiated organisational and societal levels – tend to prefer a more clearly identified and gradual approach to convergence than groups from countries with lower power distance (Nunamaker *et al.*, 1997; Watson, Ho and Raman, 1994). Therefore, in general, these studies on MIS in international contexts suggest that, based on Hofstede's (1980) measures, the main differences in use of IT are attributed to national cultural differences.

However, how does a national culture influence 'emergent' relationships between IT and organisations? Weick (1990) has suggested a useful clue to this issue with reference to Barley's (1986) work. As reviewed in the last section, Barley (1986) analysed two radiology departments that adopted CT scanners. In one department, initial expertise was held by the technicians (suburban hospital) whilst in the other expertise was lodged in radiologists (urban hospital), and in both hospitals a new IT – a Technicare 2060 whole-body computed tomography scanner – was introduced.

'Structuration', which was originally developed by Giddens (1979), is the central concept of Weick's emergent view in order to distinguish it from previous technology–structure relationships, which are defined as 'the production and reproduction of a social system through members' use of rules and resources in interaction' (Weick, 1990, p. 18). According to his interpretation, in the following manner the technology is hypothesised to affect the process of 'structuration'. At first, the new technology was exogenous. When translated into a technical system it either confirms ingrained interaction patterns or disturbs and reformulates them. These patterns are carried by scripts – 'standard plots of types of encounters whose repetition constitutes the setting's interaction order' (Barley, 1986, p. 83) – which forge reciprocal links between structure and action. It is important to understand how structures were both created and altered by interactions between radiologists and technicians, and that is possible by looking closely at the scripts that emerged from actions involving the new technology. Weick explained the process as follows:

> some of these scripts, such as direction giving, countermands, usurping the controls, direction seeking, and expected criticisms, ratified traditional institutional forms. Other scripts, such as preference stating, clandestine teaching, role reversal, and mutual execution, modified these traditional forms. Each script was built from actions evoked by the technology, but the influence of technology on structure occurred through the ratio of ratification scripts to modification scripts ... the ratio of preference stating (a modification script) to direction giving (a ratification script) was lower at Suburban than at Urban, which meant that the same technology produced more structural change at Suburban than at Urban and did so because it led to the construction of a different social order. (1990, p. 20)

For the explanation of the process of the structuration, Weick distinguishes five conceptual steps: (a) novelty of technology; (b) use of institutionalised dominance scripts; (c) proportion of decisions made by radiologist; (d) centralisation; and (e) technician's understanding of technology. According to Weick, the linkage from (c) to (d) represents action as a constraint on structure and that from (e) to (b) represents institutional constraints on action. Scripts are identified at steps (b) and (c), and either ratification or modification can occur at each of those two stages. This shows that, 'once technology provides the initial kick to the process, its effects are then dependent on how it becomes woven into the process of action' (Weick, 1990, p. 21). It is possible for cultural attributes to influence each stage from (b) to (e). For instance, the proportion of decisions made by a radiologist (step c) is dependent on how important the organisation regards such decisions – the decisions which national culture may affect. Thus centralisation (step d) may be influenced by national culture. Also, the technician's understanding of technology (step e) is open to cultural influences, since the understanding may be dependent upon a society's general perception of how the relationship between technology and organisations should be. Therefore, although Weick did not illustrate how cultural influences operate in the use of IT, the concept of structuration is useful for showing how cultural influences may feed into IT use at each step.

As discussed in the last section, Sampler (1996) has illustrated the relationship between IT and organisational structure based on the emergent view. It has been suggested that 'social norms and values' may play an important role in determining the relationship between IT and organisations. National culture can be regarded as a factor that influences the reciprocal process via some channels such as decision-making and organisational training. As Scott (1990) has argued, we need to introduce cultural factors as well as economic, political, ideological and institutional factors into the arena in terms of the reciprocal causal relations between technology and organisations under the emergent perspective. Wensley (1989) suggested that our technology embeds particular value systems and that there is a need to examine how values may be made explicit in the technology. It is people who see the ways in which technology can be used to innovate (Wensley, 1998). Land (1992, p. 12) writes in such a context:

> an information system is a social system, which has embedded in it information technology. The extent to which information technology plays a part is increasing rapidly. But this does not prevent the overall system from being a social system, and it is not possible to design a robust, effective information system incorporating significant amounts of the technology, without treating it as a social system.

However, as I have indicated, few studies if any to date have mentioned in their analysis the cultural effects on IT use based on the emergent perspective.

Specific British/Japanese cultural influences on IT use

Few studies have examined cross-national comparisons on the relationship between IT and organisations, and still fewer have mentioned specific British/Japanese *cultural* influences on IT use. The work by Hofstede (1980) indicated that along the four dimensions of national culture, compared with Britain, Japan is a country with much less 'individualism', a much higher degree of 'uncertainty avoidance', a somewhat higher degree of 'masculinity', and more or less the same extent of 'power distance'. However, as I indicated in the last section, there are no references to the effects of these national characteristics on organisational IT use in Hofstede's study.

The first study specifically of Japanese factories dates back to Abegglen's (1958) work. This was the first systematic investigation of a Japanese factory to be published in English, in which one of the characteristics of Japanese factories came to be referred to as 'lifetime commitment'. However, a systematic international comparison between a Japanese factory and others was not conducted until Dore's (1973) work. Dore's study of Hitachi and English Electric (two factories each) explored the concepts of 'market orientation' and 'organisation orientation' to refer to the types of work organisation. The former refers to the work organisation which developed in early-industrialising countries, while the latter means

> the terms and conditions of employment are less and less influenced by considerations of the price a worker might get for his skill from another employer in the external market, more and more fitted into an internal structure of relative rankings peculiar to the enterprise and predicated on the assumption of relatively stable long-term employment. (p. 12)

Dore suggested that Britain is based on a market orientation and that Japan is based on an organisational orientation, and argued that the market-oriented form of work organisation is giving way to an organisationally-oriented form. As far as national culture is concerned, however, it was maintained that

> it may well be that differences in cultural traditions – the fact that Japan is a Confucian country where education, learning and scholarship have traditionally been given a much higher place than in a more philistine culture such as Britain's – have something to do with the fact that these elements of educational neurosis are a good deal more pronounced in Japan than in England – even allowing for the British preoccupation with selection and 11-plus. But the difference in the finality of the consequences of one's type of schooling for one's life-chances is surely a more important reason. (p. 295)

Therefore, his analysis focused more on institutional than cultural aspects, though some remarks on general stereotypes of the British and of the Japanese are useful, such as, 'the British are more selfish, more irresponsible, more inclined to tell Jack that they personally are all right', while 'the Japanese are lesser individualists, are more inclined to submerge their identity in some large group to which they belong, and more likely to be obsessed by a sense of duty' (p. 297). As I discussed in Chapter 1, Dore admitted in the Preface of the Japanese translated version of Dore (1973), published in 1990, that on reflection too much emphasis had been placed on institutional aspects and the role of cultural tradition could have been examined in more detail. Based on pieces of empirical evidence in East Asian countries, he has identified that it is possible for people in two countries based on the same societal institutions to behave quite differently culturally.

Whittaker's (1990) investigation of nine pairs of matched British and Japanese factories on the pattern of use of CNC tools takes the same line of argument developed by Dore (1973). He draws on Dore's study to create two stylised forms of employment relations: an organisation-oriented employment relation (OER) and a market-oriented employment relation (MER). He draws a set of hypotheses about how OER and MER could be expected to affect skill and CNC uses before investigating actual uses. He obtained some interesting results: regarding the patterns of innovation, unmanned operating was not seen as an attraction of CNC and an operator had to be present in Britain, whereas unmanned operating was seen as an attraction of CNC and unmanned operating was carried out in Japan. With regard to training of workers, operators in Britain had considerable experience on manual machines and often had craft backgrounds, and they were chosen for CNC and given relatively more CNC-specific training, whilst in Japan operators often had little or no experience on manual machines and they were chosen for CNC and given relatively less CNC-specific training, and were sometimes required to master it themselves. In terms of division of labour, multi-machine operating was not seen as an attraction of CNC in British factories; an experienced operator had to concentrate on one machine and specialist programmers were required to have considerable machining experience, and almost all had shop-floor backgrounds. In Japanese factories, on the other hand, multi-machine operating was seen as an attraction of CNC and less experienced operators could operate more than one machine; specialist programmers were not required to have machining experience and almost none had a shop-floor background.

This may suggest a different type of CNC use due to the cultural differences between Britain and Japan. For example, Britain preferred to utilise CNC tools using operators with previous experience of manual tools, while the Japanese were trying to run their CNC tools unattended and with no previous experience of machine-tool operation. In addition, British firms were content to allocate one worker per machine whereas the Japanese were actively attempting to achieve multi-machine operation. The latter might show, in the cultural terms of Hofstede (1980), the British inclination to 'individualism' and the Japanese to 'collectivism'. However, Whittaker indicates that although Japanese culture has played an important role in the adaptation process to industrialisation and the acceptance of foreign influences, 'groupism and associated values ... cannot in themselves explain the specific institutions of employment relations which shape employer–employee interaction' (p. 32), and no consideration has been paid in his analysis to cultural influences on CNC use in order to focus upon roles that other social institutions are playing, such as the education system and the wage system, in the use of CNC tools under OER and MER.

In recent developments on business process reengineering (BPR), little attention has been paid to cultural, contextual issues other than to deal with them as obstacles to organisational change (Galliers, 1998). However, recent developments in the so-called 'Japanisation' debate should be mentioned here, as they refer to some cultural interactions involved in British industries. According to Mair (1994), European companies have long been sceptical as to whether Japanese management techniques would work outside Japan. The main fear was that European workers would reject Japanese-style workplace behaviours and practices, and thereby undermine the manufacturing methods. Western parochialism and cultural clashes might well lead to a rejection of Japanese ideas without even attempting to understand them properly (Francis and Southern, 1995).

Contrasted with an approach to Japanese manufacturing systems such as Womack, Jones and Roos (1990), who 'pay little attention to the special features of Japanese society' by devoting much attention to so-called 'lean production' (p. 9), Oliver and Wilkinson's (1992) work has some important implications for cultural influences on IT use. Oliver and Wilkinson maintain that British industry is undergoing a fundamental transformation, and it is the conditions and dimensions of this transformation that they seek to explore with the concept of Japanisation. Reviewing the various forms in which Japanese practices such as just-in-time (JIT) production are being introduced into British industries, they have reached a broad conclusion that Japanese firms have been more successful in the introduction of Japanised methods than indigenous companies through the use of greenfield sites and green labour. One of the most important conclusions they obtained is that at the heart of the success of the major Japanese corporations lies their ability to manage their internal and external dependencies in a more effective way than the vast majority of their Western counterparts have traditionally been able to do, and that they have been considerably assisted in this by a supportive set of socio-economic conditions. (p. 88)

Oliver and Wilkinson suggest that the different cultural values of the Japanese from Western people, such as the 'will to endure' and 'loyalty to a group' based on Confucian values, have partially led to the construction of teamwork – a central characteristic of the Japanese work organisation. The transformation of the traditional Western type of work organisation into a 'high-dependence' organisation thus involves political and moral dangers in the sense that the changes may well conflict with existing Western value systems. Taking into consideration the fact that most forms of JIT are based on IT (Abegglen and Stalk, 1985), such conflicts indicate that the implementation of IT in another country is subject to the influence of national cultural value systems.

Bratton's (1992) work presents another theoretical framework within which the Japanese management system can be analysed under the labour process perspective. Using case studies in manufacturing, he evaluates the potential impact of Japanisation on Western industry to explore the hypothesis that JIT production increases managerial control through the application of IT and worker-generated forms of control. As far as Japanese culture is concerned, Bratton suggests that a special 'ideological process' as a moderator is acting on the outcomes such as flexibility, minimum waste, quality and so forth, with the result that 'the employment contract goes beyond a fair day's work for a fair day's pay to mutual commitment tends to sit rather uncomfortably in a Western corporate culture' (p. 33). Again, this can be interpreted as a cultural conflict between Japanese and indigenous British manufacturers in the use of IT-based systems.

Recent works by Lam (1994, 1996, 1997) on international comparisons between British and Japanese firms are relevant to the theme of the present study. Based on a comparison of engineers' work and the relationship between the technical and managerial function in electronics firms in the two countries, Lam (1996) argues that the mechanistically structured organisation systems in British firms generate a vertical polarisation between technical and managerial roles to a relatively higher degree than is the case with Japanese firms, which inhibits knowledge-sharing and leads to the gross underutilisation of engineers in product development. Acknowledging that the divergent characteristics reflect general differences in the organisation of knowledge and technical work commonly found between electronics firms in the two countries, Lam (1997) extends the discussion and highlights the importance of knowledge structures and work systems in influencing the success of collaborative ventures. Applying and extending Polanyi's (1966) concept of 'tacit knowledge', and based on an empirical analysis of technological collaboration between British and Japanese firms, these studies clarify how differences in the organisation of knowledge and work between firms in different societal settings can inhibit collaborative work and impede effective knowledge transfer across national boundaries. She proposes to distinguish the Japanese 'organisational' from the British 'professional' model of the organisation of knowledge. Whereas the 'professional' model stresses standardised and context-free knowledge acquired through formal training, the 'organisational' model is more concerned with highly tacit and context-bounded knowledge which can be mainly obtained through firm-specific on-the-job training (OJT) on a long-term basis. Referring to such concepts as 'knowledge of experience' by Nonaka (1994) and 'the distributive nature of contextual knowledge within a community of practice' by Barley (1996), she explains a feature of the organisational model: 'the knowledge-in-use is embedded in specific organisational routines and operating procedures understood and shared by members with common experience and values' (Lam, 1997, p. 977). This insight is full of suggestions for the present study, as it indicates that organisational IT use is subject to the cultural and value systems in which the organisation is embedded. However, it cannot resolve the question of the extent to which British and Japanese firms are based on different cultural systems from each other in their operation, and the possible implications for organisational IT use.

A recent work by Bensaou and Earl (1998) on a comparison about how Western and Japanese managers frame IT management is relevant for the theme of the present study.[6] They suggest that Japanese managers have a different 'mind-set' for managing IT compared to Western counterparts. They insist that a different framing for the management of IT can be observed in terms of the following five dimensions:

1 *How do they decide what are their business needs?* In Western framing, they would develop an IT strategy that aligns their business strategy ('strategic alignment'), whereas in Japanese framing they would let

the basic way they compete, especially their operational goals, drive IT investments ('strategic instinct').

2   *How will they know whether IT investments are worthwhile*? In Western framing, they would adapt capital-budgeting processes to manage and evaluate IT investments ('value for money'), whereas in Japanese framing they would judge investments based on operational performance improvements ('performance improvement').

3   *When they are trying to improve a business process, how does technology fit into their thinking*? Western people assume that technology offers the smartest, cheapest way to improve performance ('technology solutions'), whereas Japanese people usually try to identify a performance goal and then select a technology that helps them achieve it in a way that supports the people doing the work ('appropriate technology').

4   *How should IT users and IT specialists connect in their organisation*? In Western framing, they would teach specialists about business goals and develop technically adept CIOs (chief information officers) ('IT user relations'), while in Japanese framing they would encourage integration by rotating managers through the IT function, co-locating specialists and users to executives who also oversee other functions ('organisational bonding').

5   *How can they design systems that improve organisational performance*? Western people would design the most technically elegant system possible and ask employees to adapt to it ('system design'), while Japanese people would design the system to make use of the tacit and explicit knowledge that employees already possess ('human design').

(Bensaou and Earl (1998, p. 121))

This indicates that there are some striking differences in the ways Western and Japanese managers perceive IT management. For example, Western managers assume that the most advanced form of IT offers the smartest and cheapest way to improve performance, whereas Japanese managers first identify a performance goal and then select a technology – sometimes advanced IT but sometimes simpler forms of technology – that helps them achieve it in a way that supports the people doing the work. In addition, Western managers teach IS specialists about business goals and develop technically adept, 'business-savvy' CIOs, while Japanese managers are encouraged towards integration by rotating through the IT function, co-locating specialists and users with executives who also oversee other functions. Although Bensaou and Earl (1998) do not specify reasons for the differences, these different patterns of IT design and use seem to reflect national cultural differences between Western countries and Japan, as they indicate a different underlying philosophy in framing IT management.

Overall, however, this review suggests that few studies to date have explicitly focused on British/Japanese cultural influences on IT use, based on the emergent perspective discussed in the last section.

Conclusion

This chapter has developed a review of previous studies on the theme of IT and national culture in an organisational setting. The review has been developed along three axes: the relationship between IT and organisation structure, the concept of national culture in organisational IT use, and the specific British/Japanese cultural influences on the organisational use of IT. The threefold review has illuminated the research agendas, how to approach and analyse, and to what extent the previous studies have clarified the issues. Firstly, through the review of previous studies on the relationship between technology and organisational structure it has been revealed that 'the emergent perspective' holds better for the IT era than the other two perspectives of technological determinism and organisational choice. Given such dispositions of IT as involving 'stochastic and continuous processing' (Weick, 1990, p. 9), it is important to acknowledge that the relationship between technology and organisations is an interactive one and not based on linear causality which technological/organisational determinism would hold. The emergent perspective seems to be useful in indicating some of the mechanisms through which national culture may influence IT use and, if so, what implications the influences have for its use. However, it also raises the question of whether it is possible to isolate and disentangle technological effects from other influences on organisational IT use.

Secondly, the review of national cultural influences on organisational IT use shows that relatively few studies have considered cultural effects despite international comparisons. Most studies have neglected cultural influences to focus on institutional influences in their international comparisons. Clark and Staunton's (1989) study and Sorge's (1995) study have some important suggestions on how cultural influences can be analysed, but still have not clarified what specific national cultural influences operate in the organisational use of IT. Recent developments on the effects of national culture on MIS and GDSS technologies have some implications for IT use, but these studies have been mainly based upon Hofstede's (1980) study on national cultural dimensions with little consideration of the justification of the model. The notion of 'structuration' (Giddens, 1979; Weick, 1990) has been shown to be important to confirm whether or not national culture plays an important role in the emergent process shaping organisational IT use.

Finally, through the review of specific British/Japanese cultural influences on organisational IT use, it has been revealed that national culture has been virtually neglected, or has been dealt with as a residual factor in international comparisons between the two countries. This is partly because more institutional and/or economic factors have been focused on in the analysis of the previous studies, as they have had an interest in the transferability of Japanese 'successful' systems. The discussion on the 'Japanisation' of British industries, though, has some important implications for the theme of this study. Admitting cultural uniqueness, the discussion has disclosed that the Japanisation process, such as the introduction of a JIT system, sometimes does involve cultural conflicts with existing Western values. Lam's (1994, 1996, 1997) works and Bensaou and Earl's (1998) work have also been shown to be useful for the present study. However, they have still not specified what effects national cultural values have on the use of IT.

The review of the previous studies above indicates the necessity of an analytical framework which allows for the analysis of what British/Japanese culture is, and to specify what the cultural effects are in the use of IT in an organisational setting. In other words, a model for analysis is required which makes it possible to judge that the differences resulting from the comparison between the two countries have both originated from and reflect national *cultural* differences rather than other differences, such as economic, institutional and political, between the two countries. Based on the discussion within this chapter, the following chapter will describe research methodologies used to develop the model for analysis and methodological details for collecting empirical data for the study.

3
The Analytical Model and Research Methods

Introduction

The preceding chapter has shown how the concepts of IT use and national culture have been used in an organisational context in previous studies. It has illuminated to what degree previous studies have clarified these concepts and what kinds of drawbacks have been involved in them. Based on this review, this chapter provides explanations for the analytical framework and the research methods used in our study.

I will begin by investigating what kinds of research approach are available in the discipline of IT/IS and which is appropriate for the purpose of this study. My analysis will make clear that the survey approach is well-suited for the topic being pursued. I will discuss how I approach IT use in an organisational setting and the analytical levels of IT use which are to be examined, and in the following section focus on how to operationalise national culture in the study including a review and discussion of some previous studies on conceptualisation and operationalisation of national culture. Then, specifying patterns of IT use which are sensitive to cultural influences, I develop a model of cultural influences on organisational IT use. The whole analytical framework used for the study is presented, and explanations of methodological details follow. Some preliminary work for the field study and the pilot study done before the survey are also given and the chosen techniques of data collection and the structure of the collected data are illustrated in the final section.

The relevance of a survey-based approach for the study

The survey as opposed to case study approach

A number of research approaches have been identified in the general field of IS and IT. Galliers (1992) indicated that it is possible to divide the approaches into two camps: the scientific approach and the interpretivist approach. The former comprises laboratory experiments, field experiments, surveys, case studies, theorem proof, forecasting and simulation. The latter includes subjective/argumentative research, action research, descriptive/interpretative research, futures research and role/ game-playing. Despite such varieties of approaches, however, surveys and case studies are among the most often employed approaches in the discipline (Panteli, 1995; Vitalari, 1985; Hamilton and Ives, 1982). Also, Orlikowski and Baroudi (1991) found that, having reviewed 155 research articles in four major journals on information systems[1] published from 1983 to 1988, 49.1 per cent of them were surveys, 27.1 per cent were laboratory experiments, and 13.5 per cent were case studies.

A survey is an approach that aims to take a general view of a phenomenon, in which 'snapshots of practices, situations or views at a particular point in time [are undertaken] using questionnaires or (structured) interviews from which inferences may be made' (Galliers, 1992, pp. 153–4). On the other hand, a case study approach is defined as 'an attempt at describing the relationships which exist in reality, usually within a single organisation or organisational grouping' (p. 151). As such, both approaches have strengths and weaknesses. In the survey approach, a greater number of variables can be studied thus providing a general description of situations in the real world from a variety of viewpoints. Adopting the survey approach increases the ability to generalise the phenomenon; however, it also reduces the insight obtained regarding the causes and processes behind the phenomena under study. On the other hand, a case study approach makes it possible to capture reality in greater detail through an in-depth investigation of a phenomenon in a single organisation or a small number of organisations. However, generalisation becomes difficult because of its restriction to a single event/organisation. Different interpretations of the events by individual researchers are also possible.

There are two main reasons for the present study adopting a survey rather than a case study approach. Firstly, because national culture is a fairly diffuse phenomenon over a nation, the focus on national culture makes it necessary to collect considerably diffuse data, for which a survey approach is best suited. It is not appropriate to judge a feature, for example, which is obtained from a single company, as a truly cultural phenomenon in the nation because of the small sample size. For instance, if in a comparison of managerial preferences in Rover and Honda we find Rover's hierarchical control system and Honda's flat and lean production system, we cannot regard the former as being based on British culture and the latter on Japanese culture. Rather, they should be regarded as exhibiting organisational sub-cultures or their company strategy. Under the perspective of organisational determinism, which was reviewed in the last chapter, a single case study on the relationship between technology and organisational structure would be sufficient, as the main purpose of the perspective is illustrating the possibility for an organisation to choose and design technologies and organisational entities at will according to its requirements. The viewpoint from the 'emergent perspective' on which my analytical framework has been built makes it necessary to take a rather different approach from a single case study, especially considering the research theme of national culture. A survey approach, which is an effective way to obtain fairly diffuse data, is therefore relevant to the study here.

Secondly, this study aims to identify some possible organisational mechanisms through which national culture may influence the emergent relationships between IT and organisations, rather than the more detailed questions of how and why national culture conditions the emergent process. As Panteli (1995) claims, a concern for the 'what' question of a phenomenon is, generally speaking, likely to favour the use of a survey approach, whilst 'how and why' questions are better answered via a case study approach. Thus, the question 'what are the organisational mechanisms through which national culture may influence IT–organisation relationships' is better pursued via the survey approach rather than through the case study approach. As specified in Chapter 1, the aim of this research is not so much to investigate the workings of these organisational mechanisms, but to identify, by indicating such organisational mechanisms, whether cultural influences are an important or unimportant element in the reciprocal emergent processes through which IT use is shaped. A survey approach is rather advantageous to provide answers to such a question, particularly when the research goal is to describe the incidence or prevalence of a phenomenon rather than to describe its processes (Yin, 1984).

It should be noted, however, that the case study approach is actually more popular in the analysis of IT–organisation relationships in terms of an emergent paradigm (Markus and Robey, 1988; Weick, 1990; Orlikowski and Robey, 1991). This is partly because an interpretive methodology is often regarded as useful to understand perceptions in context. However, taking into account the fact that few studies have been conducted which analyse national cultural influences on IT use, and thus little is known about the organisational mechanisms through which cultural effects are channelled, the survey method is necessary to understand the general picture of the possible organisational channels that cultural effects feed into IT use. Arguably, the case study approach should be employed as the next step of analysis which clarifies *how* the wider culture influences IT use in more detail.

Furthermore, the survey approach is more appropriate in order to grasp broadly-based cultural *contextual* influences on the process of interactive IT–organisation developments and the emergent outcomes. Indeed, researching culture in terms of contextual influence is not to suggest that culture's effects are direct or linear, but that they feed into the process of the interaction between IT and organisations through values, that is managerial preferences. The contextual effects of national culture are subtle and indirect (Scarbrough, 1998), which makes it necessary to collect a very broad and large sample and to take a comparative approach. National culture is a macro-level phenomenon – not amenable to micro-level observation.[2]

Techniques for collecting data in the survey

There are several techniques for collecting data from respondents – by postal mail, telephone, email, or face-to-face interviews. I have used the postal mail approach, as this seems the most appropriate way of gathering data from a large number of respondents at low cost. A survey through email is a very cost-effective approach as well, but this is still less common and email is not necessarily available for all respondents in a company. Using the telephone or face-to-face interviews may be effective when the researcher's ability in oral communication is reasonably high, but in an international survey like this study, telephone or face-to-face interviews are not necessarily good research strategies. Despite the drawbacks of the postal mail approach, such as a presumption of respondents' good literacy skills, non-completion by respondents, and relatively low response rates (Glastonbury and MacKean, 1991; Bryman, 1989), the postal mail type of survey still seems a most relevant approach to the present study.

The analytical levels of organisational IT use

In this section, I examine my approach to 'organisational IT use'. The levels of analysis to be discussed are firstly the hierarchical levels of an organisation, and secondly the differentiation of the concept of 'national culture'.

Two hierarchical levels for the analysis: shop-floor and management

In this study I analyse organisational IT use at the shop-floor level and at the line-manager level, there being two main reasons for this choice. Firstly, as reviewed in the preceding chapter, discussions on IT use in organisational settings are developed at both levels. For example, at the shop-floor level, changes in the job content of blue-collar workers under IT have been discussed from various points of view since Braverman (1974); that is, for instance, whether they are upgraded or deskilled/ degraded by the introduction of IT in the workplace. At the management level in the organisation, it is asserted by both academic researchers and practitioners that the roles of middle managers have been changing greatly with the introduction of IT (Osterman, 1991; Applegate, Cash and Quinn-Mills, 1988). It has also been suggested that the number of levels of hierarchy is decreasing, and a flatter organisation or a network organisation is predicted to be emerging (Bessant, 1993; Drucker, 1989; Grootings, 1989). There seem to be few pieces of work in which discussions have been developed at both levels of analysis, which is what I am trying to do in this study.

Secondly, from experiences in my previous study (Kambayashi, 1996a) I was aware that IT affected organisational structure and employees' job content separately at the shop-floor level and at the management level. I found that at the shop-floor level IT made possible more team-oriented design and job boundaries were blurred, but at the management level hierarchical structure was still maintained and frequencies of checks and instructions by superiors to their subordinates increased. These findings suggest that IT use at each level is different and thus it is appropriate to set two levels of analysis.

Managerial preferences and actual practices

In approaching the organisational use of IT, both managerial preferences for IT use and actual practices are focused on. I asked in the questionnaire not only current patterns of IT use in factories in each country, but also their managerial preferences for using IT. It is insufficient to merely investigate current patterns of IT use. As the research objective lies in the possibility of national cultural influences on organisational IT use, data on national culture is required as well as data on current practices of IT use, which I am measuring as 'managerial preferences' in each factory.

As indicated in the introductory chapter, factors other than national culture may influence organisational IT use including the national and/or international economy, decisions made by competitors, foreign intervention, decisions made by suppliers and/or customers, politics, national institutions, national laws and regulations, technologies, trade unions, and/or organisational culture (Mead, 1998). It is important to differentiate mainly national cultural influences from these other factors which might otherwise feed into the analysis. As Tayeb (1988) criticises, many researchers have simply compared a group of managers in each country and observed some differences in the way they view certain aspects of their work, and then have attributed those differences to national culture. As discussed in the last chapter, the emergent view of IT and organisations, on which I am attempting to develop my analysis, raised the question of how far it is possible to isolate technological effects from other influences on IT use. However, the disentanglement of national culture from other factors is made possible to some extent through asking in the questionnaire managerial preferences as proxies for national culture separately from actual practices on IT use. More details on the form of differentiation will be indicated in later sections of this chapter – summarised in Table 3.5.

The operationalisation of national culture and the patterns of IT use

This section discusses how to approach and operationalise national culture and its possible influences on organisational IT use. As I reviewed in the preceding chapter, some studies have suggested possible ways for national culture to affect IT use in an either explicit or implicit way. In this section I develop a more detailed examination of the concept of national culture and how previous studies operationalise the concept in order to obtain suggestions on what kind of approach to national culture is relevant for the study.

Cultural orientations by Kluckhohn and Strodtbeck

As shown in the last chapter, some previous studies have tried to operationalise national culture through analysing its dimensions. Probably the first widely influential attempt to show a systematic comparative model between nations through the concept of culture is that of Kluckhohn and Strodtbeck (1961). The model distinguishes six basic cultural orientations, which reveal the group's perceptions of human conditions:

1 Nature of the people: good/evil/a mixture of good and evil;
2 Person's relationship to nature: dominant/in harmony/subjugation;
3 Person's relationship to other people: lineal(hierarchical)/collateral (collectivist)/individualist;
4 Modality of human activity: doing/being/containing;
5 Focus of human activity: future/present/past;
6 Conception of space: private/public/mixed.

(Kluckhohn and Strodtbeck, 1961, p. 12)

Each orientation includes a range of variations which have implications for management. For example, in terms of the first cultural orientation, the nature of people, the variation 'good' is claimed to be associated with optimism about other people's motivations and capacities, with participation encouraged and direct communication valued, whilst 'evil' is associated more with pessimism and suspicion of peers and subordinates and of negotiation partners. Also, in respect to the third orientation or relationship to others, the variation 'lineal or hierarchical' is said to be associated with respect for authority, 'tall' organisations and communication on a hierarchical basis, whereas 'collateral or collectivist' relates more to relationships within the group and how they influence attitudes towards work, superiors and other groups – members of other groups may be treated with suspicion; and structures and systems that remove the individual from the group and that break down group boundaries are disliked. 'Individualist' implies for management that people primarily perceive themselves as individuals rather than as members of a group, with a corresponding need for systems that maximise opportunities for personal achievement and status – interesting work is more likely to be valued, competition encouraged, with an egalitarian self-image.

Cultural contexts by Hall

The notion of 'cultural contexts' developed by Hall (1976) is another useful approach to analysing national culture. Hall shows how cultures vary in the way their members define and utilise the context when communicating and developing relationships, and he distinguishes between 'high-context' and 'low-context' cultures. According to him, high-context cultures depend heavily on the external environment, situation, and non-verbal behaviour in creating and interpreting communications. People in the cultural group learn from birth to interpret the covert clues given in these contexts when they communicate, so much meaning is conveyed indirectly. For people in low-context cultures, however, the environment is less important and non-verbal behaviour is often ignored; therefore communicators have to provide more explicit information. Thus, in low-context cultures, a direct style of communication is highly valued and uncertainty is disliked in management communications, whilst in high-context cultures, such as Japanese and Arabic, an indirect style of communication is valued (Hall, 1976; Mead, 1998). Some cultural dimensions and characteristics of each culture are summarised below:

1 *Relationships*: long-lasting and deep personal involvement with others in high-context cultures, while shorter in duration and less deep personal involvement with others in low-context cultures;
2 *Messages*: communicated by shared code and a wider range of expressions in high-context cultures, while communicated by explicit, and direct and 'blunt' style in low-context cultures;
3 *Authority*: personally responsible for subordinates' actions in high-context cultures, whereas diffused throughout the bureaucratic system in low-context cultures;
4 *Agreements*: spoken rather than written in high-context cultures, and written rather than spoken in low-context cultures;
5 *Insiders/outsiders*: closely distinguished in high-context cultures, while less closely distinguished in low-context cultures;
6 *Cultural patterns*: ingrained and slow to change in high-context cultures, while faster to change in low-context cultures.
                                                              (Hall, 1976, pp. 105–16)

It is inappropriate to rank different countries based on Hall's model, as it is built on qualitative insights rather than quantitative data. However, according to Hall, generally speaking, high-context cultures include Japan, Korea, China and other Asian countries, compared with low-context cultures such as the USA, Scandinavian countries and Germany.[3]

Hofstede's cultural dimensions

Since Hall's work, the most influential study on national culture has been that of Hofstede (1980, 1991), whose dimensional approach has been used for empirical studies on international comparison by many researchers. As discussed in previous chapters, Hofstede (1980) defined national culture as 'the collective programming of the mind which distinguishes the members of one human group from another' (p. 25) and identifies its four dimensions: 'power distance', 'uncertainty avoidance', 'individualism/collectivism' and 'masculinity/femininity'.[4] In his investigations into the work-related attitudes and values of managers working in subsidiaries of one multinational company in 39 countries, he identified these four main cultural dimensions along which a country can be illustrated to differ from another. According to Hofstede, 'power distance' indicates the extent to which a society accepts that power in institutions and organisations is distributed unequally. 'Uncertainty avoidance' indicates the lack of tolerance in a society for uncertainty and ambiguity. 'Individualism' refers to a loosely-knit social framework in which people are supposed to take care only of themselves and their immediate families; 'collectivism' is defined as a society in which they can expect their relatives, clan or work organisation to look after them. 'Masculinity' is the opposite of femininity in that it stands for a society in which social gender roles are clearly distinct: men are supposed to be assertive, tough and focused on material success; women are supposed to be more modest, tender and concerned with the quality of life.

Hofstede outlined managerial implications for these four cultural dimensions, and Table 3.1 indicates the four cultural dimensions along which Britain and Japan are located by his study. The table shows that considerable differences can be found between the two countries in terms of each dimension. This is especially so with regard to 'uncertainty avoidance' and 'individualism/collectivism', with the differences here being over 40 points in the two dimensions, whereas in the other two dimensions the differences are relatively smaller.

Although Hofstede has made a significant contribution to the study of national culture in organisations in the sense that he has identified its main dimensions and has operationalised the concept, his approach also has some flaws. Firstly, in his investigation he attempted to control corporate/organisational culture by conducting his questionnaire survey on a single multinational company, which has brought about

Table 3.1   Britain and Japan along Hofstede's four cultural dimensions

	Britain	Japan	Average	Standard deviation
Power distance	35(42)	54(33)	52	20
Uncertainty avoidance	35(47)	92(7)	64	24
Individualism/collectivism	89(3)	46(22)	50	25
Masculinity/femininity	66(9)	95(1)	50	20

Note: Adapted from Hofstede (1980, p. 315). Score for each dimension is shown in each cell. The score ranking in each dimension among the 53 countries investigated is indicated within parentheses. 'Average' and 'standard deviation' have been calculated from the 53 countries studied.

suspicions on the national representativeness of the sample. He explains it as follows:

> studying subsidiaries of multinational corporations represents a narrow-sample strategy, but with the advantage that the functional equivalence of the samples is clear. That these samples are atypical does not matter as long as they are atypical in the same way from one country to another.   (Hofstede, 1980, p. 39)

Secondly, Hofstede saw the origin of cultural differences in values, that is the 'mental programmes' that control behaviour in the most diverse areas of the life of an individual. As Sorge and Warner (1986) indicate, it is doubtful whether locating cultural differences in value systems is compatible with his survey-based questionnaire, in which he asked only for values or preferences in each individual. Value differences can thus only be used to explain cultural differences 'to the degree that conscious reference to values or preferences controls their behaviour *ex ante*' (p. 41). There may be some behaviours that cannot be explained by value systems measured through a retrospective survey questionnaire. He thus arrived, according to Tayeb (1988), at his conclusions about the overwhelming influences of cultural factors on organisational behaviour on the basis of speculations rather than hard evidence.

Despite the difficulties and weaknesses indicated above, the point is that the dimensional approach identified by Hofstede has been so influential that many subsequent researchers have used his dimensions to analyse national culture and to conduct international comparisons. In fact, most of the studies that followed Hofstede (1980) have referred to his work and actually used these four dimensions in the operationalisation of national culture for authors' own analyses in many fields (see for example Jaeger, 1986; Kedia and Bhagat, 1988; Smith, 1992, 1994; Hoppe, 1993; Peterson, 1993; Shane, 1994; Chow, Kato and Shields, 1994; Straub, 1994; Griffith, 1996; Mejias *et al.*, 1997; Katz and Townsend, 1998).[5] As Smith (1994) concludes, in spite of such drawbacks and stringent criticisms of Hofstede's work, 'there are no indications that the cultural diversity mapped by Hofstede is in the process of disappearing' (p. 10).

Tayeb's cultural dimensions

As noted above, since Hofstede's influential work most researchers who have focused on national culture have referred to his work or used his dimensional approach, and thus not many studies have developed their own operationalisation of the concept. Tayeb's (1988) work on organ-isational behaviour in India and Britain, however, attempted to find a definition and approach to the notion of national culture. She tackled Hofstede's second problem mentioned above and tried to solve it by using a different questionnaire survey in order to specify what 'a cultural effect' really means. According to her, Hofstede did not empirically investigate cultural effects, that is the relationships between the four dimensions of values and the structures of organisations whose managers participated in the study: 'the relationships are conceptual and specula-tive' (Tayeb, 1994, p. 435). In order to solve the problem, she conducted her fieldwork in three independent stages in India and England: first a comparison between socio-cultural features of Indian and English people; secondly, work-related attitudes held by a sample of Indian and English employees; and thirdly organisational structure and management systems of a sample of carefully selected companies whose employees had participated in the second stage. She explains:

> the first stage aimed at establishing the salient cultural factors attrib-uted to the two peoples. On the basis of the findings of this stage, a series of hypotheses were constructed about the likely work-related values and attitudes which Indian and English employees would be expected to hold . . . then the second and third stages of the study were carried out and the hypotheses were tested against the findings of the first stage. (Tayeb, 1994, p. 436)

Through these stages of selection it was possible to examine the consist-ency between culture and management and to assess what genuine Indian/English culture was and to identify how the sample really reflected the respective cultural values. As a result, she identified six main cultural aspects, some of which are similar to those in Hofstede's work: 'power and authority relationship', 'ambiguity and uncertainty', 'commitment' consisting of 'motivation' and 'individualism', 'trust', 'expectation from a job', and 'management philosophy' (Tayeb, 1988, pp. 104–5).

Cultural attitudes by Adler, Campbell and Laurent

Adler, Campbell and Laurent (1989) is another work which attempted to examine cultural attitudes in different countries following Hofstede's work. They examined attitudes to power and relationships in order to analyse the values of managers in 13 countries (Switzerland, Germany, Denmark, Sweden, Britain, Netherlands, Belgium, Italy, France, the United States, China, Indonesia and Japan).[6] They used four parameters: perceptions of the organisation as political systems; authority systems; role formulation systems; and hierarchical relationship systems. The research focused on (a) how far the manager carries his/her status into the wider context outside the workplace; (b) the manager's capacity to bypass levels in the hierarchy; and (c) the manager as expert in contrast to the manager as facilitator. Table 3.2 shows the percentage in *disagreement* in response to the statement 'in order to have efficient work relationships, it is often necessary to bypass the hierarchical line', whilst Table 3.3 shows the percentages in *agreement* responding to the statement 'it is important for a manager to have at hand precise answers to most of the questions that his subordinates may raise about their work'.

The data in these tables suggest that cultural values ascribed to the hierarchical structuring in an organisation and the role of managers vary among countries. For instance, as indicated in Table 3.2, Swedish employees have a strong tendency to bypass hierarchical lines when direct contact with knowledge sources located elsewhere in the organisation may produce greater efficiency and speed. Table 3.3 shows that it is more important for a manager in Sweden to be able to tap sources of expert power than to be able to give all the technical answers to subordinates by themselves. The Swedish manager uses hierarchical structuring to facilitate problem-solving and organisation. On the other hand,

Table 3.2   Disagreement in bypassing levels in a hierarchy by Adler, Campbell and Laurent

Nation	Percentage
Sweden	22%
Britain	31%
The United States of America	32%
Denmark	37%
Netherlands	39%
Switzerland	41%
Belgium	42%
France	42%
Germany	46%
China	66%
Italy	75%

Note: Adapted from Laurent (1983, p. 86) and Adler, Campbell and Laurent (1989, p. 64).

Table 3.3 Agreement on the idea of the manager as facilitator by Adler, Campbell and Laurent

Nation	Percentage
Sweden	10%
Netherlands	17%
The United States of America	18%
Denmark	23%
Britain	27%
Switzerland	38%
Belgium	44%
Germany	46%
France	53%
Italy	66%
Indonesia	73%
China	74%
Japan	78%

Note: Adapted from Adler, Campbell and Laurent (1989, p. 69).

at the opposite extreme, the Japanese value hierarchical structuring as a means of signalling who has authority over whom.

Trompenaars' cultural dimensions

Trompenaars (1993) is another whose work has provided a set of parameters for analysing national cultural differences. He drew together and applied ideas contributed by some of those discussed earlier in this section to identify seven parameters: (1) interpersonal relationship and rules (universal versus particular); (2) the group and the individual (individualism versus collectivism); (3) feeling and relationship (affective versus neutral); (4) how far we get involved (specific versus diffuse); (5) how we accord status (achievement basis versus age, class, gender, education, and so on); (6) how we manage time (past- and present-oriented versus future-oriented); (7) how we relate to nature (inner-directed, that is controlling nature, versus outer-directed, that is letting it take its course).

As we see, the work of Kluckhohn and Strodtbeck is influential throughout particularly on the first, sixth and seventh parameters. Hofstede's thinking on individualism/collectivism is also reflected in the first and the second, and power distance in the fifth parameters. Adler, Campbell and Laurent's work influences the fourth and the fifth, and Hall's the sixth (Mead, 1998). As Trompenaars himself admits, his work focuses more on the practical problems of dealing with members of other national cultures than on academic needs, which seems a disadvantage in applying his parameters to operationalise the notion of national culture for the study here. Figure 3.1 outlines locations of Britain, Japan and the United States along each parameter.

The discussion so far has examined various models making cross-cultural comparisons on a range of dimensions, and some parameters of national culture have been clarified by these previous studies. Although they are not necessarily exhaustive, they cover the main approaches to national culture and provide some clues for operationalisation of the notion.[7] As the next step, it is necessary to argue which dimensions should be focused upon for the theme here. In other words, it is required to develop a discussion on which cultural dimensions are most relevant to organisational IT use.

Developing a model of cultural influences on IT use

The discussion developed in the preceding section is useful for finding and specifying what patterns of IT use in an organisational setting are sensitive to cultural influences, and Table 3.4 summarises various dimensions of national culture discussed so far. The table shows that the dimensions of national culture vary according to researchers, but share some parameters in common, which suggests some clues as to

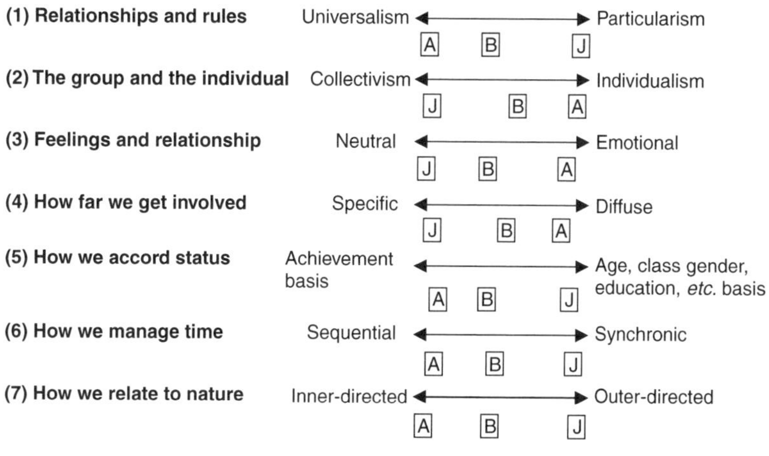

Figure 3.1   Britain, Japan and the USA along Trompenaars' seven dimensions
Note: Approximate location of each country is signified along each parameter. A, B, and J stand for the USA, Britain, and Japan respectively.
Source: Adapted from Trompenaars (1993), pp. 8–11.

Table 3.4 Various dimensions of national culture

Researchers	Indicated dimensions of national culture
Kluckhohn and Strodtbeck (1961)	Nature of people; person's relationship to nature; person's relationship to other people; modality of human activity; focus of human activity; conception of space
Hall (1976)	Relationships to people; means of messages; authority; agreements; insiders/outsiders; cultural patterns
Hofstede (1980)	Power distance; uncertainty avoidance; individualism/collectivism; masculinity/femininity
Tayeb (1988)	Power and authority relationship; ambiguity and uncertainty; commitment (divided into motivation and individualism); trust; expectation from a job; management philosophy
Adler, Campbell and Laurent (1989)*	Perceptions of the organisation as political systems; authority systems; role formulation systems; hierarchical relationship systems
Trompenaars (1993)	Interpersonal relationship and rules; the group and the individual; feeling and relationship; how far we get involved; how we accord status; how we manage; how we relate to nature

Note: * originated from Laurent (1983).

which aspects of national culture are likely to have wider validity in an organisational setting and which therefore may influence organisational IT use.

These various dimensions may be broadly classified into two main categories which I will term a 'control' dimension and a 'relationship' dimension, both of which can be theoretically supported by previous studies as dimensions that are likely to influence organisational IT use. The classification is outlined in Figure 3.2.

Each of the studies suggests that national culture consists of more or less similar dimensions to the summary typology of 'control' and 'relationship' dimensions. Each model shares the two dimensions in common as its components of national culture, which suggests that these dimensions reflect more generally-accepted aspects of national culture than others. Of course, each model includes some dimensions which do not directly relate to the two dimensions: 'conception of space' in Kluckhohn and Strodtbeck's (1961) work and 'perceptions of the organisation

National culture

Control dimension	Relationship dimension
• Linear/hierarchical relationship to other people	• Collectivist/individualist relationship to other people
• Authority	• High/low content cultures
• Power distance; uncertainty avoidance	• Individualism/collectivism
• Power and authority relationship	• Individualistic commitment
• Ambiguity and uncertainties	• The group and the individual
• Authority systems	
• Hierarchical relationship systems	
• Interpersonal relationship and rules	

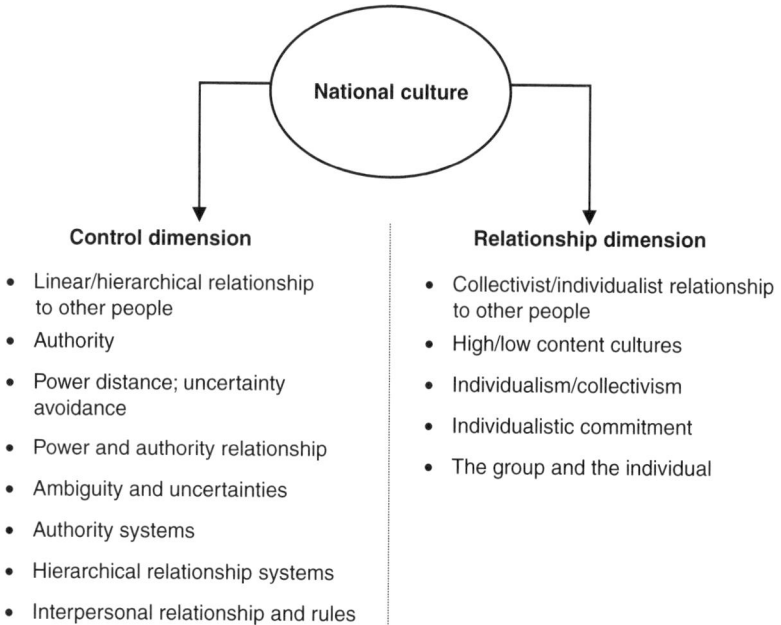

Figure 3.2   Two main dimensions of national culture

as political systems' in Adler, Campbell and Laurent's (1989) work, for instance. However, while the 'control' and 'relationship' dimensions are common to *each* cultural model in broad terms, they are reflected differentially in each. Therefore, my analysis below will clarify in detail the attributes of the two main dimensions of national culture and their relationships with patterns of IT use.

The control dimension and components

As shown in Figure 3.2, the first group is a set of dimensions which are thought to be associated with organisational hierarchy and/or authority system. Hall's (1976) parameter of 'authority', Hofstede's (1980) 'power distance' and 'uncertainty avoidance', Tayeb's (1988) 'power and authority relationship', and Adler, Campbell and Laurent's (1989) 'authority system' and 'hierarchical relationship system' seem to represent different but related aspects of hierarchy and control. According to Hall (1976), while authority is diffused throughout the bureaucratic hierarchical system and personal responsibilities are difficult to pin down in 'low-context cultures', people in authority are personally responsible for the actions of subordinates in 'high-context cultures'. Hofstede (1980) maintained that 'power distance' refers to the distance between individuals at different levels of a hierarchy, and suggested that in an 'uncertainty avoidance' culture clear rules and regulations are welcomed, managers are prone to issue clearer instructions and subordinates' initiatives are more tightly controlled through a hierarchical authority system.

Tayeb's (1988) concepts of 'power and authority relationship' and 'ambiguity and uncertainty' also address organisational hierarchy. She argues that if in a society there is a wide power and authority gap between seniors and juniors, the same pattern is reflected in an unequal power relationship between superiors and subordinates in an organisation in that society, in the form of high centralisation and low consultation through a hierarchy. In a society with low tolerance for uncertainty, organisational members are more likely to display mechanisms by which they can buffer themselves against the uncertainty. Such mechanisms manifest themselves 'in greater use of rules and regulations and detailed definitions of areas of discretion and responsibility' (Tayeb, 1988, p. 45). Adler, Campbell and Laurent's (1989) empirical examination of a manager's capacity to bypass levels in the hierarchy and on the manager's role as expert versus facilitator, obviously also relates to the organisational hierarchical system.

Characterising these parameters in terms of possible influence on IT use suggests that one likely expression of their influence is to do with the use of IT for purposes of hierarchical control and the imposition of authority. Although it is problematic to move from the plane of culture to that of IT applications, the above-mentioned analyses suggest that for exploratory purposes the variable of 'control-oriented IT use' (CIU) can be proposed as a reasonably important indicator of possible cultural influences at the appropriate level of abstraction. CIU will be defined as a pattern of organisational IT use in which IT is deployed primarily for the purposes of controlling activities in a hierarchical fashion. The process of the operationalisation of national culture and its relationships with CIU is provided in Figure 3.3.

As shown in the figure, the cultural models developed by the various authors tend to support my view that the variable of CIU is likely to reflect cultural influences. The parameters which the above-mentioned cultural models indicate can be reasonably expected to operate as a hierarchical pattern of IT use. Managerial preferences which are highly control-oriented can be usefully operationalised in terms of information flows and job content (Francis, 1986): important information will be

| Cultural models | Kluckhohn and Strodtbeck (1961)
Hall (1976)
Hofstede (1980)
Tayeb (1988)
Adler, Campbell and Laurent (1989)
Trompenaars (1993) |

| Cultural dimension | 'Control' dimension |

Linear/hierarchical relationship to other people
Authority
Power distance; uncertainty avoidance
Power and authority relationship; ambiguity and uncertainties
Authority systems; hierarchical relationship systems
Interpersonal relationship and rules, etc.

| The variable | Control-oriented IT use (CIU) |

| Questions | Managerial preferences (*cf.* Table 3.5)
Actual practices (*cf.* Table 3.5) |

Note: ■▶ denotes operationalising process ; ┅▶ denotes possible intervening factors.

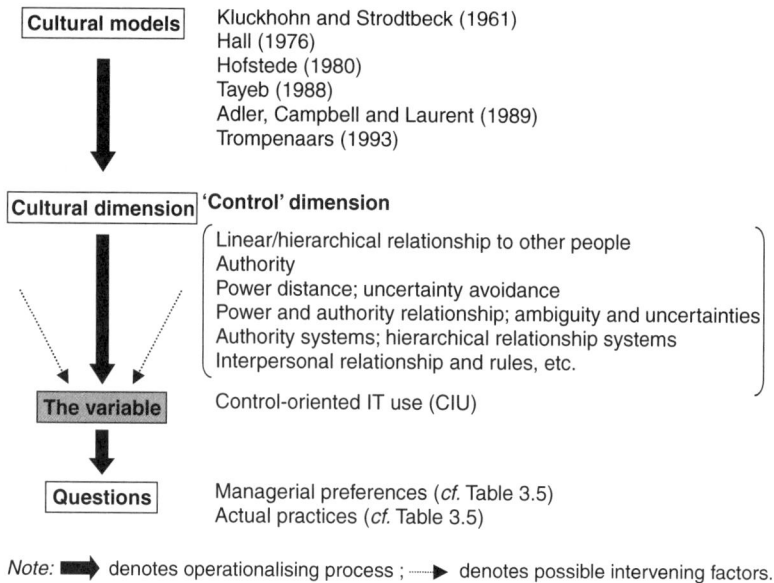

Figure 3.3 Operationalising process of national culture and its relationship with CIU

concentrated in top management (Q5a in the survey questionnaire discussed later in this chapter; see Appendix and Table 3.5); information will flow on a top-down basis reflected in the organisational hierarchy (Q5b); and job contents of employees will be designed as simply as possible (Q5c). In practical terms, the managerial preferences are likely to develop as follows at the shop-floor level: the preference for the concentration of important information for top management would operate as, for instance, limited access for a shop-floor worker to strategic information databases such as sales forecasts (Q6a, *cf.* Kambayashi, 1996b, 1998). In order to minimise uncertainty at work, workers would be given more quantitative information, such as production target rates, than qualitative information like briefings on company performance (Q6c,d). Many checks and instructions through hierarchical control would be provided to eliminate abnormalities (Q6b), resulting in little sharing of information with other workers at lateral levels (Q6e, *cf.* Susman, 1990). As a result, shop-floor workers would have jobs that are as simplified and standardised as possible (Q7c, *cf.* Davis and Wacker, 1987), and it might be impossible for them to be engaged in 'unusual operations' to deal with problems and changes flexibly (Q7d, *cf.* Koike, 1988).

At the management level, the managerial preference for the concentration of important information for top management would operate in a similar way to the shop-floor level, including limited access for line managers to strategic information databases (Q9a). The preference for top-down information flow may need hierarchical control of information in a factory (Q10b), which tends to make a line manager's job a 'liaison role' centring on communicating instructions to subordinates (Q10a), as was shown in Adler, Campbell and Laurent's (1989) work. The preference for simple job design, coupled with the parameter of top-down information flow, would lead a factory, for example, to gain less information from across different functional boundaries (Q9c). Also it is presumed that a higher control-orientation may well need rapid access to information databases when problems occur on the line (Q9b), thus requiring a line manager to report the problems to a senior manager (Q10c). The relationship between managerial preferences and their operational forms, that is actual practices of IT use, will be summarised later in Table 3.5.

As indicated in Figure 3.3, however, it should be noted that some intervening factors other than national culture, such as management systems and societal institutions, can intrude in the operationalising process. For example, traditional Tayloristic management, incorporating principles of 'scientific management' for avoiding 'uncertainties' and systematic soldiering at the shop-floor, which have prevailed in many nations beyond cultural differences (Warner, 1994), requires the concentration of information at the top management level which Frederick W. Taylor calls the 'planning department'. The information is then distributed via the organisational hierarchy, resulting in simple job design, expressed as a 'one-man, one-job' system (Francis, 1986). In this sense, the effects of national culture cannot be unmediated and may be diluted with other influences. Nevertheless, the effects of national culture still exist and the way intervening factors influence actual practices depends in part on their assimilation and adaptation within the particular national culture. As Scarbrough and Terry (1998) suggest, such systematic and institutional innovation tends to be selectively reinvented within its particular social contexts and the wider contextual influences are important in shaping the changes.

The relationship dimension and components

Referring to Figure 3.2, the second group of dimensions of national culture identified in Table 3.4 is associated with the person's relationship to other people. As discussed earlier, Kluckhohn and Strodtbeck (1961) suggested that there are three ways in which a person develops a relationship with other people: lineal or hierarchical, collateral or collectivist, and individualist. Similar parameters can be identified in other authors' works as well: Hall's concept of 'relationship to people' suggests that relationships are relatively long-lasting and individuals feel a deep personal involvement with each other in high-context cultures, whilst relationships between individuals are relatively shorter in duration and in general deep personal involvement with others is valued less in low-context cultures. Also, he suggests that *insiders* and *outsiders* are closely distinguished in the former cultures whilst they are less closely distinguished in the latter cultures: here *outsiders* refer to non-members of the family, clan, organisation and so forth.

Hofstede's (1980) dimension of 'individualism/collectivism' is a similar concept to Hall's. According to Hofstede, in collectivist cultures the distinction made between in- and out-groups means that altruism may be restricted to members of a group; a higher premium is placed on group loyalty which is valued above efficiency. Employees in collectivist cultures expect organisations to look after them like a family member, and organisational procedures are based on loyalty and a sense of duty (Watson and Brancheau, 1992). On the other hand, individualist cultures are claimed to stress individual achievements and rights and expect the individual to focus on satisfying their own needs; individual decisions are valued over and above group decisions and thus individuals show loyalty as long as it suits their interests. As shown in the last section, both Tayeb (1988) and Trompenaars (1993) point out approximately similar parameters to Hofstede's concept.

These parameters can be reasonably expected to influence the pattern of organisational IT use. The above-mentioned analyses suggest that for exploratory purposes the variable of 'individual-oriented IT use' (IIU) can be proposed as another important indicator of possible cultural influences at the appropriate level of abstraction, which indicates the extent to which a person's relationship with other people in the use of IT shows an individualist pattern. This means that IIU will be defined as a pattern of organisational IT use in which an organisational member uses IT on an individual basis rather than on a group basis. The relationships between national culture and IIU are illustrated in Figure 3.4.

It is possible to propose that IIU reflects the cultural attributes discussed above and influences managerial preference for IT use in the following form: individual instead of group-based transmission of infor-

| Cultural models | Kluckhohn and Strodtbeck (1961)
Hall (1976)
Hofstede (1980)
Tayeb (1988)
Adler, Campbell and Laurent (1989)
Trompenaars (1993) |

| Cultural dimension | **'Relationship' dimension**
Collectivist/individualist relationship to other people
High/low context cultures
Individualism/collectivism
Individualistic commitment
The group and the individual: collectivism/
individualism, etc. |

| The variable | Individual-oriented IT use (IIU) |

| Questions | Managerial preferences (*cf.* Table 3.5)
Actual practices (*cf.* Table 3.5) |

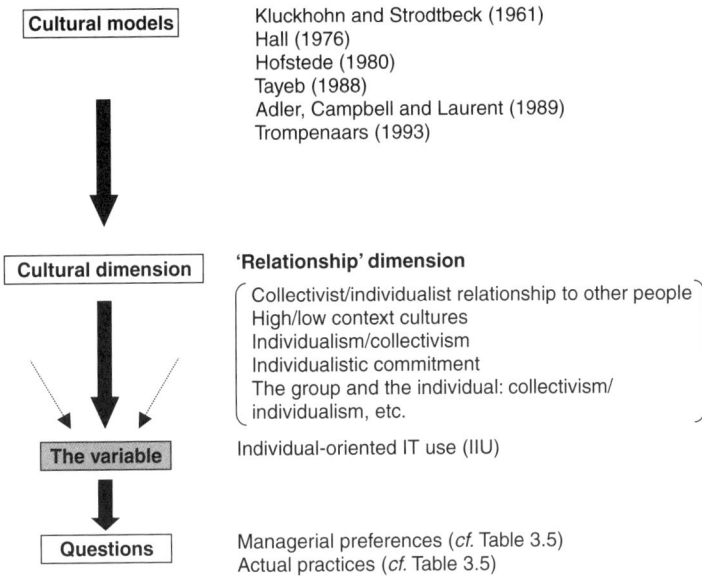

Note: ▶ denotes operationalising process ; ┈▶ denotes possible intervening factors.

Figure 3.4   Operationalising process of national culture and its relationship with IIU

mation; team-based rather than individual-based use of IT; and sticking to a particular job using a single IT-based system rather than frequent job rotation. Under IIU, it is possible to postulate that individual transmission of information is preferred to the collectivistic method of transmission where the distribution of information to each individual is up to the group (Q5d); employees prefer an individualistic way of work rather than in team/group formation under IIU (Q5e); and each employee would stick to a single individual job and frequent rotation would not be a good idea, as the job would be specified in terms of the individual (Q5c). In actual terms, these managerial preferences will operate as follows at the shop-floor level: the preference for individual transmission instead of group-oriented transmission of information would make a factory choose a strategy to give each employee their own computer passwords (Q6f). As indicated in Chapter 2 (p. 30), much previous literature suggests that teamwork may involve conflict among members when a Japanese company, whose value system is based on groupism/collectivism, constructs factories in a Western society in which individualist values prevail in every part (Oliver and Wilkinson, 1992; Elger and Smith, 1994; Womack, Jones and Roos, 1990). The preference for teamwork would lead a factory to adopt teamwork as the usual way of organisation (Q7a). Also, as suggested by Okubayashi (1995), it is possible to presume that in a highly individualised society each worker would stick to his/her individual role, so that there would be little incentive to help each other at work (Q7b) and there would be little job rotation (Q7e).

At the management level, the managerial preference for individual transmission of information would likely involve a factory providing individual managers with their own computer passwords for gaining access to information databases (Q9d). The managerial preference for teamwork may lead a factory to use a group-oriented work system such as GDSS particularly in the context of IT use (Q10d, *cf.* Briggs, Nunamaker and Sprague, 1998). In the use of GDSS, information-sharing in the group may be achieved through regular/irregular exchanges of information among members on line (Q9e). The managerial preference for a fixed job system may well bring about a line manager's sticking to a particular section and frequent job rotations may not be practised (Q10e). As with CIU, some intervening factors other than national culture may influence actual practices. Nevertheless, the effects of national culture still exist and the way such intervening factors influence actual practices depends in part on their assimilation and adaptation within the particular national culture (Scarbrough and Terry, 1998).

The relationship between CIU and IIU

As shown above, CIU and IIU are patterns of organisational IT use which are arguably sensitive to national cultural influences with respect to the previous studies. These variables are more likely to display the influence of the cultural context in the form of CIU and IIU, if such influences operate in the use of IT in a factory in each country.

Although CIU and IIU have been conceptualised independently in the above discussion, it seems possible for the two patterns of IT use to relate to each other. For instance, the preference for the concentration of important information for top management would operate as limited access for an employee to strategic information databases – that is the aspect of CIU – but may also help develop individual access to information databases rather than adopt team/group access – the aspect of IIU. Indeed, Hofstede (1980) admits that a weak correlation has been found in his sample between the 'uncertainty avoidance' and 'individualism' indices.

However, my analysis below will treat the two patterns of IT use independently and thus present the data on the dimensions of CIU and IIU separately. Although there may be a case for analysing the relationship between CIU and IIU, the main focus of the present study lies in clarifying the broad hypothesis that national culture influences the patterns of IT use rather than analysing the relationship between CIU and IIU in detail. Taking into account the fact that little is known about cultural influences on IT use (*cf.* Chapter 2, pp. 17–26), it is necessary to examine in the first place whether cultural influences are an important or unimportant factor in organisational IT use. The analysis of the detailed relationship between CIU and IIU might lead to a failure to see the broad picture of cultural influences. Arguably, the detailed relationship should be analysed as the next step of analysis after some cultural influences are shown to be evident in the data collected.

What I will present in subsequent chapters is different CIU and IIU tendencies which can be found in British factories, Japanese factories and Japanese factories located in Britain (JFB). A number of possible influences apart from national culture may be investigated. As I will discuss in Chapter 4, some of these, such as types of IT/systems and industry, will be controlled for. Other possible differences between countries, such as economic, institutional and political influences, may be present in the data collected. However, taking into consideration the importance of CIU and IIU as explanatory factors which were developed from cultural models in previous studies discussed above, some national cultural influences will be expected to be evident in the data collected.

The analytical model and the hypothesis

Incorporating the above-mentioned discussions, the whole analytical framework for the present study on the influences of national culture upon organisational IT use is summarised in Figure 3.5. As indicated in this figure, my analysis tries to examine national cultural influences on organisational IT use, mediated by contextual factors (shown in square brackets in the middle of the figure). Another factor considered to be controlled for is the kind of IT/systems in use. These factors correspond to the factors discovered by Sorge *et al.* (1983) to have a key influence on CNC use. These factors should be controlled for, or their influences should be minimised, in the analysis of the influences of national

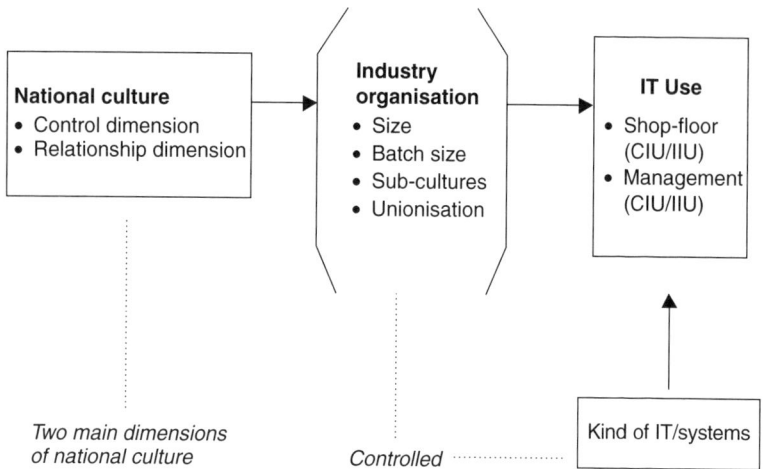

Figure 3.5 shows a flow diagram with the following boxes:

National culture
- Control dimension
- Relationship dimension

→

Industry organisation
- Size
- Batch size
- Sub-cultures
- Unionisation

→

IT Use
- Shop-floor (CIU/IIU)
- Management (CIU/IIU)

Two main dimensions of national culture

Controlled

Kind of IT/systems

Figure 3.5   The analytical model

culture on organisational IT use in order that mainly national cultural effects are differentiated.

Firstly, IT use depends on the kind of IT/systems installed in the organisation; the technologies/systems used are expected to be more or less similar in the nations concerned (Clark, 1987; Clark and Newell, 1993). Secondly, IT use also depends upon contextual factors such as industry and organisation. An identical industry shares its competitors and suppliers which might influence organisational IT use. The characteristics of an individual organisation, for instance its size, the batch size in the factory, its special organisational sub-cultures and the level of unionisation, might also influence the pattern of organisational IT use. By controlling for these factors it is possible to specify the effects of national culture on IT use in a factory.[8] Through comparisons on CIU and IIU among British factories, Japanese factories, and JFB, it is possible to examine whether national culture influences organisational IT use.

As mentioned in Chapter 2, the preceding chapter and earlier in this chapter, a large number of previous studies on national culture have built some hypotheses focusing on a few cultural dimensions based on Hofstede's (1980, 1991) work, for example 'uncertainty avoidance', and have attempted to test them. For instance, this has involved a hypothesis that 'the higher the "uncertainty avoidance" of a society, the more people in the society prefer to ensure that champions work within the organisation's rules and standard operating procedures to develop the innovation' (Shane, Venkataraman and MacMillan, 1995, p. 936). Also, Katz and Townsend (1998), in an article discussing the influence of national culture on organisational structure, set and test some hypotheses such as:

> in cultures where high levels of 'power distance' and/or 'uncertainty avoidance' exist, more effective organisations will be characterised by decision-making, low levels of delegation, low levels of job autonomy, and information systems that are less intrusive to the non-managerial worker. In such cultures, functional structures will be the most commonly used organisational structures. (p. 9)

However, I am not constructing a hypothesis to be tested only on the basis of the dimensions of national culture suggested by Hofstede's work. That might involve a methodological danger, as Hofstede's cultural dimensions have been measured by some specific variables. For instance, 'uncertainty avoidance' is a concept measured in his questionnaire survey with a scale of the degree of preference for rule orientation, employment stability and work stress. The rule orientation item in the questionnaire is: 'company rules should not be broken – even if the employee thinks it is the company's best interest', with a five-point scale from 'strongly agree' to 'strongly disagree' (Hofstede, 1980, pp. 161–2). Also, his 'individualism' index is based on mean answer scores on 14 'work goals' questions in the questionnaire, such as: 'how important is it to you to have an opportunity for high earnings?'; and 'how important is it to you to fully use your skills and abilities on the job?' (*ibid.*, p. 220). The problem of using cultural dimensions developed by Hofstede in our investigations is that they grasp only one part of the features of a society. This leads me to question whether Hofstede's categories are really appropriate and relevant to the dimensions that we are to measure.

Furthermore, taking account of the fact that, as indicated in the introductory chapter, there have not been many previous studies on national cultural influences on IT use, the present study here should be more exploratory. As was indicated in the concepts of CIU and IIU, the empirical data gathered through the survey should be about the patterns of IT use instead of cultural dimensions. My focus lies on clarifying the broad hypothesis that national culture influences the patterns of IT use, and my analysis is more data-driven and does not test Hofstede's model as such. I report my data to suggest explanations in an exploratory and propositional way rather than in a model-testing and deductive way.

Preliminary work for the field study

Before this study began, in 1994, I had engaged in a research project with my colleagues in which we investigated the influences of IT on organisational structure in Japanese factories in Japan. Although some findings were presented (Kambayashi, 1995, 1996a, 1996b, 1998; Okubayashi *et al.*, 1994), there were some methodological shortcomings in the project. Firstly, coupled with ambiguity on definitions of the concepts IT and organisation structure, its analytical framework could not examine the real 'influences' of IT on organisation structure. Under its framework it was difficult to differentiate true IT effects, as all the questions asked in the questionnaire were just how firms perceived the changes in the last five years of some features of work organisation and of personnel management system. Secondly, industrial differences were not taken into consideration in the analysis. Samplings of non-manufacturing firms as well as manufacturing firms were included to get a general picture of Japanese firms, and little effort was made to avoid industrial differences. Thirdly, despite the fact that the initial objective of the project had been to clarify features of *Japanese* work organisation as opposed to their counterparts in other countries, no international comparison was conducted.

These drawbacks of my previous research project led me to an international research project on the relationship of IT and organisation structure. For this project, it seemed that it was necessary to solve the shortcomings mentioned above; not only refining key concepts such as IT and organisation structure, and so forth, but also constructing an analytical model to control for sector differences. The national cultural differences should be targeted in a single aspect: national culture, in order to explore how the national difference may affect IT use in organisational contexts. All these considerations led me to construct the analytical model developed in the previous section.

Pilot study

A pilot study was carried out separately before the British and Japanese surveys, after the development of the conceptual framework already discussed and the initial version of the questionnaire. This was an important process to illuminate possible weaknesses of the analytical framework and concepts which were not necessarily familiar to business practitioners, as getting data from firms through questionnaires was vital for my study. A pilot study in Britain was conducted with a small group of managers (a production director, an operations director and a manufacturing manager) employed in the British manufacturing sector. A pilot study was also conducted in Japan with a production director and two production managers filling in the Japanese translated version of the questionnaire.[9] Attention was paid not only to comments and suggestions on the content of the questionnaire and the cover letter, but also to the length of time taken to fill in the questionnaire.

Both in the British and Japanese pilot studies, the structure of the questionnaire was generally supported. Most of the concepts used were easily understood, and no radical changes were needed. Also, it took about 10 minutes to fill in the questionnaire both in the British and Japanese pilot studies, which was the length of time originally intended. However, the following suggestions were made in the British pilot study. Firstly, the term 'middle manager' was suggested to be ambiguous for business practitioners, and changed to 'line manager' – this term also being used in the Japanese survey. Secondly, although 10 questions on work systems for the shop-floor and management levels were prepared for in the initial version of the questionnaire, the pilot study revealed that it was necessary to categorise these questions into a few groups in order to make it easier for a respondent to reply. Thirdly, other minor revisions to improve the response rate were made, such as aligning check boxes in an identical column and shortening the length of each statement.

In the Japanese pilot study, it was difficult to make radical changes from the British survey questionnaire, since the data from both countries would be compared with each other.[10] However, some parts of the questionnaire did need modifications to fit the Japanese situation. For example, a different classification of industries is employed in Japan, therefore the question on belonging to an industrial classification in the questionnaire (*cf.* Q14a in Appendix) was modified into the Japanese standard industrial classification (SIC) code. One of the biggest problems was, however, the translation of the English version of the questionnaire into Japanese. It was necessary for the questionnaire to be written in Japanese in the Japanese survey, as it was expected that few respondents would reply to an English version. In the pilot study in the Japanese survey, the translation was checked carefully and revised many times until the Japanese became clear and straightforward. One of the most important things to keep in mind during the translation was that the Japanese should not be a word-for-word translation of the English version, but be equivalent in terms of its meanings. Although differences in languages in an international comparison is a factor which is quite difficult to be controlled for, I have attempted to minimise the difference in the meanings and nuances through a back-translation from Japanese into English, with the help of a colleague whose native language is English.

These pilot studies were needed to improve response rates which were one of the key factors for a successful survey-based research project. Based on the comments received and suggestions noted above, I reformulated the final version of questionnaire which is given in the Appendix.

The structure of the survey

After the improvement of the questionnaire based on the suggestions and comments received during the pilot studies, the questionnaire was sent to each sampled company. This self-administered postal question- naire was the main source of data in the study. Methodological details such as the construction of the questionnaire, sampling procedures and the structure of the samples are explained in this section. I begin by illustrating the construction of the questionnaire sent, to indicate how each question reflects each concept developed in the previous sections, such as managerial preferences, actual practices, CIU and IIU.

The design of the questionnaire

As shown in the Appendix in this volume, the questionnaire consisted of 14 questions, which can be classified into three main groups: ques- tions on the technologies/systems installed (Q1 to Q4); on patterns of organisational IT use (Q5 to Q13); and on company/factory profiles (Q14). The main focus of the questionnaire lies in the patterns of organ- isational IT use, but the questions on the technological basis used in each factory are also required to understand what kind of technologies are used and to understand the necessity to control for the factor if appropriate. Question 14 is also needed to understand the institutional aspects of each respondent, such as the line of business, size of the com- pany and the factory/plant, and the year established and the unionisa- tion of the workforce. Each question, except the space for free comments at the end, was designed in the form of simple box-checking or number-circling, to enable the respondent to complete the question- naire with minimum effort.

The questions on the patterns of organisational IT use consisted of questions on managerial preferences for IT use (Q5) and actual practices on IT use (Q6 to Q12). The questions on actual practices consisted of questions for the shop-floor level (Q6, 7, 8 and 11) and for the management level (Q9, 10 and 12). (Regarding the process of development of each question and the theoretical justifications from previous literature, see above, pp. 51ff.) The overall relationship between each question in the questionnaire is shown in Table 3.5.

Sampling procedures

The survey was conducted at the establishment level of three types of manufacturing firm: British firms, Japanese firms, and Japanese firms located in Britain. The following databases were used to check how many firms exist in each country: 'One Source for Windows, volume 1, March 1997 version' for the surveys of British factories and JFB (hereafter 'the British survey'), and 'the Digital Data Service' by Diamond Corporation for the survey of Japanese factories (hereafter 'the Japanese survey'). All the firms on the databases were stratified into two bands by their size in terms of the number of employees: 'less than 200' and '200 or more'. The group of '200 or more' was selected as the object of sampling, as our focus lay in organisational IT use in large firms rather than in small- and medium-sized firms. This has the benefit of substantially increasing the homogeneity of the sample, as compared with the diversity that would arise if small- and medium-sized firms were included. The largest factory for each firm in terms of its size (that is the number of employees) was specified and selected as the object of sampling according to the databases.[11]

Five industries were particularly targeted for the survey: chemicals/pharmaceuticals, machinery, electrical engineering, transportation, and rubber/plastic products. There were several reasons for this selection. Firstly, according to the databases the number of firms in each country was relatively higher in these industries than in other industries, which made it possible to make comparisons within each sector among the three groups of factories. According to the databases, the number of British factories, Japanese factories or JFB was rather limited in other industries – this was particularly the case with JFB. Considering that the larger the sample, the greater the prospect of generalisation and statistically valid results (Glastonbury and MacKean, 1991), it is appropriate to sample the five largest industries.

Secondly, these industries have relatively greater reputations for innovation in organisation design on the back of IT. For example, chemicals in Britain is a capital-intensive industry with a reputation

Table 3.5 Patterns of IT use, managerial preferences and actual practices

Patterns of IT use	Managerial preferences	Actual practices	
		Shop-floor level	Line-manager level
Control-oriented IT use (CIU)	• Concentration of important information at the top (5a) • Top-down information flow (5b) • Simple job design (5c)	• Accessibility to strategic information (6a)* • Use of information provided by managers (6b) • Amount of quantitative information (6c) • Amount of qualitative information (6d)* • Sharing information with other workers (6e)* • Simplified and predetermined jobs (7c) • Dealing with daily problems of the line (7d)*	• Accessibility to strategic information (9a)* • Rapid access to information databases in a problematic situation (9b) • Gaining less information from across different functional boundaries (9c)* • Liaison as the main job (10a) • Communicating instructions as the most important role (10b) • Need to report major problems to senior managers (10c)
Individual-oriented IT use (IIU)	• Individual transmission of information (5d) • Teamwork (5e)* • Fixed job system (5f)	• Having individual password for gaining access to relevant databases (6f) • Organised in teams (7a)* • Helping each others to finish their work (7b)* • Job assignment on an individual basis (7e)	• Having individual password for gaining access to relevant databases (9d) • Sharing of information to attain group consensus (9e)* • Use of GDSS (10d)* • Being stuck in a particular section (10e)

Note: The question number in the questionnaire is shown in parenthesis. * indicates items measured by a 'reversed scale' along which it is presumed that the higher the score, the lower the extent of the corresponding pattern of IT use. For example, the preference for 'teamwork' (5e), instead of that for 'individualised work system', was actually measured for calculating the IIU score.

for such innovation (Edwards, 1987) – this is also the case in Japan (Tidd, Bessant and Pavitt, 1997). Machinery, electrical engineering, transportation and rubber/plastic products in Japan have strong reputations for their IT-based innovations, and are most commonly chosen as a target of survey-based research on IT (Shimada, 1991; Okubayashi *et al.*, 1994).

Thirdly, relatively higher response rates were achieved in these five industries in a research project I had conducted previously (see p. 60), which led me to expect a higher response rate in these sectors in this project as well. The higher response rates might suggest that factories in these particular industries had a relatively higher interest in the introduction of IT-based systems. According to the databases, 949 British firms, 123 Japanese firms located in Britain, and 2701 Japanese firms in Japan exist which have '200 or more' employees in the five industries, and the largest factory of each firm was in fact sampled.

The British survey was conducted during May–June 1997, during which I was studying at the University of Warwick as a research student. The Japanese survey was conducted during October–November 1997 when I was back in Japan. In the British survey, the questionnaire was sent under my own name through Warwick Business School Research Bureau. In the Japanese survey, although the survey itself was designed and conducted by myself, it was sent with the cooperation of the School of Business Administration, Kobe University, for which I had been working, and three collaborators' names together with my own name were printed on the envelope as sender's names, in order to achieve a higher response rate.[12]

In the British survey, the questionnaire was written in English and entitled 'The Design and Use of IT in Manufacturing Industry: A Comparative Survey of Britain and Japan', with a Japanese translation for the Japanese survey. The questionnaire was sent to the production/operations director in each factory/plant in each nation. It was necessary to send the questionnaire to the person who possessed the most knowledge of IT-based systems, as the questions consisted of IT use concerning both shop-floor production processes and managerial uses. Production/operations directors were thought to be the best positions for satisfying the requirement. It was quite possible, however, that these directors could not answer for reasons such as time constraints. On the cover letter, therefore, a note was given which said that in the case of unavailability of the directors themselves, the questionnaire should be passed on to a person with knowledge of shop-floor production processes and of management information processing, such as the production, operations or logistics manager, to complete. A personal name was able to be specified and printed on a label on envelopes in the Japanese survey through the Digital Data Service, whilst a personal name was not available in the British survey, as all the available names are limited to managing director's and/or secretaries' names in One Source. Also, when a survey project is conducted in Japan, generally speaking, it is highly recommended to specify the name to whom a questionnaire is sent, otherwise very few respondents would be ready to cooperate with the project (Okubayashi *et al.*, 1994).[13] The firms' lists available in the Digital Data Service in the Japanese survey were relatively exhaustive, but the lists in One Source in the British survey were limited, as the information was based on the registration with Companies House. However, in Britain, One Source, which is updated monthly and covers more than 50 000 establishments in the UK, still seems to be one of the most comprehensive and reliable data sources on factories in the UK, and therefore appeared to be acceptable for use in the sampling.

In the British survey, the initial mailing of the questionnaire, with the cover letter and the return envelope, to 949 British factories and 123 JFB was conducted on 6 May 1997. The deadline of the reply was set as 30 May. As the by-the-deadline response was not as high as I had initially expected – at least 20 per cent considering response rates in other postal questionnaire surveys (Hitt, Ireland and Stadter 1982; Carter, 1984) – I sent a reminder letter together with the questionnaire and the return envelope, firstly on 6 June and secondly on 30 June, to all non-respondent factories. All the questionnaires were sent by second-class mail because of its relatively lower cost. Further, during 30 June–4 July, follow-up telephone calls were made to all the remaining non-respondents whose telephone numbers were available from One Source. The questionnaires from respondents were collected at Warwick Business School Research Bureau, through Freepost. The process of the collection of questionnaires from respondents is shown in the upper half of Figure 3.6, which may suggest that the reminders, the first reminder in particular, functioned quite well and contributed to the improvement of the response rate.

On the other hand, the initial mailing to 2701 Japanese factories was conducted on 8 October 1997, and the deadline set for return, through standard-class mail, was 31 October. The research project on the Japanese survey was funded by a Research Grant from the Japanese Education Ministry. No reminders were mailed in the Japanese survey, as I was able to achieve reasonably high response rates by the deadline. However, follow-up telephone calls were made to all non-respondents during 4–7

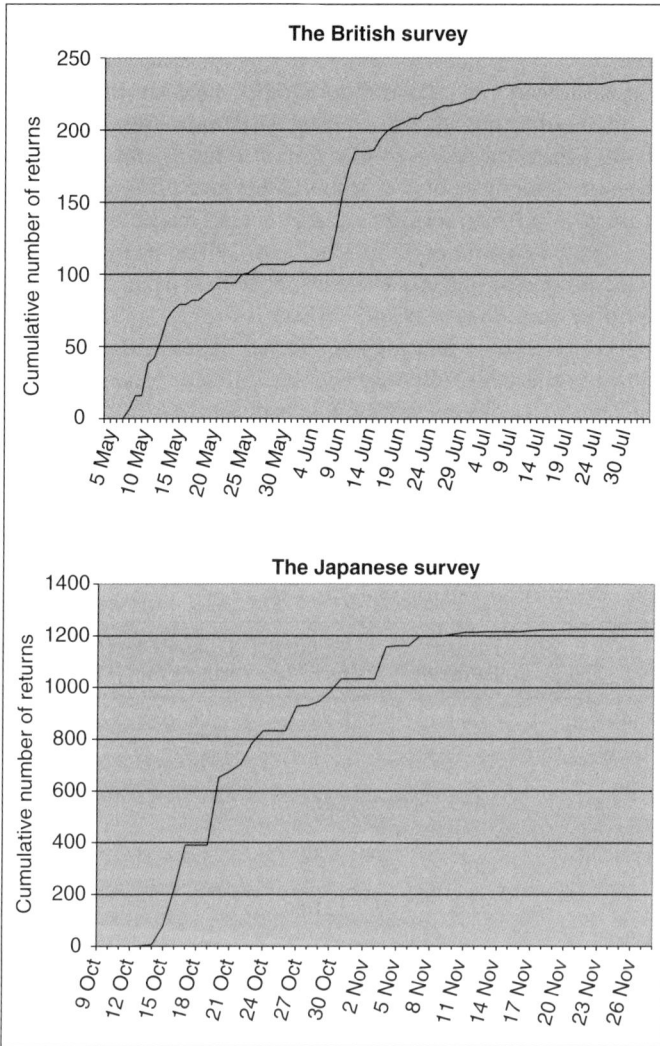

Figure 3.6 The process of collection of questionnaires in the surveys

November to further improve the figure. The questionnaires from respondents were collected at the School of Business Administration, Kobe University, through Freepost. The whole process of collecting the questionnaires is shown in the lower half of Figure 3.6.

The structure of the samples

Response rates

Much literature on research methodologies suggests that one of the most fundamental drawbacks of postal questionnaires as used in this study is that they are prone to low response rates, and that they may introduce an element of bias as respondents and non-respondents can differ from each other in regard to characteristics relevant to the research (Bryman, 1989; Glastonbury and MacKean, 1991). To make the matter worse, Goyder (1988) suggests some evidence that people's preparedness to respond to questionnaires and surveys is declining. Table 3.6 shows the details of attempted mailings of questionnaires in the survey.

As shown in this table, response rates are different between groups. The response rates of the British survey, that is of British factories and JFB, are lower than that of the Japanese survey. The following reasons are conceivable for the respective response rates: the British survey was conducted as my personal research project, whereas the Japanese survey was con-

Table 3.6 Response rates in each survey

	British factories	Japanese factories	Japanese factories in Britain (JFB)	Total
Total number of questionnaires sent (a)	949	2 701	123	3 773
Valid responses (b)	199	1 226	36	1 461
Invalid responses (c)	30	147	3	180
• do not answer[1]	5	118	3	126
• cannot answer[2] (d)	19	29	0	48
• whole blank	6	0	0	6
Addresses gone away and returned (e)	46	2	4	52
No responses[3]	674	1 326	80	2 080
Percentage of valid responses[4]	22.5%	45.9%	30.3%	39.8%

Note: [1]includes 'not participating policy', 'too busy'; [2]includes 'factory/plant closed down', 'no manufacturing sector', 'IT not introduced'; [3]calculated by: (a) – (b) – (c) – (e); [4]calculated by: [(b)/{(a) – (d) – (e)}] × 100.

ducted with the collaboration of three senior professors which might have made the respondent feel they were responding to a bona-fide project. Also, no specific names were printed on the envelope in the British survey due to unavailability from the database, whilst the name of the director was specified on the envelope in the Japanese survey, which may well have motivated the Japanese respondents to answer.[14] In the case of the postal questionnaire survey, instances of low response rates are evident even in major journals in organisational research: according to Bryman's (1989) research, studies by Hitt, Ireland and Stadter (1982) achieved a 25 per cent response rate in a survey of US industrial firms; and Carter (1984) achieved 21 per cent in a survey of US newspaper organisations. Also, as stated above, given that people's willingness to respond to questionnaires and surveys has been recently declining (Goyder, 1988), the study's overall response rates (39.8 per cent) appear to be a generally acceptable level for this kind of survey, especially for an international survey.

Possible biases

A major reason for the failure to return was the time constraint of the respondent in both countries, but in the British survey in particular – this was addressed through the process of making telephone follow-up calls. The second major reason was that the company took a non-partic-ipating policy on any social research and/or market research of such kinds. Thus most of the cases of 'no responses' in the table are considered to be due to reasons of pressure of time on respondents or for policy reasons. The entry of 'cannot answer' in Table 3.6 shows the number of returned questionnaires in which the reasons for non-answers were written. They indicated there were some other reasons for non-answers, including 'factory/plant closed down', 'no manufacturing sector', and 'IT not introduced'. It is possible that some bias has been introduced: if there are some large or systematic differences between those firms which participated in the survey and those which did not, bias may well be involved in the sample. In the present study, for example, if the non-respondents are more likely to be firms who are reluctant to intro-duce IT than other respondents, the results drawn from the sample will exaggerate the positive aspects of IT. However, taking into consideration the fact that major reasons for the refusal were simply lack of time and a non-participating policy in *any* social research, it seems unlikely that large or systematic biases were involved in the sample.

Although the reminder letters, the first one in particular, were very effective in improving response rates in the British survey (*cf.* Figure 3.6), their use also raises the question of bias. If there are large or systematic differences between the firms which responded before the reminder and those after the reminder, bias may well be involved in the sample. For example, in the case that the reminder might have put pressure on busy respondents to fill in the questionnaire very quickly, the results drawn from the early sample and the late sample will differ from each other. It is also possible that respondents who took an interest in the contents of the questionnaire were early respondents, while those who found them uninteresting were late respondents. Table 3.7 shows differences on average between non-respondents and respondents, and between early and late respondents in the British survey, in terms of (a) turnover and (b) the number of full-time employees of the wider corporation.

Table 3.7 Differences in turnover and number of employees between non-respondents and respondents and between early and late respondents

Differences between non-respondents and respondents
(a) Turnover

	Non-respondents	Respondents	*t*-value
British factories	£120 251 000	£79 868 000	.88 ($p < .399$)
Japanese factories	£997 965 000	£884 945 000	.60 ($p < .700$)
Japanese factories in Britain (JFB)	£60 623 000	£71 577 000	−.39 ($p < .841$)

(b) Number of employees

	Non-respondents	Respondents	*t*-value
British factories	3 901.7	2 008.5	1.09 ($p < .201$)
Japanese factories	7 425.8	5 010.3	1.26 ($p < .135$)
Japanese factories in Britain (JFB)	9 985.7	12 407.5	−.56 ($p < .495$)

Note: Calculated 1 UK pound sterling as 200 Japanese yen, according to the approximate exchange rate in March 1997. Data used from 'One Source: March 1997 Version' for British factories and JFB; *Kaisha Shikihou* [*Annual Book of Japanese Companies*], 1998 (in Japanese), for Japanese factories.

Differences between early and late respondents
(a) Turnover

	Early respondents	Late respondents	*t*-value
British factories	£83 621 000	£65 688 000	.39 ($p < .712$)
Japanese factories in Britain (JFB)	£69 594 000	£72 701 000	−.10 ($p < .897$)

(b) Number of employees

	Early respondents	Late respondents	t-value
British factories	1 955.9	2 231.1	$-1.00\,(p<.191)$
Japanese factories in Britain (JFB)	13 991.5	11 003.4	.88 $(p<.402)$

Note: 'Early respondents' ($N = 102$ in British factories and $N = 10$ in JFB) refer to companies which responded before 6 June 1997 on which date the first reminder was sent to non-respondents. 'Late respondents' ($N = 97$ in British factories and $N = 26$ in JFB) are defined as the rest of the respondents.

According to these tables, no statistically significant differences are identified either between non-respondents and respondents or between early and late respondents in terms of turnover and the number of employees of the wider corporation. Also, no significant differences have been found between early and late respondents in terms of each question in the questionnaire. This justifies taking the two groups together in statistical analyses. However, the possibility of some bias still has to be recognised here, since those who are willing to help may always differ from those who are not in any research requiring the cooperation of informants, whether these be case study subjects or respondents to questionnaires.

Features of the samples

Turnovers of the wider corporation of each group of respondent factories should also be taken into consideration as shown in Table 3.8 which shows that the average turnover of Japanese factories is bigger than that of British factories and JFB. This indicates that there is a difference with regard to the distribution of company size among each group of factories. (I will discuss the population data on the number of full-time employees of respondents in the next chapter, which will be summarised in Table 4.5.)

Table 3.9 indicates the job status of respondents in each group of factories. According to this table, most respondents are either 'directors' or 'managers' in each group, although there are some differences. For example, respondents in JFB include more managers than in British factories and Japanese factories.[15] Although not shown in the table, 12 directors in British factories and one in Japanese factories belonged to the Finance department; 13 managers in Japanese factories belonged to the Personnel department, but all others in the two entries of directors and of managers belonged to the Production, Operations or IT department. Therefore it is possible to conjecture that most respondents are assumed

Table 3.8   Turnovers of the wider corporation of respondent factories

	British factories	Japanese factories	Japanese factories in Britain (JFB)
Minimum	£1 628 000	£15 385 000	£4 275 000
Maximum	£8 341 000 000	£4 552 396 000	£324 294 000
Average	£79 868 000	£884 945 000	£71 577 000
Standard deviation	£610 574 000	£2 870 810 000	£78 503 000
N	188	1 131	35
Missing	11	95	1

Note: Calculated 1 UK pound sterling as 200 Japanese yen, according to the approximate exchange rate in March 1997. Data used from 'One Source: March 1997 Version' for British factories and JFB; *Kaisha Shikihou [Annual Book of Japanese Companies]*, 1998 (in Japanese), for Japanese factories.

to have enough knowledge of IT use both at shop-floor and management levels in each organisational setting to fill in the questionnaire.

Conclusion

A good model for analysis and a systematic methodology are vital for the successful completion of any research project. This chapter has developed the analytical framework and methodological details in the study. After examining the relevance of a survey-based approach instead of a case study approach to the theme, the levels of analysis of

Table 3.9   Respondents by job status

	British factories	Japanese factories	Japanese factories in Britain (JFB)
Managing directors	11 (5.6%)	4 (0.3%)	0 (0.0%)
Deputy managing directors	0 (0.0%)	86 (7.1%)	2 (5.7%)
Directors	103 (52.6%)	902 (74.4%)	11 (31.4%)
Managers	77 (39.3%)	208 (17.2%)	20 (57.1%)
Others	5 (2.6%)	12 (1.0%)	2 (5.7%)
N	196 (100.0%)	1 212 (100.0%)	35 (100.0%)
Missing	3	14	1

Note: The percentage of each cell to N is shown in parentheses. 'Managing directors' include chief executives and presidents; 'Deputy managing directors' in Japanese factories include '*senmu*' and '*joumu*'. 'Directors' in Japanese factories refers to '*bucho*'; 'Managers' in Japanese factories mainly refer to '*kacho*' (section chief). 'Others' mainly consists of company secretaries.

organisational IT use have been set. Two hierarchical levels in a factory – shop-floor and line management – have been targeted. Both managerial preferences for, and actual practices of, IT use have been set for the analysis. Then, how to operationalise national culture has been examined by referring to previous studies on national cultural dimensions. Two patterns of IT use have been conceptualised, both of which are justified as likely to display cultural influences: control-oriented IT use (CIU) and individual-oriented IT use (IIU). Although most previous studies on empirical examinations of national cultural influences in organisational studies have tried to construct hypotheses based on Hofstede's (1980) work, this study does not take such an approach to national culture. A new research theme like cultural influences on IT use makes it appropriate for me to take an exploratory rather than hypothesis-testing approach. Instead of testing Hofstede's model as such, I attempt to explore the broad hypothesis that national culture influences organisational IT use.

After detailing the whole picture of the analytical model, methodological details on the study have been given. The preliminary work for the field study and the structure of the survey have also been explained in detail. Although some biases may exist in the sample, the data seems as a whole to indicate that the samples have few large or systematic biases, which justifies the sample selection. In addition, no significant differences can be identified between early and late respondents. It has been shown that, given the chosen techniques of data collection and the structure of the samples, analysis based on the data that I collected makes it possible to understand national cultural influences on organisational IT use.

In the next chapter I will analyse data on some contextual factors indicated in Figure 3.5, which should be controlled for in the present study in order to differentiate mainly cultural effects from others.

4
The Analysis of the Context

Introduction

As discussed in the last chapter, one of the issues to be considered in an international comparison on the organisational use of IT is how to construct an analytical model which makes it possible to differentiate the effect of one specific factor (that is, national culture) from others and to explain differences among nations which the empirical data suggest. Therefore, some factors should be controlled for in the present study so as to differentiate national cultural effects from other contextual factors. In this chapter I examine the possible factors which may affect results other than national cultural influences and ways to minimise these influences.

Some suggestions from Sorge *et al.*'s work

As reviewed in Chapter 2, Sorge and his colleagues (1983) investigated the influence of national socio-economic conditions on the development and use of computerised numerical control (CNC), in which they make a comparison of comparable engineering firms between two countries. The research shows that in the face of similar developments of CNC technologies, the reactions of firms differ in different national contexts which are shaped by unchanging socio-technical traditions. The factors discovered to have had a key influence were:

1 Company or plant size;
2 Batch size, or time needed to machine a batch;
3 Type of cutting and machinery;

4   National institutions and habits of technical work, management and training; and

5   Socio-economic conditions of the present situation, regarding shortage of natural resources, limitation of mass markets and slow growth.

(p. 148)

It is possible that these factors could influence the results of our study, so it is necessary to exclude their effects in examining national cultural influences on IT use. I propose to organise and summarise such factors in the following way: kinds of technology/systems; industry to which each factory belongs; and factors relating to an individual organisation such as company/factory size, unionisation, and *organisational* sub-cultures.[1] Although unionisation and organisational sub-cultures have not been covered in Sorge *et al.*'s (1983) work, they are also important factors in the theme here. I will discuss this point later in the chapter. With regard to point 4, I have tried to show that CIU and IIU are the methods of organisational IT use in which mainly national cultural, rather than national institutional, influences are likely to be displayed. Regarding point 5, although the Japanese survey was conducted approximately five months after the British survey – the sampling procedure was explained in the previous chapter – there appear to be no vital differences in the two countries with respect to their socio-economic conditions, such as shortage of natural resources and limitation of mass markets. Therefore, in the following sections, by using our sample data, I examine whether or not it is necessary to control for the other factors, that is, factors 1, 2 and 3 in Sorge *et al.*'s (1983) work as well as factors of unionisation and organisational sub-cultures.

Control for kinds of technologies/systems

The shop-floor level

All manufacturing firms have their own technologies/systems which they use to manufacture goods in their factories. Kinds of technologies/ systems are one of the main factors to be controlled for, as this study focuses on influences of national cultural differences upon organisational use of IT. If the technological bases in each country were different from each other it could be difficult, or even impossible, to make an international comparison on IT use because of the differences in the independent variable. Figure 4.1 shows what types of information technologies/ systems have been installed at the shop-floor level of a factory in each set, that is British factories, Japanese factories and JFB. Table 4.1 shows the results of chi-square tests concerning the null hypothesis that each type of technology and nation (that is British factories and Japanese factories) are independent from each other.[2] This is the factor to be controlled for which Sorge *et al.* (1983) indicated as 'type of cutting and machinery'.

Figure 4.1 indicates that there are considerable differences in terms of the content of IT systems adopted among each group, particularly between British factories and Japanese factories. For instance, CAD (65.8 per cent) and MRP (61.2 per cent) are major technologies used in British samples as opposed to CAD (50.8 per cent) and NC (48.7 per cent) in Japanese samples. As suggested by Clark (1987) and Clark and Newell (1993), MRP and MRP2 are adopted far less in Japanese factories, which may suggest different variants of IT have existed, with different societal embedding of these ITs in each country. The result of chi-square tests concerning the null hypothesis that type of IT and nation (that is, Britain and Japan) are independent indicates the rejection of the null hypothesis, in terms of most IT/systems with the significance level $p < .01$. The

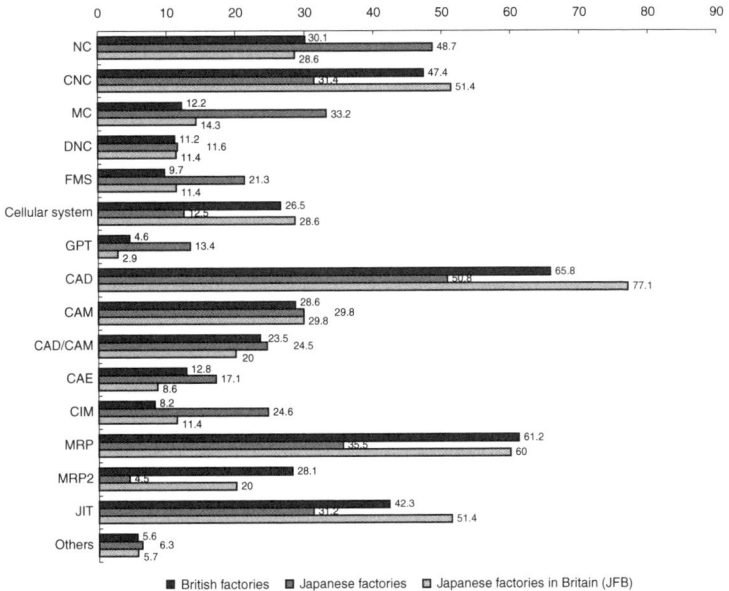

Figure 4.1   Technologies and systems used (all samples)
Note: Multiple answers. The percentage of each technology/system to *N* is shown.

Table 4.1 Pearson chi-square test for the independence of technologies/systems from nations (all samples)

	Value	Significance
NC	23.060	.000
CNC	19.541	.000
MC	34.809	.000
DNC	0.022	.881
FMS	14.105	.000
Cellular system	27.171	.000
GPT	12.121	.000
CAD	15.429	.000
CAM	0.117	.732
CAD/CAM	0.086	.770
CAE	2.307	.129
CIM	26.078	.000
MRP	47.363	.000
MRP2	129.789	.000
JIT	9.669	.002
Other(s)	0.120	.729

null hypothesis has not, however, been rejected for the following five IT/systems: DNC, CAM, CAD/CAM, CAE and Other(s). This suggests that nations and the types of IT/systems used are not independent from each other. Concerning the group JFB, Figure 4.1 shows that its distribution is more or less similar to that of British factories. This different distribution of IT/systems among each group needs controlling for in an international comparison.

It is possible to divide each sample into types of industries in order to reduce the effects of technologies/systems, as it is thought that firms in the same industry adopt more or less similar types of technologies/systems. For example, continuous process technology is thought to be more typically adopted in the chemicals/pharmaceuticals industry. Figure 4.2 shows the distribution of every IT/system in each sampled industry – that is, chemicals/pharmaceuticals, machinery, electrical engineering, transportation and rubber/plastic products. The results of Pearson chi-square tests are summarised in Table 4.2. All chi-square tests exclude the sample of JFB again, as the sample sizes are not big enough to execute the tests.

According to Table 4.2, the levels of significance of Pearson chi-square tests in each industry have been a little reduced in comparison with those in all industries shown in Table 4.1. It means that more or less similar technologies/systems are used in firms within an industry. For

Chemicals/pharmaceuticals

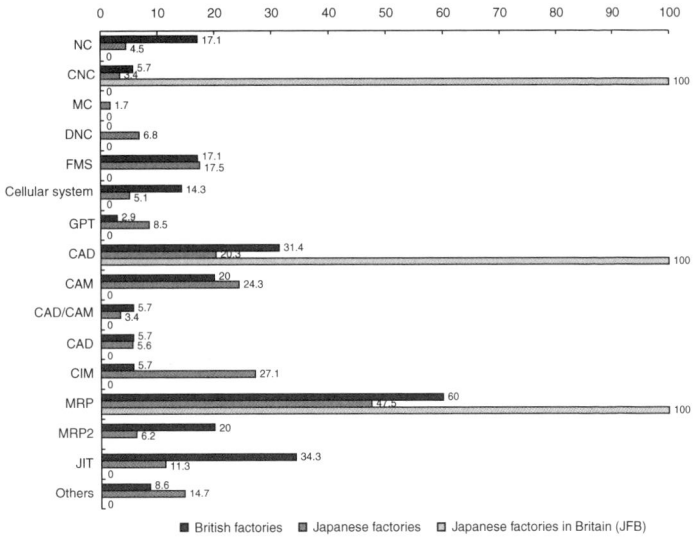

NC	British: 17.1; Japanese: 4.5; JFB: 0
CNC	British: 5.7; Japanese: 3.4; JFB: 100
MC	British: 1.7; Japanese: 0; JFB: 0
DNC	British: 6.8; Japanese: 0; JFB: 0
FMS	British: 17.1; Japanese: 17.5; JFB: 0
Cellular system	British: 14.3; Japanese: 5.1; JFB: 0
GPT	British: 8.5; Japanese: 2.9; JFB: 0
CAD	British: 31.4; Japanese: 20.3; JFB: 100
CAM	British: 24.3; Japanese: 20; JFB: 0
CAD/CAM	British: 5.7; Japanese: 3.4; JFB: 0
CAD	British: 5.7; Japanese: 5.6; JFB: 0
CIM	British: 27.1; Japanese: 5.7; JFB: 0
MRP	British: 60; Japanese: 47.5; JFB: 100
MRP2	British: 20; Japanese: 6.2; JFB:
JIT	British: 34.3; Japanese: 11.3; JFB: 0
Others	British: 14.7; Japanese: 8.6; JFB: 0

■ British factories ▨ Japanese factories ☐ Japanese factories in Britain (JFB)

Machinery

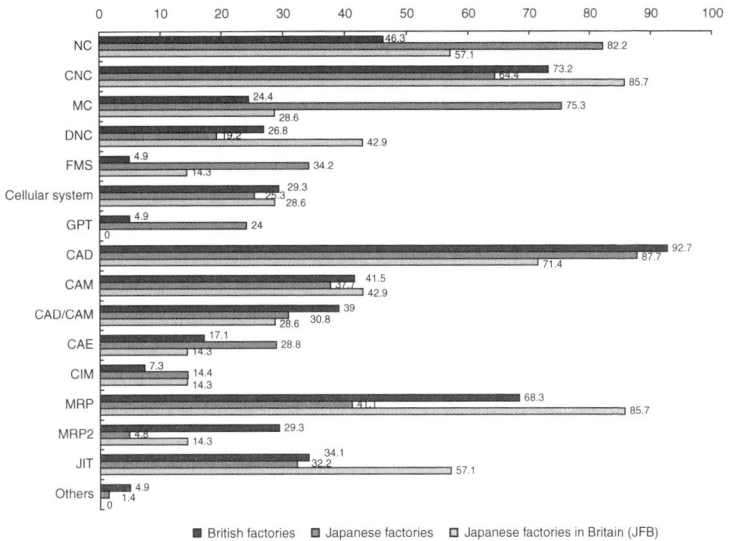

NC	British: 46.3; Japanese: 57.1; JFB: 82.2
CNC	British: 65.9; Japanese: 73.2; JFB: 85.7
MC	British: 24.4; Japanese: 28.6; JFB: 75.3
DNC	British: 19.2; Japanese: 26.8; JFB: 42.9
FMS	British: 4.9; Japanese: 14.3; JFB: 34.2
Cellular system	British: 29.3; Japanese: 25.3; JFB: 28.6
GPT	British: 4.9; Japanese: 0; JFB: 24
CAD	British: 92.7; Japanese: 87.7; JFB: 71.4
CAM	British: 41.5; Japanese: 37.7; JFB: 42.9
CAD/CAM	British: 39; Japanese: 28.6; JFB: 30.8
CAE	British: 17.1; Japanese: 14.3; JFB: 28.8
CIM	British: 7.3; Japanese: 14.4; JFB: 14.3
MRP	British: 68.3; Japanese: 41.1; JFB: 85.7
MRP2	British: 29.3; Japanese: 4.8; JFB: 14.3
JIT	British: 34.1; Japanese: 32.2; JFB: 57.1
Others	British: 4.9; Japanese: 1.4; JFB: 0

■ British factories ▨ Japanese factories ☐ Japanese factories in Britain (JFB)

Figure 4.2

Electrical engineering

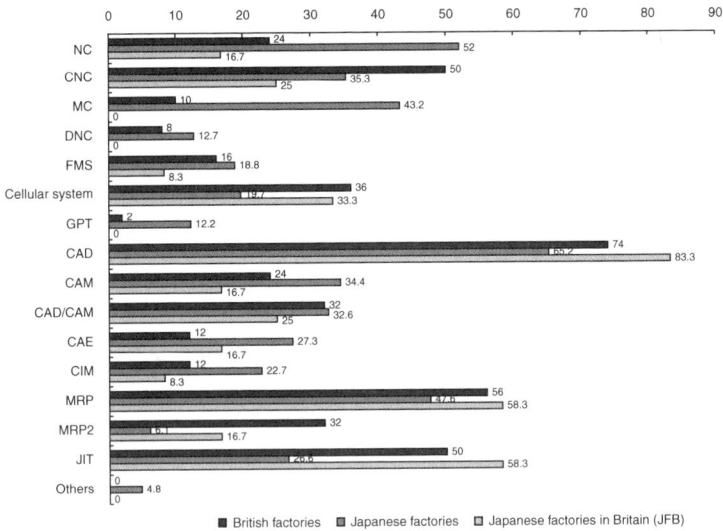

NC — British factories: 24; Japanese factories: 52; JFB: 16.7
CNC — British factories: 50; Japanese factories: 35.3; JFB: 25
MC — British factories: 10; Japanese factories: 43.2; JFB: 0
DNC — British factories: 8; Japanese factories: 12.7; JFB: 0
FMS — British factories: 16; Japanese factories: 18.8; JFB: 8.3
Cellular system — British factories: 36; Japanese factories: 19.7; JFB: 33.3
GPT — British factories: 2; Japanese factories: 12.2; JFB: 0
CAD — British factories: 74; Japanese factories: 66.7; JFB: 83.3
CAM — British factories: 24; Japanese factories: 34.4; JFB: 16.7
CAD/CAM — British factories: 32; Japanese factories: 32.6; JFB: 25
CAE — British factories: 12; Japanese factories: 27.3; JFB: 16.7
CIM — British factories: 12; Japanese factories: 22.7; JFB: 8.3
MRP — British factories: 56; Japanese factories: 47.6; JFB: 58.3
MRP2 — British factories: 32; Japanese factories: 16.1; JFB: 16.7
JIT — British factories: 50; Japanese factories: 26.6; JFB: 58.3
Others — British factories: 0; Japanese factories: 4.8; JFB: 0

■ British factories ▨ Japanese factories ▢ Japanese factories in Britain (JFB)

Transportation

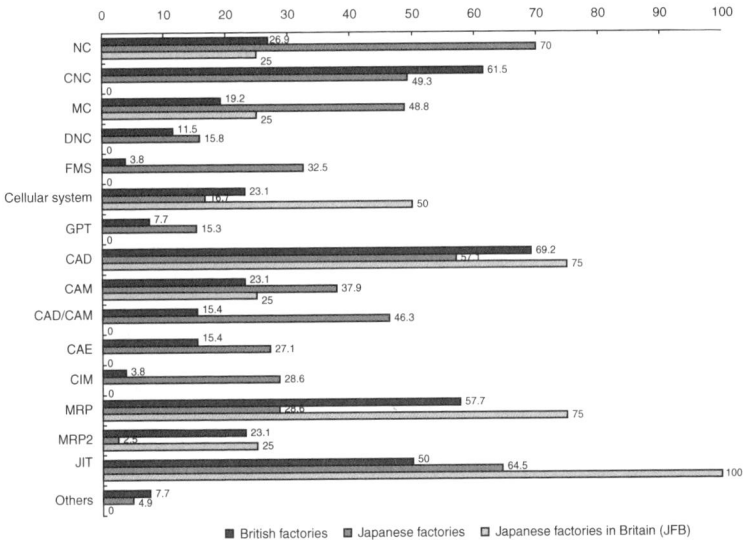

NC — British factories: 70; Japanese factories: 26.9; JFB: 25
CNC — British factories: 61.5; Japanese factories: 49.3; JFB: 0
MC — British factories: 48.8; Japanese factories: 19.2; JFB: 25
DNC — British factories: 15.8; Japanese factories: 11.5; JFB: 0
FMS — British factories: 32.5; Japanese factories: 3.8; JFB: 0
Cellular system — British factories: 23.1; Japanese factories: 16.7; JFB: 50
GPT — British factories: 15.3; Japanese factories: 7.7; JFB: 0
CAD — British factories: 69.2; Japanese factories: 57.1; JFB: 75
CAM — British factories: 37.9; Japanese factories: 23.1; JFB: 25
CAD/CAM — British factories: 46.3; Japanese factories: 15.4; JFB: 0
CAE — British factories: 27.1; Japanese factories: 15.4; JFB: 0
CIM — British factories: 28.6; Japanese factories: 3.8; JFB: 0
MRP — British factories: 57.7; Japanese factories: 26.5; JFB: 75
MRP2 — British factories: 23.1; Japanese factories: 2.5; JFB: 25
JIT — British factories: 64.5; Japanese factories: 50; JFB: 100
Others — British factories: 7.7; Japanese factories: 4.9; JFB: 0

■ British factories ▨ Japanese factories ▢ Japanese factories in Britain (JFB)

Figure 4.2 (*Cont'd overleaf*)

Rubber/plastic products

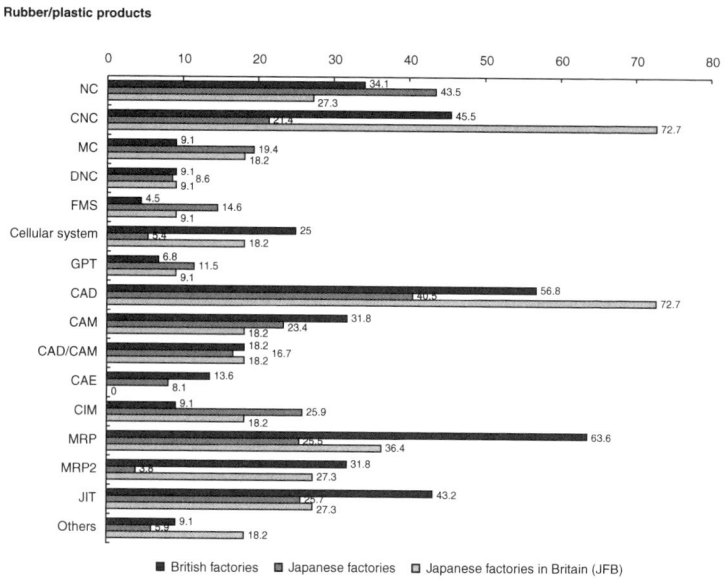

Figure 4.2   Technologies and systems used in each industry
Note: Multiple answers. The percentage of each technology/system to *N* in each industry is shown.

example, Table 4.2 shows that factories in the chemicals/pharmaceuticals industry are inclined to adopt MRP, CAM and CAD, not having significant levels of chi-square variance, which indicates that these technologies/systems are used in both British factories and Japanese factories.

Some of the results of the chi-square tests do not show that the technologies/systems used and nations are perfectly independent even in sub-samples divided by industry. However, in spite of such limitations, the results of chi-square tests shown in Table 4.2 in general indicate that by dividing the samples into an industrial group, it is possible to provide *some* control for the influence of technologies/systems.

The management level

As discussed in Chapter 1, examples of IT/IS installed at the management level are PC, LAN, VAN, WAN, DSS, GDSS, EIS, SIS and so on. Table 4.3 shows a comparison among British factories, Japanese factories and JFB in the sample on the scope and focus of the management information system (MIS). As shown in the table, there are few large differences identified in terms of the scope of the MIS. About 70 per cent of respondents

Table 4.2 Pearson chi-square tests for the independence of IT from nations in each industry

Kinds of technologies	Chemicals/ pharmaceuticals		Machinery		Electrical engineering		Transportation		Rubber/plastic products	
	Value	Significance	Value	Significance	Value	Significance	Value	Significance	Value	Significance
NC	7.549	.006	21.563	.000	12.886	.000	18.773	.000	1.440	.230
CNC	0.435	.510	1.106	.293	3.728	.054	1.390	.238	12.864	.000
MC	0.602	.438	36.145	.000	19.384	.000	8.112	.004	2.812	.094
DNC	2.515	.113	1.135	.287	0.856	.355	0.318	.573	0.014	.904
FMS	0.003	.958	13.753	.000	0.212	.645	9.151	.002	3.297	.069
Cellular system	4.011	.045	0.255	.613	6.275	.012	0.640	.424	23.087	.000
GPT	1.322	.250	7.354	.007	4.609	.032	1.073	.300	0.887	.346
CAD	2.083	.149	0.807	.369	1.613	.204	1.387	.239	4.354	.037
CAM	0.299	.585	0.194	.659	1.901	.168	2.201	.138	1.539	.215
CAD/CAM	0.435	.510	0.980	.322	0.002	.996	9.001	.003	0.066	.798
CAE	0.000	.988	2.264	.132	5.059	.024	1.652	.199	1.555	.212
CIM	7.428	.006	1.429	.232	2.857	.091	7.367	.007	6.135	.013
MRP	1.839	.175	9.504	.002	1.159	.282	9.000	.003	28.413	.000
MRP2	7.147	.008	21.005	.000	28.657	.000	21.418	.000	52.719	.000
JIT	12.047	.001	0.056	.814	10.505	.001	2.085	.149	6.188	.013
Others	0.926	.336	1.882	.170	2.500	.114	0.355	.551	0.726	.394

in each set of factories use either networked PC or companywide integrated MIS. With regard to the focus of the MIS, however, my data show some differences between countries. For example, 62.0 per cent of British factories use MIS which provide information to individual managers like executive information systems (EIS), whilst only 29.6 per cent of British factories use Lotus Notes and/or group decision support systems (GDSS) where information is provided to groups of managers. On the other hand, 31.6 per cent of Japanese factories adopt EIS and 68.4 per cent adopt Lotus Notes and/or GDSS – I will return to this issue in Chapter 7.

At the management level, the technological basis is more ambiguous than at the shop-floor level thus there is less need to control for the technologies/systems.[3] It is thought that the main IT used at this level is information communication technology which I call management information system (MIS) technology. Email systems and some packaged software applications such as Lotus Notes and GDSS are examples of these MIS technologies (Ciborra, 1996; Shimada, 1991). Taking into consideration the fact that such MIS technologies are well-standardised in terms of their structures and functions, and thus fewer differences are observed among companies than IT machines/equipment installed at the shop-floor level,[4] it is less necessary at the management level to control for technologies/systems in the following analysis.

Control for industry

Within an industry, the suppliers and competitors of firms should be controlled for in the analysis. Although 'industry' is not on the list in Sorge *et al.*'s (1983) work because of the single focus upon the machine-tool industry in their analysis, this is one of the key factors to be controlled for where sampling is conducted from several different industries (Edwards, 1987). Table 4.4 shows the industrial composition of the samples that I collected in the survey.

According to this table, firstly, the number of total samples in the group of JFB is relatively smaller than that of the other two groups. The number of factories which belong to the chemicals/pharmaceuticals group in JFB is only one, for instance, which is not a sufficient sample size to execute a meaningful statistical analysis, say a *t*-test, based on the industrial groups. Although no lower limit on sample size has been suggested to conduct statistical methods, this suggests that the sample size in JFB is too small and thus the group should be dealt with separately from the others in the following comparison. Secondly, the distribution

Table 4.3 The scope and focus of the MIS in British factories, Japanese factories and Japanese factories in Britain (JFB)

The scope of the MIS

	Not integrated	PC distributed	Network PC	Companywide	Others	Total
British factories (N = 198)	12.9	9.1	37.9	40.4	0.5	100.0
Japanese factories (N = 1 225)	3.8	26.4	26.7	42.9	0.2	100.0
Japanese factories in Britain (JFB) (N = 36)	8.3	11.1	36.1	41.7	2.8	100.0

The focus of the MIS

	Individuals	Groups	Others	Total
British factories (N = 179)	62.0	29.6	8.4	100.0
Japanese factories (N = 1 207)	31.6	68.4	0.0	100.0
Japanese factories in Britain (JFB) (N = 31)	48.4	45.2	6.5	100.0

Note: The percentage to N is given in each cell. Refer to Qs 3 and 4 in the questionnaire in the Appendix.

of the samples by industry is quite different in each group. For instance, 'electrical engineering' is the highest percentage in British samples (25.1 per cent) whereas 'rubber/plastic products' is the highest in Japanese samples (37.7 per cent).[5]

Table 4.4 indicates that the composition of industries in each nation is very different from each other. This suggests that it is necessary to control for the industry's effects in analysing organisational IT use.

Control for individual organisations

As illustrated in Figure 3.5 in the previous chapter, the characteristics of an individual organisation should be controlled for, such as its size, the batch size in the factory, its special organisational sub-cultures and level of unionisation.

Table 4.4 Distribution of samples by industry

	British factories	Japanese factories	Japanese factories in Britain (JFB)	Total
Chemicals/ pharmaceuticals	36 (18.1%)	185 (15.1%)	1 (2.8%)	222 (15.2%)
Machinery	41 (20.6%)	147 (12.0%)	7 (19.4%)	195 (13.3%)
Electrical engineering	50 (25.1%)	229 (18.7%)	13 (36.1%)	290 (19.8%)
Transportation	26 (13.1%)	203 (16.6%)	4 (11.1%)	235 (16.1%)
Rubber/plastic products	46 (23.1%)	462 (37.7%)	11 (30.6%)	519 (35.5%)
N	199 (100.0%)	1 226 (100.0%)	36 (100.0%)	1 461 (100.0%)
Missing	0	0	0	0

Note: The percentage of each cell to N is shown in parentheses.

Size of organisations

Not only at the level of industry but also at that of each organisation, some factors such as size of organisation,[6] unionisation and organisational culture may affect IT use. Table 4.5 shows the distribution of the number of employees of the wider corporation of respondent factories and the number of factory full-time employees. This table shows that, both at the wider corporation level and at the factory level, the number of employees is distributed unevenly among each group. In the JFB group, 37.1 per cent of the group are in the category of 'greater than 25 000', whilst in the British factories group only 2.5 per cent falls into the category. Some 79.9 per cent of British factories have less than 1000 employees whereas 27.2 per cent of Japanese factories are in the identical category. The same tendency can be observed at the factory level: the British factories group have relatively fewer employees than the other two groups. Pearson chi-square tests of these cross-tabulations suggest that the number of employees distributes unevenly among groups.[7] These statistics indicate that it is necessary to control for organisational size in the subsequent analyses.

In the following, I will analyse data by dividing all samples into two groups by the size of factory: 'less than 200 employees' and '200 or more employees'. One of the reasons for the classification is that a small- and medium-sized establishment (factory, plant, etc.) in Japanese manufacturing customarily refers to an establishment whose employees are less than 200, and is distinguished from a larger one. Furthermore,

Table 4.5   The distribution of the number of employees of respondents

Of the wider corporation

	British factories	Japanese factories	Japanese factories in Britain (JFB)
Less than 1 000	159 (79.9%)	334 (27.2%)	5 (14.3%)
1 000–1 999	13 (6.5%)	195 (15.9%)	3 (8.6%)
2 000–4 999	14 (7.0%)	247 (20.1%)	3 (8.6%)
5 000–9 999	4 (2.0%)	136 (11.1%)	7 (20.0%)
10 000–24 999	4 (2.0%)	168 (13.7%)	4 (11.4%)
Greater than 25 000	5 (2.5%)	146 (11.9%)	13 (37.1%)
N	199 (100.0%)	1 226 (100.0%)	35 (100.0%)
Missing	0	0	1

Of factories

	British factories	Japanese factories	Japanese factories in Britain (JFB)
Less than 200	127 (63.8%)	359 (29.4%)	11 (30.6%)
200–499	60 (30.2%)	374 (30.6%)	10 (27.8%)
500–999	9 (4.5%)	205 (16.8%)	9 (25.0%)
1 000–1 499	1 (0.5%)	106 (8.7%)	5 (13.9%)
1 500–1 999	1 (0.5%)	57 (4.7%)	0 (0.0%)
Greater than 2 000	1 (0.5%)	121 (9.9%)	1 (2.8%)
N	199 (100.0%)	1 222 (100.0%)	36 (100.0%)
Missing	0	4	0

Note: The percentage of each cell to *N* is shown in parentheses.

Table 4.5 shows that the number of British factories who have 500 or more employees is negligible against the total sample, which suggests that it is appropriate to divide the sample into the two size groups, 'less than 200' and '200 or more'. Therefore, I call the former 'small factory' and the latter 'large factory' hereafter in the present study.

Batch size

In Sorge *et al.* (1983), batch size was indicated to be an important factor having a key influence on results. Table 4.6 shows the relationship between batch size in each factory and industry to which the factory belongs. The table indicates that the batch size of a factory is unevenly distributed among industries: for example, 54.1 per cent of factories that adopted the mass production process belong to transportation; 52.3 per cent that adopted the continuous process belong to 'rubber/plastic

Table 4.6   Batch size and industry

	Custom	Small batch	Large batch	Mass production	Continuous
Chemicals/ pharmaceuticals	23 (5.0%)	61 (16.9%)	89 (31.9%)	3 (1.2%)	46 (41.6%)
Machinery	98 (21.4%)	67 (18.5%)	10 (3.6%)	19 (7.8%)	0 (0.0%)
Electrical engineering	109 (23.7%)	91 (25.1%)	22 (7.9%)	65 (26.6%)	3 (2.7%)
Transportation	56 (12.2%)	25 (6.9%)	16 (5.7%)	132 (54.1%)	4 (3.6%)
Rubber/plastic products	173 (37.7%)	118 (32.6%)	142 (50.9%)	25 (10.2%)	58 (52.3%)
Total	459 (100.0%)	362 (100.0%)	279 (100.0%)	244 (100.0%)	111 (100.0%)

Note: N =1455. The percentage of each cell to column total is shown in parentheses. Refer to Q1 in the Questionnaire shown in the Appendix.

products'; 41.6 per cent that adopted the continuous process belong to chemicals/pharmaceuticals. 'Rubber/plastic products' shows the highest percentages in custom, small batch and large batch processes.[8] This suggests that, though batch size cannot be controlled for sufficiently even by dividing into each industrial group, the analysis through the data classified by industrial group provides some level of control for batch size.

Unionisation

Unionisation is one of the most important factors to be controlled for amongst institutional factors, as a considerable amount of previous research suggests there is a relationship between trade unions and IT use. For example, unions have, understandably enough, identified fears in regard to several key features of the introduction of IT, such as threatened job losses, work reorganisation through skill squeeze, and the introduction of teamwork (Beirne and Ramsay, 1992; Cressey, 1992). Table 4.7 shows (i) to what extent the workforce is unionised in organisations in each group, and (ii) the percentages of factories whose workforces are unionised against those non-unionised in each country, classified by industry and size of the factory.

According to Table 4.7, 94.1 per cent of workforces in Japanese factories are unionised compared with 27.0 per cent in British factories, which suggests that it is necessary for this factor to be controlled for in the present study. However, large factories (in the lower part of the table) show reasonably higher percentages of unionisation than those of small factories in most industries. This means that the workforce

Table 4.7 The rate of unionisation of workforces

Whole sample

	British factories	Japanese factories	Japanese factories in Britain (JFB)
Unionised	27.0%	94.1%	50.0%
Non-unionised	73.0%	5.9%	50.0%
N	100.0%	100.0%	100.0%
Missing	3	4	0

By industry and size

Industry	Size	British factories	Japanese factories	Japanese factories in Britain (JFB)
Chemicals/pharmaceuticals	Large	73.3%	93.2%	(...)
	Small	23.8%	85.4%	0.0%
Machinery	Large	33.3%	94.5%	57.1%
	Small	12.5%	88.9%	0.0%
Electrical engineering	Large	18.8%	96.0%	66.7%
	Small	15.2%	75.5%	0.0%
Transportation	Large	70.0%	98.9%	50.0%
	Small	31.3%	100.0%	0.0%
Rubber/plastic products	Large	31.6%	98.3%	60.0%
	Small	16.0%	89.6%	50.0%

Note: 'Large' and 'small' in the second column indicate factories with 200 or more employees and factories with less than 200 employees. Refer to Q14(d) in the Questionnaire in the Appendix.

tends to be more unionised in large factories than in small factories in each industry. For example, the workforce of 73.3 per cent of large British factories in chemicals/pharmaceuticals is unionised as opposed to 23.8 per cent of small British factories in that industry. The tendency holds particularly good in JFB. However, the differences between large and small factories are relatively smaller in Japanese factories than in the other two groups of factories. This suggests that the analysis through the data classified by size provides some control for the factor of unionisation, though the factor cannot be controlled for perfectly even by dividing into each size group.

Organisational sub-cultures

Another important factor which should be controlled for in the analysis is organisational sub-cultures. As I mentioned in the last chapter, a considerable number of previous studies indicate that *organisational* culture affects IT use in an organisation. For instance, it is suggested that MIS use depends on the organisational culture where it is used (Raman and Watson, 1994). Cooper (1994) claims that when IT conflicts with an organisational culture, the implementation and use of IT is resisted by users of the organisation.

Some difficulties may involve the control for *organisational* subcultures in the analysis of the influences of *national* culture on organisational use of IT, as culture is intangible and it is difficult to grasp cultural influences in concrete terms. It is difficult to distinguish national culture from organisational culture when we find a new phenomenon in an organisational context. It does not necessarily mean, however, that control is impossible. Firstly, some influences of organisational culture may be eliminated by collecting fairly extensive and diffused data from the population. It is difficult to judge that an organisation in Japan truly has a so-called Japanese culture in the case of smaller samples. However, if a big sample size is available in each country, it is possible to tell to some degree what is the Japanese-ness by comparing it statistically with British samples. The sample sizes that I have collected from British factories ($N = 199$) and from Japanese factories ($N = 1226$) seem large enough to reduce the effect of organisation sub-cultures in the analysis. With regard to the sample of JFB, the relatively smaller sample size ($N = 36$) indicates a necessity to deal with the sample separately from the other two samples.

Secondly, though organisational sub-culture is one of the important factors to affect IT use, some previous studies show that organisational sub-culture itself is being affected by the national culture in which the organisation exists. For example, Raman and Watson (1994) claim that national culture is *the* dominant culture, and that organisational culture is itself subject to the influences of national culture. Thus even if organisational culture may affect IT use in each organisation, it also reflects the national culture in which the organisation exists. In the case of large samples, therefore, the influences of organisational sub-cultures on IT use could be expected to be minimised.

Conclusion

Factors to be controlled for in an international comparison have been discussed in this chapter: kind of technologies/systems; industry; organisational size; unionisation; batch size; and organisational sub-cultures.

The data of the sample show that it is necessary for these factors to be controlled for, but technologies/systems at the shop-floor level and the batch size of a factory have been found to be represented by industrial group to some extent. My analysis has indicated that there is less need to control for the technologies/systems at the management level, as the technological basis is more or less similar as compared to the shop-floor level. Unionisation has been identified to be controlled for to some extent by dividing all samples into sub-groups classified by industry and represented by organisational size, or the number of employees. However, it must be acknowledged that still these factors cannot be perfectly controlled for in my study. All I have claimed in this chapter is that the above-mentioned approach provides *some* control for these contextual factors and thus provides an opportunity to show more explicitly national cultural influences on organisational IT use.

In the following three chapters, empirical findings on national cultural influences on organisational IT use will be reported and discussed in detail. First, I will focus attention in the next chapter on differences in managerial preferences among each set of factories to look for empirical evidence for national cultural influences on organisational IT use.

5
Some Evidence of Cultural Influences on IT Use

Introduction

Based on the analytical framework developed in the previous chapter, this chapter looks for some empirical evidence in our data for national cultural influences on IT use. As already discussed, data has been gathered regarding two types of organisational IT use – CIU and IIU – to examine the broad hypothesis that national culture affects IT use. In this chapter, data on the two patterns of IT use are reported respectively. National culture predicts managerial preferences for IT use in each factory. I look for empirical evidence for different patterns of IT use from the data on managerial preference in terms of CIU and IIU, firstly between British factories and Japanese factories; then, together with data on JFB, I examine a situation where JFB can be situated, that is either closer to the pattern of British factories/Japanese factories or between the two.

Findings on control-oriented IT use

General view

As explained in Chapter 3, CIU has been defined to consist of three factors: the concentration of important information at the top; top-down information flow; and simple job design. In an organisation in which the degree of CIU is high, hierarchical control of information is presumed. It is possible to presume that a traditional Taylorist management, which serves for avoiding uncertainties at the shop-floor, requires the concentration of information at the top management level, so that information is distributed via the organisational hierarchy resulting in a simple

Table 5.1 Measures of managerial preferences for CIU

Pattern of IT use	Managerial preference
Control-oriented IT use (CIU)	• Concentration of important information at the top • Top-down information flow • Simple job design

Alpha = .62 for British factories; .51 for Japanese factories; and .49 for JFB.

job design like the 'one-man, one-job' system. The relationship between CIU and the measures of managerial preferences is illustrated in Table 5.1, with results of reliability tests of these measures (that is, Cronbach's alpha).

As shown in the table, CIU in managerial preference has been measured through the following three items: concentration of important information at the top; top-down information flow; and simple job design. Statistical tests of the data, however, show that there was not high consistency among the items of the 'composite' measures, and the items cannot be used collectively as a scale. Therefore, I present data based on each item individually, instead of calculating the overall average scores on CIU.

Figure 5.1 shows the general trend of these managerial preferences in each set of factories. According to these illustrations, each set of factories has shown rather strong disagreement to limited access for a shop-floor worker to important information, top-down information flow and simple job design, although different degrees of preference can be observed among each set of factories. Each set of factories has indicated disagreement to the statement on top management's exclusive access to strategically important information. Nearly half of the respondents' factories in each set have shown disagreement whereas 30–40 per cent in each set have agreed. Each set has less preference for top-down information flow, though Japanese factories have shown stronger preference than the other two sets. With regard to the preference for simple job design, the agreement to the statement looks rather small in comparison with the other two items, although, again, Japanese factories' preference seems stronger than the other two.

Comparison between British factories and Japanese factories

Some statistical tests have been done to examine differences among each set in detail. Table 5.2 indicates descriptive statistics in each set

92

Preference for limited access to important information

British
factories
(N=199) | 52.2 | 17.1 | 30.7

Japanese
factories
(N=1224) | 49 | 19 | 32

Japanese
factories
in Britain
(N=34) | 50 | 11.8 | 38.2

0%   20%   40%   60%   80%   100%

Top management should have exclusive access to the most important kinds of information

▨ Disagree   ■ Neither agree nor disagree   ☐ Agree

Preference for top-down information flow

British
factories
(N=199) | 57.3 | 20.6 | 22.1

Japanese
factories
(N=1222) | 43.3 | 30.8 | 26

Japanese
factories
in Britain
(N=34) | 50 | 23.5 | 26.5

0%   20%   40%   60%   80%   100%

Information flow should always reflect the management hierarchy in any situation

▨ Disagree   ■ Neither agree nor disagree   ☐ Agree

Preference for simple job design

British
factories
(N=199) | 52.8 | 28.1 | 19.1

Japanese
factories
(N=1221) | 40 | 26.7 | 33.3

Japanese
factories
in Britain
(N=34) | 50 | 38.2 | 11.8

0%   20%   40%   60%   80%   100%

Lower-graded employees should have the simplest jobs

▨ Disagree   ■ Neither agree nor disagree   ☐ Agree

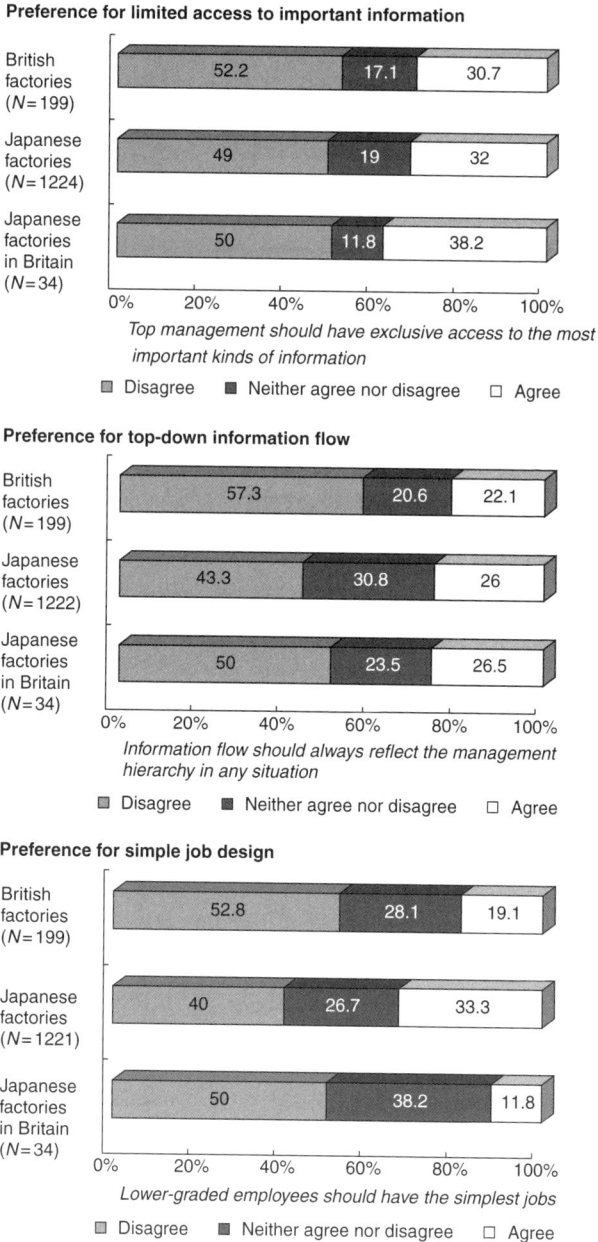

Figure 5.1 Managerial preferences for CIU – general view

Table 5.2 Managerial preferences for CIU in British factories and Japanese factories
Concentration of important information at the top management level
Main effect of nation: $F = .59$ (covariates: size $F = .11$; industry $F = .42$)

		British factories			Japanese factories			t-value
		Average	Standard deviation	N	Average	Standard deviation	N	
All samples		2.64	1.37	199	2.72	1.17	1224	-0.72
All large factories		2.61	1.41	72	2.71	1.17	863	-0.58
All small factories		2.66	1.36	127	2.73	1.16	358	-0.52
All chemicals/pharmaceuticals		2.69	1.41	36	2.75	1.17	185	-0.21
All machinery		2.76	1.43	41	2.58	1.12	147	0.74
All electrical engineering		2.66	1.36	50	2.62	1.20	229	0.23
All transportation		2.38	1.13	26	2.83	1.17	203	-1.82
All rubber/plastic products		2.63	1.47	46	2.75	1.17	460	-0.55
Chemicals/pharmaceuticals	Large	2.67	1.54	15	2.79	1.20	103	-0.29
	Small	2.71	1.35	21	2.70	1.13	82	0.60
Machinery	Large	2.89	1.27	10	2.70	1.08	110	0.43
	Small	2.72	1.49	31	2.22	1.17	36	1.54
Electrical engineering	Large	2.59	1.54	17	2.55	1.18	176	0.12
	Small	2.70	1.29	33	2.83	1.22	53	-0.48
Transportation	Large	2.40	1.08	10	2.81	1.17	178	-1.18
	Small	2.38	1.20	16	2.92	1.19	25	-1.42
Rubber/plastic products	Large	2.57	1.50	21	2.72	1.19	296	-0.54
	Small	2.68	1.46	25	2.79	1.13	162	-0.44

Table 5.2 (Cont'd)
Top-down information flow
Main effect of nation: $F = 14.57^{***}$ (covariates: size $F = 2.69$; industry $F = .03$)

		British factories			Japanese factories			t-value
		Average	Standard deviation	N	Average	Standard deviation	N	
All samples		2.43	1.26	199	2.73	1.08	1222	-3.19**
All large factories		2.38	1.32	72	2.70	1.07	861	-2.01*
All small factories		2.46	1.23	127	2.80	1.09	358	-2.81*
All chemicals/pharmaceuticals		2.69	1.41	36	2.75	1.12	185	-1.63
All machinery		2.61	1.20	41	2.67	1.05	147	-0.33
All electrical engineering		2.42	1.34	50	2.60	1.09	229	-0.92
All transportation		2.35	1.06	26	2.64	1.10	201	-1.28
All rubber/plastic		2.28	1.29	46	2.81	1.05	460	-2.69**
Chemicals/pharmaceuticals	Large	2.27	1.44	15	2.86	1.16	103	-1.54
	Small	2.62	1.28	21	2.76	1.06	82	-0.45
Machinery	Large	2.67	1.22	10	2.65	1.02	110	0.05
	Small	2.59	1.21	31	2.75	1.15	36	-0.54
Electrical engineering	Large	2.24	1.30	17	2.60	1.10	176	-1.13
	Small	2.52	1.37	33	2.62	1.08	53	-0.40
Transportation	Large	2.20	1.03	10	2.61	1.10	176	-1.21
	Small	2.44	1.09	16	2.84	1.11	25	-1.15
Rubber/plastic products	Large	2.52	1.47	21	2.76	1.02	296	-1.00
	Small	2.08	1.12	25	2.90	1.10	162	-3.41**

Simple job design

Main effect of nation: $F = 20.84$*** (covariates: size $F = 1.73$; industry $F = .31$)

		British factories			Japanese factories			t-value
		Average	Standard deviation	N	Average	Standard deviation	N	
All samples		2.47	1.17	199	2.85	1.12	1 221	-4.47***
All large factories		2.32	1.22	72	2.84	1.12	860	-3.74***
All small factories		2.55	1.13	127	2.89	1.14	358	-2.92**
All chemicals/pharmaceuticals		2.67	1.07	36	2.78	1.12	184	-0.55
All machinery		2.61	1.14	41	2.79	1.14	147	-0.89
All electrical engineering		2.50	1.13	50	2.86	1.10	229	-2.09*
All transportation		2.00	1.06	26	2.90	1.11	201	-3.90***
All rubber/plastic		2.41	1.33	46	2.88	1.14	460	-2.62**
Chemicals/pharmaceuticals	Large	2.33	1.23	15	2.63	1.13	102	-0.87
	Small	2.90	0.89	21	2.96	1.08	82	-0.26
Machinery	Large	2.67	1.22	10	2.78	1.13	110	-0.27
	Small	2.59	1.13	31	2.83	1.21	36	-0.84
Electrical engineering	Large	2.53	1.33	17	2.86	1.12	176	-1.00
	Small	2.48	1.03	33	2.85	1.03	53	-1.59
Transportation	Large	1.70	1.06	10	2.94	1.07	176	-3.61***
	Small	2.19	1.05	16	2.60	1.35	25	-1.10
Rubber/plastic products	Large	2.29	1.19	21	2.85	1.14	296	-2.10*
	Small	2.52	1.45	25	2.93	1.16	162	-1.60

Note: 'Large' and 'small' in the second column indicate large factories with 200 or more employees and small factories with less than 200 employees. It is presumed that the higher the average CIU score, the higher the extent of the control-oriented use. *T*-value indicates the result of the *t*-test on average values between British factories and Japanese factories. The significant levels are * $p < .05$, ** $p < .01$ and *** $p < .001$.

and the results of *t*-tests on the average score between British factories and Japanese factories, classified by industry and factory size[1] in order to avoid their effects. First of all, to test overall differences controlling for factory size and industry, analysis of variance (ANOVA) was carried out with factory size and industry as covariates. Below the title of each table are shown the results of the ANOVA.

The ANOVA results show significant differences between nations (that is, British factories and Japanese factories) in terms of 'top-down information flow' and 'simple job design', but factory size and industry are not significant covariates in terms of all items. As shown in these tables, the set of Japanese factories shows stronger preference for CIU in general. Although no statistically significant difference can be observed in each subset between British factories and Japanese factories with regard to the preference for concentration of important information at the top management level, in terms of the other two items, that is the preference for top-down information flow and that for simple job design, some significant differences can be observed. Regarding 'top-down information flow', Japanese factories got higher scores than British factories in all samples and in all large and in all small factories. Small 'rubber/plastic products' particularly show a higher significant difference. Regarding 'simple job design', Japanese factories again got higher scores than British factories in all samples. Japanese large 'transportation' factories in particular got higher scores with a higher significant difference. These results suggest that, generally speaking, Japanese factories have a greater preference for CIU than British factories.

Japanese factories in Britain

Table 5.3 shows where JFB is situated in terms of each item on CIU. The table indicates the descriptive statistics for the JFB. ANOVA was conducted to explore the differences between average scores for each item among JFB, British factories and Japanese factories. Where the overall ANOVA is significant, the results of *post hoc* Scheffe's tests are shown to indicate where (that is, either between British factories/JFB or between JFB/Japanese factories) significant differences can be observed.[2] Below the title of each table are shown the results of a two-way ANOVA to look for interaction effects having factory size or industry as a variable.[3]

The results of a two-way ANOVA show significant differences among nations (that is, British factories, Japanese factories and JFB) in terms of 'top-down information flow' and 'simple job design', but no significant interactions both between factory size and nation and between industry and nation in terms of all items. Also, they show that the main effect of

Table 5.3 Managerial preferences for CIU in Japanese factories in Britain (JFB)
Concentration of important information at the top management level
(i) Main effect of nation $F = .88$; size $F = .17$; interaction (nation/size) $F = .05$
(ii) Main effect of nation $F = .87$; industry $F = .44$; interaction (nation/industry) $F = .90$

	Japanese factories in Britain (JFB)			British factories' average	Japanese factories' average	F-value	Scheffe's test	
	Average	Standard deviation	N				British factories/ JFB	JFB/Japanese factories
All samples	2.91	1.38	34	2.64	2.72	0.80	(...)	(...)
All large factories	2.87	1.46	23	2.61	2.71	0.44	(...)	(...)
All small factories	3.00	1.26	11	2.66	2.73	0.44	(...)	(...)
All chemicals/ pharmaceuticals	3.00	(...)	1	2.69	2.75	(...)	(...)	(...)
All machinery	3.33	1.63	6	2.76	2.58	(...)	(...)	(...)
All electrical engineering	3.00	1.65	12	2.66	2.62	0.55	(...)	(...)
All transportation	3.25	0.96	4	2.38	2.83	(...)	(...)	(...)
All rubber/plastic products	2.45	1.13	11	2.63	2.75	0.52	(...)	(...)

Table 5.3 (Cont'd)
Top-down information flow
(i) Main effect of nation $F = 7.09$***; size $F = 1.45$; interaction (nation/size) $F = .18$
(ii) Main effect of nation $F = 5.26$**; industry $F = 1.34$; interaction (nation/industry) $F = 1.10$

	Japanese factories in Britain (JFB)			British factories' average	Japanese factories' average	F-value	Scheffe's test	
	Average	Standard deviation	N				British factories/ JFB	JFB/Japanese factories
All samples	2.68	1.22	34	2.43	2.73	6.35**	–	–
All large factories	2.57	1.12	23	2.38	2.70	2.96	(...)	(...)
All small factories	2.91	1.45	11	2.46	2.80	4.55*	–	–
All chemicals/ pharmaceuticals	2.00	(...)	1	2.47	2.82	(...)	(...)	(...)
All machinery	3.50	1.05	6	2.61	2.67	(...)	(...)	(...)
All electrical engineering	2.67	1.07	12	2.42	2.61	0.59	(...)	(...)
All transportation	2.50	0.58	4	2.35	2.64	(...)	(...)	(...)
All rubber/plastic products	2.36	1.57	11	2.28	2.81	5.73**	–	–

Simple job design

(i) Main effect of nation $F = 11.56***$; size $F = 6.67**$; interaction (nation/size) $F = 2.25$

(ii) Main effect of nation $F = 10.54***$; industry $F = .46$; interaction (nation/industry) $F = 1.16$

	Japanese factories in Britain (JFB)			British factories' average	Japanese factories' average	F-value	Scheffe's test	
	Average	Standard deviation	N				British factories/ JFB	JFB/Japanese factories
All samples	2.50	0.96	34	2.47	2.85	11.25***	–	*
All large factories	2.32	1.22	23	2.32	2.84	10.07***	–	*
All small factories	3.09	1.14	11	2.55	2.89	4.59*	–	–
All chemicals/ pharmaceuticals	3.00	(...)	1	2.67	2.78	(...)	(...)	(...)
All machinery	2.33	0.82	6	2.61	2.79	(...)	(...)	(...)
All electrical engineering	2.75	1.06	12	2.50	2.86	2.20	(...)	(...)
All transportation	2.50	0.58	4	2.00	2.90	(...)	(...)	(...)
All rubber/plastic products	2.27	1.10	11	2.41	2.88	4.72**	–	–

Note: 'Large' and 'small' indicate large factories with 200 or more employees and small factories with less than 200 employees. It is presumed that the higher the average CIU score, the higher the extent of the control-oriented use. The column of 'F-value' shows the results of one-way ANOVA to explore the differences between average scores for each item among JFB, British factories and Japanese factories. Significant levels are $* p < .05$, $** p < .01$ and $*** p < .001$. An asterisk in the last two columns indicates a significant difference ($p < .05$) and '–' indicates no significant difference. '(...)' indicates either no test being conducted or it being impossible to show the value.

nation is greater than that of size or industry with regard to all items. In terms of the concentration of important information at the top, JFB show no significant differences among each set of factories. In terms of 'top-down information flow', the *F*-value shows some differences between average scores among each set of factories in some subsets, but the results of Scheffe's tests indicate no significant differences either between British factories and JFB or between JFB and Japanese factories. The results of the tests suggest that significant differences can be observed only in terms of the preference for simple job design between Japanese factories and JFB. It seems difficult to articulate a consistent pattern on CIU in JFB, but the data suggests that JFB in general have a lesser preference for simple job design than Japanese factories. A more or less similar pattern can be observed in large and small factories, although the difference between large Japanese factories and large JFB with respect to the preference for simple job design is quite notable.

Findings on individual-oriented IT use

General view

As explained in the previous chapter, IIU has been defined to consist of three factors: individual transmission of information; individualised work; and a fixed job system. Under IIU, it is possible to postulate that individual transmission of information is preferred to the collectivistic method of transmission where the distribution of information to each individual is up to the group. It is preferred for employees to use an individualistic way of working rather than team/group work under IIU. Each employee would stick to an individual job and frequent rotation would not be used, as the job would be thought to be owned exclusively by the individual. The relationship between IIU and the measures of managerial preferences are provided in Table 5.4. Again, the results of reliability test of these measures are provided below the table. As shown,

Table 5.4   Measures of managerial preferences for IIU

Pattern of IT use	Managerial preference
Individual-oriented IT use (IIU)	• Individual transmission of information • Teamwork * • Fixed job system

Alpha = .59 for British factories; .21 for Japanese factories; and .25 for JFB.
Note: * shows that the item is measured by a reversed scale.

IIU in managerial preferences has been measured through the following three items: individual transmission of information; teamwork; and fixed job system. As with the CIU, the reliability test indicates that there was not a high consistency among the items of the 'composite' measures, and the items cannot be used collectively as a scale. Therefore, again, I present data based on each item individually, instead of calculating the overall average scores on IIU.

Figure 5.2 shows these managerial preferences in each set of factories. The preference for individualised work has been asked along a reversed scale in the questionnaire (*cf.* Table 3.5), that is, the preference for teamwork. According to this figure, all sets of factories have a general preference for group-oriented IT use. Each has shown more disagreement than agreement to the statements on the preference for the individual transmission of information and individualised fixed job system, and rather stronger preference for teamwork in general. However, some differences can be observed among each set of factories on some items. In regard to the individual transmission of information, Japanese factories seem to indicate stronger preference for individual transmission than the other two sets of factories. Also, in regard to the preference for the fixed job system, Japanese factories look to show a rather weaker preference for the fixed job system.

Comparisons between British factories and Japanese factories

Table 5.5 indicates descriptive statistics in each set and the results of the *t*-tests on the average score between British factories and Japanese factories, classified by industry and factory size to avoid their effects. For the item of 'individualised work', the preference for 'teamwork' was in fact measured through a reversed scale, but a modification has been made to calculate descriptive statistics to show the extent of the 'individualised' pattern of IT use. Again, to test overall differences controlled for by factory size and industry, ANOVA was conducted with factory size and industry as covariates. Below the title of each table are shown the results.

The ANOVA results show significant differences between nations (that is, British factories and Japanese factories) in terms of all items, but again factory size and industry are not significant covariates in terms of all items. As shown in this table, preferences for IIU between British factories and Japanese factories are not consistent in each item. Japanese factories generally indicate stronger preference than British factories for the individual transmission of information, and less preference for teamwork. With regard to the preference for the fixed job system,

Preference for individual transmission of information

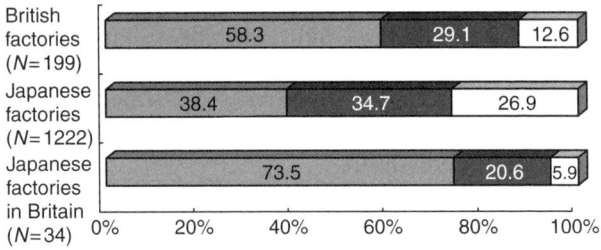

British
factories
(N=199)

Japanese
factories
(N=1222)

Japanese
factories
in Britain
(N=34)

58.3	29.1	12.6
38.4	34.7	26.9
73.5	20.6	5.9

0%   20%   40%   60%   80%   100%

*Information should be communicated individually to
each employee rather than to teams or groups*

☐ Disagree   ■ Neither agree nor disagree   ☐ Agree

Preference for teamwork

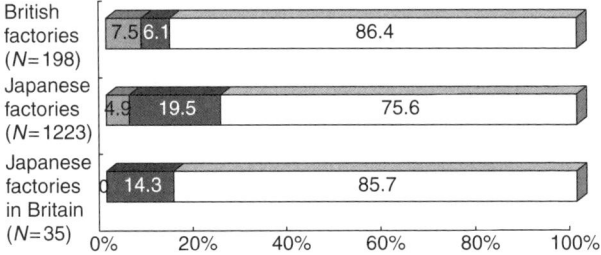

British
factories
(N=198)

Japanese
factories
(N=1223)

Japanese
factories
in Britain
(N=35)

7.5	6.1	86.4
4.9	19.5	75.6
	14.3	85.7

0%   20%   40%   60%   80%   100%

*Team working and/or GDSS are generally the best way for
achieving company goals*

☐ Disagree   ■ Neither agree nor disagree   ☐ Agree

Preference for fixed job system

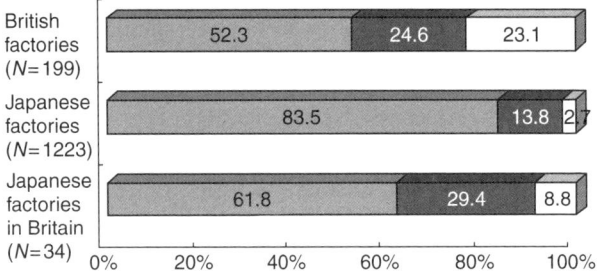

British
factories
(N=199)

Japanese
factories
(N=1223)

Japanese
factories
in Britain
(N=34)

52.3	24.6	23.1
83.5	13.8	2.7
61.8	29.4	8.8

0%   20%   40%   60%   80%   100%

Each employee should stick to their assigned role

☐ Disagree   ■ Neither agree nor disagree   ☐ Agree

Figure 5.2   Managerial preferences for IIU – general view

Table 5.5 Managerial preferences for IIU in British factories and Japanese factories
Individual transmission of information
Main effect of nation: $F = 47.37$*** (covariates: size $F = .32$; industry $F = .07$)

		British factories			Japanese factories			t-value
		Average	Standard deviation	N	Average	Standard deviation	N	
All samples		2.29	1.04	199	2.85	1.01	1222	-7.25***
All large factories		2.22	1.05	72	2.87	1.00	861	-5.29***
All small factories		2.33	1.04	127	2.81	1.04	358	-4.51***
All chemicals/pharmaceuticals		2.11	1.06	36	2.78	0.92	185	-3.88***
All machinery		2.61	1.09	41	2.77	1.03	147	-0.86
All electrical engineering		2.26	1.03	50	3.01	1.07	229	-4.56***
All transportation		2.54	0.86	26	2.95	0.98	202	-2.02*
All rubber/plastic		2.04	1.03	46	2.79	1.01	459	-4.77***
Chemicals/pharmaceuticals	Large	2.13	1.30	15	2.89	0.94	103	-2.78**
	Small	2.10	0.89	21	2.63	0.88	82	-2.49*
Machinery	Large	2.67	1.00	10	2.87	1.04	110	-0.59
	Small	2.59	1.13	31	2.44	0.94	36	0.59
Electrical engineering	Large	2.05	1.03	17	2.99	1.05	176	-3.50***
	Small	2.36	1.03	33	2.85	1.03	53	-3.02**
Transportation	Large	2.60	0.52	10	2.89	0.96	177	-0.95
	Small	2.50	1.03	16	3.32	1.03	25	-2.49*
Rubber/plastic products	Large	2.05	1.07	21	2.78	0.98	295	-3.28***
	Small	2.04	1.02	25	2.81	1.05	162	-3.44***

Table 5.5 (Cont'd)
Teamwork (reversed scale: adjusted)
Main effect of nation: $F = 45.10$*** (covariates: size $F = 3.25$; industry $F = .02$)

		British factories			Japanese factories			t-value
		Average	Standard deviation	N	Average	Standard deviation	N	
All samples		1.77	1.00	198	2.15	0.73	1 223	-5.16***
All large factories		1.62	0.76	71	2.14	0.71	862	-5.58***
All small factories		1.86	1.10	127	2.19	0.78	358	-3.15**
All chemicals/pharmaceuticals		1.92	1.11	36	2.11	0.66	185	-1.01
All machinery		2.05	1.28	40	2.18	0.79	147	-0.63
All electrical engineering		1.64	0.85	50	2.18	0.80	229	-4.27***
All transportation		1.77	0.86	26	2.12	0.70	202	-2.01*
All rubber/plastic		1.57	0.81	46	2.17	0.72	460	-5.31***
Chemicals/pharmaceuticals	Large	1.87	0.74	15	2.10	0.65	103	-1.26
	Small	1.95	1.32	21	2.12	0.67	82	-0.57
Machinery	Large	2.00	1.41	10	2.15	0.73	110	-0.51
	Small	2.06	1.27	31	2.31	0.95	36	-0.90
Electrical engineering	Large	1.35	0.61	17	2.13	0.78	176	-3.99***
	Small	1.79	0.93	33	2.34	0.86	53	-2.91**
Transportation	Large	1.80	0.63	10	2.13	0.67	177	-1.51
	Small	1.75	1.00	16	2.08	0.86	25	-1.12
Rubber/plastic products	Large	1.43	0.51	21	2.17	0.71	296	-4.67***
	Small	1.68	0.99	25	2.17	0.74	162	-2.91**

Fixed job system

Main effect of nation: $F = 120.48$*** (covariates: size $F = 3.15$; industry $F = .25$)

		British factories			Japanese factories			t-value
		Average	Standard deviation	N	Average	Standard deviation	N	
All samples		2.59	1.14	199	1.83	0.77	1223	9.10***
All large factories		2.54	1.22	72	1.79	0.77	862	7.52***
All small factories		2.62	1.10	127	1.92	0.78	358	7.81***
All chemicals/pharmaceuticals		2.44	1.13	36	1.86	0.79	185	2.94**
All machinery		2.76	1.20	41	1.84	0.79	147	5.84***
All electrical engineering		2.44	1.16	50	1.82	0.77	229	3.62***
All transportation		2.69	0.97	26	1.70	0.73	202	5.02***
All rubber/plastic		2.67	1.17	46	1.88	0.78	460	4.51***
Chemicals/pharmaceuticals	Large	2.33	1.35	15	1.85	0.80	103	1.35
	Small	2.52	0.98	21	1.88	0.78	82	2.80**
Machinery	Large	3.22	1.20	10	1.83	0.80	110	3.42**
	Small	2.63	1.18	31	1.86	0.76	36	3.11**
Electrical engineering	Large	2.18	1.19	17	1.76	0.75	176	1.42
	Small	2.58	1.15	33	2.00	0.81	53	2.52*
Transportation	Large	2.90	0.88	10	1.67	0.72	177	5.19***
	Small	2.56	1.03	16	1.92	0.81	25	2.22*
Rubber/plastic products	Large	2.52	1.24	21	1.85	0.78	296	2.43*
	Small	2.80	1.12	25	1.93	0.77	162	3.77***

Note: 'Large' and 'small' in the second column indicate large factories with 200 or more employees and small factories with less than 200 employees. Reversed scales have been adjusted, thus it is presumed that the higher the average IIU score, the higher the extent of the individual-oriented use. *T*-value indicates the result of the *t*-test on average values between British factories and Japanese factories. Significant levels of statistical tests are * $p < .05$, ** $p < .01$ and *** $p < .001$.

however, Japanese factories generally show less preference than British factories. In other words, as far as managerial preference goes, British factories show stronger preference for teamwork in the use of IT-based system than Japanese factories, but job rotation is not thought to be a good system in British factories in general. This general pattern is quite consistent among subsets classified by industry and factory size, although the difference of the average value between British factories and Japanese factories is considerable in specific industries and factory sizes: electrical engineering, rubber/plastic products and machinery with regard to the individual transmission of information; electrical engineering and rubber/plastic products with regard to teamwork; small factories in each industry and large factories in transportation, machinery and rubber/plastic products with regard to the fixed job system. All industries except machinery show significant differences between British factories and Japanese factories regarding individual transmission of information, and electrical engineering and rubber/plastic products show considerably higher differences between British factories and Japanese factories concerning individualised work. With regard to the fixed job system, all industrial groups show statistically significant differences, but machinery, transportation and rubber/plastic products indicate relatively higher significant differences than other industries.

Japanese factories in Britain

Table 5.6 shows where JFB can be situated in terms of each item on IIU, and indicates the descriptive statistics for the JFB. ANOVA was carried out to explore the differences between average scores for each item among JFB, British factories and Japanese factories. Where the overall ANOVA is significant, the results of *post hoc* Scheffe's tests are shown in the last two columns. Again, below the title of each table are shown the results of a two-way ANOVA to look for interaction effects having (i) factory size, and (ii) industry as variables.

The results of a two-way ANOVA show that there are significant differences among nations (that is, British factories, Japanese factories and JFB) in terms of all items, but no significant interactions either between factory size and nation or between industry and nation in terms of all items. Also, they show that the main effect of the nation is greater than that of size or industry with regard to all items. This table shows that the overall tendency on IIU of JFB is rather closer to British factories, as statistically significant differences can be generally observed between JFB and Japanese factories. With regard to individual transmission of information, large factories in JFB show significant differences

Table 5.6 Managerial preferences for IIU in Japanese factories in Britain (JFB)
Individual transmission of information
(i) Main effect of nation $F = 35.57$***; size $F = .98$; interaction (nation/size) $F = 1.15$
(ii) Main effect of nation $F = 27.40$***; industry $F = 1.07$; interaction (nation/industry) $F = 1.50$

	Japanese factories in Britain (JFB)			British factories' average	Japanese factories' average	F-value	Scheffe's test	
	Average	Standard deviation	N				British factories/ JFB	JFB/Japanese factories
All samples	1.94	1.01	34	2.29	2.85	37.53***	–	*
All large factories	2.09	1.08	23	2.22	2.87	19.95***	–	*
All small factories	1.64	0.81	11	2.33	2.81	15.80***	*	*
All chemicals/ pharmaceuticals	3.00	(...)	1	2.11	2.78	(...)	(...)	(...)
All machinery	1.50	0.55	6	2.61	2.77	(...)	(...)	(...)
All electrical engineering	2.25	1.29	12	2.26	3.01	12.18***	–	*
All transportation	1.75	0.96	4	2.54	2.95	(...)	(...)	(...)
All rubber/plastic products	1.82	0.87	11	2.04	2.79	15.72***	–	*

Table 5.6 (Cont'd)
Teamwork (reversed scale: adjusted)
(i) Main effect of nation $F = 33.15$***; size $F = .64$; interaction (nation/size) $F = 1.21$
(ii) Main effect of nation $F = 19.52$***; industry $F = 1.52$; interaction (nation/industry) $F = 1.82$

	Japanese factories in Britain (JFB)			British factories' average	Japanese factories' average	F-value	Scheffe's test	
	Average	Standard deviation	N				British factories/ JFB	JFB/Japanese factories
All samples	1.49	0.74	35	1.77	2.15	31.58***	–	*
All large factories	1.50	0.72	24	1.62	2.14	25.53***	–	*
All small factories	1.45	0.82	11	1.86	2.19	9.86***	–	*
All chemicals/ pharmaceuticals	3.00	(...)	1	1.92	2.11	(...)	(...)	(...)
All machinery	1.43	0.53	7	2.05	2.18	(...)	(...)	(...)
All electrical engineering	1.50	0.80	12	1.64	2.18	12.11***	–	*
All transportation	1.25	0.50	4	1.77	2.12	(...)	(...)	(...)
All rubber/plastic products	1.45	0.82	11	1.57	2.17	18.37***	–	*

Fixed job system

(i) Main effect of nation $F = 59.11$***; size $F = .09$; interaction (nation/size) $F = .98$

(ii) Main effect of nation $F = 69.96$***; industry $F = 1.02$; interaction (nation/industry) $F = 1.07$

	Japanese factories in Britain (JFB)			British factories' average	Japanese factories' average	F-value	Scheffe's test	
	Average	Standard deviation	N				British factories/ JFB	JFB/Japanese factories
All samples	2.21	1.04	34	2.59	1.83	72.67***	*	*
All large factories	2.30	1.15	23	2.54	1.79	31.06***	–	*
All small factories	2.00	0.77	11	2.62	1.92	30.74***	*	–
All chemicals/ pharmaceuticals	3.00	(...)	1	2.67	2.78	(...)	(...)	(...)
All machinery	2.33	0.82	6	2.61	2.79	(...)	(...)	(...)
All electrical engineering	2.75	1.06	12	2.50	2.86	11.37***	–	–
All transportation	2.50	0.58	4	2.00	2.90	(...)	(...)	(...)
All rubber/plastic products	2.27	1.10	11	2.41	2.88	20.34***	–	–

Note: 'Large' and 'small' indicate large factories with 200 or more employees and small factories with less than 200 employees. It is presumed that the higher the average IIU score, the higher the extent of the individual-oriented use. The column of 'F-value' shows the results of one-way ANOVA to explore the difference between average scores for each item among JFB, British factories and Japanese factories. Significant levels are $* p < .05$, $** p < .01$ and $*** p < .001$. An asterisk in the last two columns indicates a significant difference ($p < .05$) and '–' indicates no significant differences. '(...)' indicates either no test being conducted or it being impossible to show the value.

compared with Japanese factories, but small factories in JFB indicate significant differences compared with British factories as well, which means small factories in JFB have the lowest score among the three sets of factories. As far as descriptive statistics are concerned, the tendency holds true in machinery in particular. Concerning teamwork, the results of Scheffe's test show the difference not between JFB and British factories, but between JFB and Japanese factories in all subsets. With regard to the fixed job system, the descriptive statistics and the results of Scheffe's test indicate that both large and small factories in JFB are situated in between British factories and Japanese factories, although large factories in JFB indicate significant difference with Japanese factories, but small factories with British factories. This suggests large factories in JFB have closer managerial preference for the fixed job system to British factories, but small factories in JFB are closer to Japanese factories.

Conclusion

This chapter has attempted to find from the data some evidence for national cultural influences on organisational IT use. CIU and IIU have been examined separately. Regarding CIU, all sampled factories do not prefer a highly controlling method of use of IT-based systems. They have shown rather strong disagreement to top managers' exclusive access to important information, top-down information flow and simple job design, although different degrees of preference can be observed among each set of factories. However, the degree of the preferences between British factories and Japanese factories is different in terms of top-down information flow and simple job design. In these dimensions of CIU, Japanese factories show higher managerial preferences with statistically significant levels.

   With regard to IIU, all sampled factories indicate a rather strong general disagreement to the individualised pattern of IT use. Each set of factories has shown more disagreement than agreement to the statements on the preference for individualised transmission of information and individualised fixed job systems, and rather stronger preference for teamwork in general. Comparing data on British factories and Japanese factories with each other, however, a considerable difference in each item concerning the degree of preferences is observed. Japanese factories indicate a much higher preference regarding individualised transmission of information, and a lesser preference for teamwork and for the fixed job system. These data suggest that Japanese factories have more preference for job rotation than British factories, but the degree of preference for teamwork is not as high as in British factories. These findings are more or less consistent in each subset classified by industry and factory size.

The sample size of JFB is not big enough to divide into subsets by size *and* industry. However, all sampled factories and subsets classified by size *or* industry suggest that JFB can be located as having the least preference in IIU, though overall data in IIU suggests JFB have managerial preferences rather closer to British factories than to Japanese factories. Concerning CIU, it is difficult to judge where JFB are situated, as they do not show statistically significant differences except for the preference for simple job design, in which JFB show lower scores than Japanese factories with significant difference, and rather closer preference to British factories. Taking all of these findings into consideration, Japanese factories have rather stronger preferences than British factories for CIU and IIU in general; JFB have rather closer preference for IIU to British factories in general.

National culture predicts managerial preferences in each factory. What I have outlined above is different CIU and IIU tendencies to be found in British factories, Japanese factories and JFB. A number of possible influences apart from national culture might have been investigated. As indicated in the last chapter, some of these have been controlled for. Other possible differences between countries, such as economic, institutional and political influences may be present in the data. However, taking all the evidence into account, the extent of the differences in IT use discussed above, the fact that that they are found at a national – not sectoral – level with regard to most items measured, and the importance of CIU and IIU as explanatory factors which were developed from cultural models in previous studies, lead towards the conclusion that some national cultural influences are evident in my data.

In the following two chapters, my analysis will clarify how these cultural influences operate in actual terms in each set of factories.

6
How Cultural Influences Operate at the Shop-floor Level

Introduction

The preceding chapter depicted the managerial preferences for IT use in British factories, Japanese factories, and JFB – the proxies for national culture. Some differences could be observed among each set of factories both for CIU and for IIU. This chapter describes how these differences in managerial preferences are developing in actual terms at the shop-floor level of a factory. The main reason for describing actual practices of patterns of IT use as well as managerial preferences is that the score of the latter may or may not reflect that of the former. It is possible that cultural dispositions may not really be displayed in an organisation for some reason: in which case some other factors such as economic, institutional or political factors may be involved in determining actual IT use.

Findings on control-oriented IT use

General view

As discussed in Chapter 3, CIU at the shop-floor level has been presumed to develop in seven specific areas. The relationship between CIU and the measures of actual practices at the shop-floor level is given in Table 6.1. As with managerial preferences shown in the last chapter, the results of a reliability test of these measures are provided below the table.

As shown in the table, managerial preferences for CIU are presumed to appear as concrete phenomena on the shop-floor in an organisation. For example, the managerial preference for the concentration of important information at the top management level might operate as limited access for a shop-floor worker to strategic information databases like

Table 6.1   Measures of actual practices in CIU at the shop-floor level

Pattern of IT use	Actual practices
Control-oriented IT use (CIU)	• Accessibility to strategic information* • Use of information provided by managers • Amount of quantitative information • Amount of qualitative information* • Sharing information with other workers* • Simplified and predetermined jobs • Dealing with daily problems of the line*

Alpha = .06 for British factories; .26 for Japanese factories; and .05 for JFB.
Note: * indicates that the item is measured by a reversed scale.

sales forecasts (Kambayashi, 1998). In order to minimise uncertainty at work, workers would be given more quantitative information such as production target rates, rather than qualitative information like a briefing on company performance. Many checks and instructions through a hierarchical control would be provided to eliminate abnormalities, resulting in little sharing of information with other workers at lateral levels (Susman, 1990). As a result, shop-floor workers would have jobs as simplified and standardised as possible (Davis and Wacker, 1987), and it might be impossible for them to engage in 'unusual operations' to deal with problems and changes flexibly (Koike, 1988).

Statistical tests of the data, however, show that there was poor consistency among the items of the 'composite' measures, and the items cannot be used collectively as a scale. Therefore, again, I present data based on each item individually, instead of calculating the overall average scores on actual practices in CIU at the shop-floor level.

Figure 6.1 shows the general trend of each dimension of actual practices in terms of CIU at the shop-floor level. According to the figure, most aspects of actual practice in CIU look different from each other. Comparing British factories and Japanese factories, my data suggest that more Japanese factories than British factories have actually limited access to strategic information databases; used information given by managers; have provided workers with more quantitative and less qualitative information; or simplified and predetermined a worker's job. This suggests Japanese factories' stronger tendency towards CIU. However, more Japanese factories workers can deal with the daily problems of the line. It is difficult to read specific JFB's tendencies, but, at least, JFB have actually given workers more quantitative *and* more qualitative information.

Accessibility to strategic information

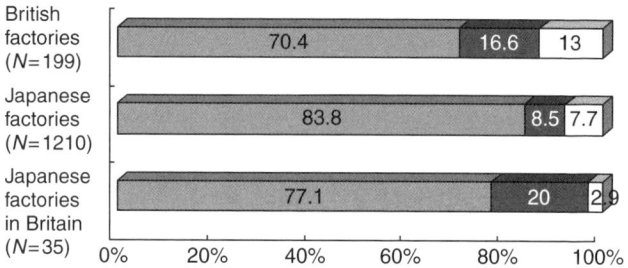

It is possible for workers to gain access to strategic
information (e.g. sales forecasts)

▨ False ■ Neither true nor false ☐ True

Use of information provided by managers

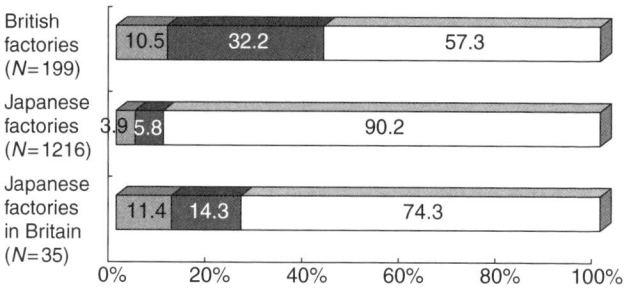

Workers usually use information provided by managers

▨ False ■ Neither true nor false ☐ True

Figure 6.1

Amount of quantitative information

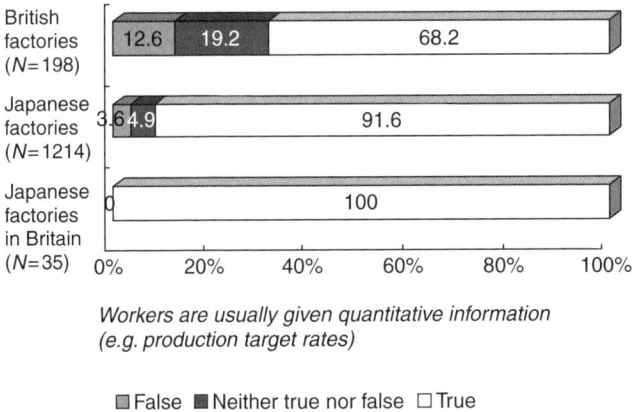

Workers are usually given quantitative information (e.g. production target rates)

☐ False ■ Neither true nor false ☐ True

Amount of qualitative information

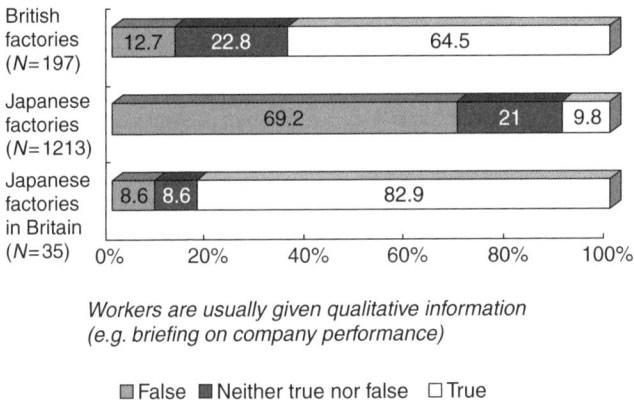

Workers are usually given qualitative information (e.g. briefing on company performance)

☐ False ■ Neither true nor false ☐ True

Figure 6.1   (Cont'd overleaf)

Sharing information with other workers

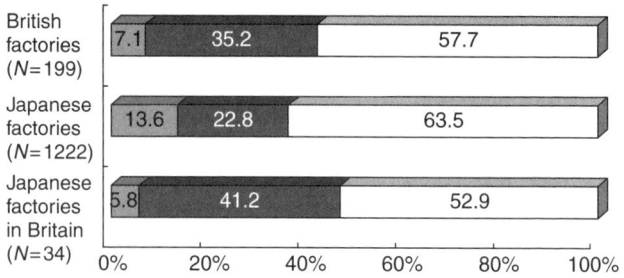

British
factories
(N=199) | 7.1 | 35.2 | 57.7

Japanese
factories
(N=1222) | 13.6 | 22.8 | 63.5

Japanese
factories
in Britain
(N=34) | 5.8 | 41.2 | 52.9

Workers usually share information with other workers

☐ False ■ Neither true nor false ☐ True

Simplified and predetermined jobs

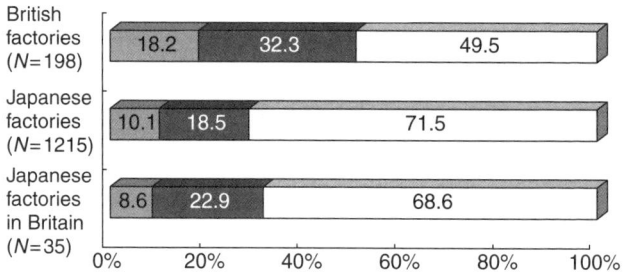

British
factories
(N=198) | 18.2 | 32.3 | 49.5

Japanese
factories
(N=1215) | 10.1 | 18.5 | 71.5

Japanese
factories
in Britain
(N=35) | 8.6 | 22.9 | 68.6

*Workers' jobs are simplified and predetermined
as much as possible*

☐ False ■ Neither true nor false ☐ True

Figure 6.1

Dealing with daily problems of the line

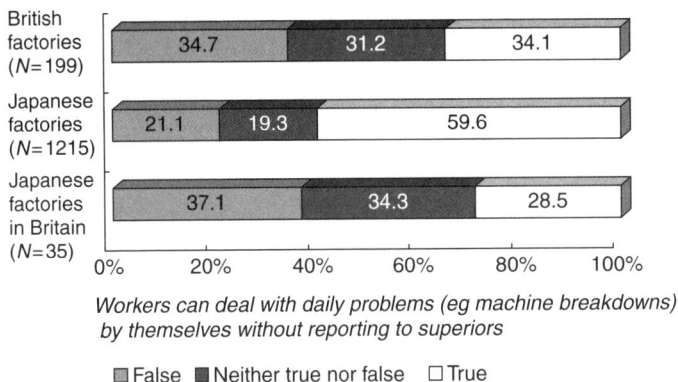

Figure 6.1 Actual practices in CIU at the shop-floor level – general view

Comparison between British factories and Japanese factories

Table 6.2 shows descriptive statistics regarding British factories and Japanese factories and the results of *t*-tests in terms of the difference between the two average scores in each dimension of CIU. As with the presentation of the data developed in the last chapter, below the title of each table are shown the results of ANOVA tests to assess whether factory size and/or industry are significant covariates. The ANOVA results show significant differences between nations (that is, British factories and Japanese factories) in terms of all items except 'sharing information with other workers', in which the type of industry is a significant covariate. Factory size and/or industry are significant covariates in terms of some items, for example 'amount of quantitative information' and 'simplified and predetermined jobs', but the *F*-value of the main effect of nation is still greater than the covariates in terms of most cases.

According to this table, regarding most dimensions of CIU, Japanese factories have achieved, generally speaking, higher average scores than British factories with significant statistical differences. With regard to the access to strategic information databases, Japanese factories in general actually limit worker access and the tendency holds good for machinery and electrical engineering in particular. Regarding the use of information provided by managers, Japanese factories again indicate much higher scores than British factories in most subsets, but the trend is particularly

Table 6.2 Actual practices in CIU in British factories and Japanese factories at the shop-floor level
Accessibility to strategic information (reversed scale: adjusted)
Main effect of nation: F = 6.52** (covariates: size F = 2.14; industry F = 11.65**)

		British factories			Japanese factories			t-value
		Average	Standard deviation	N	Average	Standard deviation	N	
All samples		4.04	1.23	199	4.30	0.96	1210	−2.82**
All large factories		4.00	1.24	72	4.34	0.94	854	−2.25*
All small factories		4.06	1.23	127	4.22	1.01	353	−1.25
All chemicals/pharmaceuticals		4.42	0.91	36	4.15	1.07	184	1.39
All machinery		3.59	1.38	41	4.24	1.04	147	−2.85**
All electrical engineering		3.72	1.28	50	4.18	0.98	229	−2.41*
All transportation		4.31	1.16	26	4.40	0.96	197	−0.43
All rubber/plastic		4.35	1.14	46	4.39	0.88	453	−0.26
Chemicals/pharmaceuticals	Large	4.20	0.77	15	4.19	1.02	103	0.21
	Small	4.57	0.98	21	4.10	1.14	81	1.75
Machinery	Large	3.56	1.67	10	4.25	1.05	110	−1.22
	Small	3.59	1.32	31	4.31	0.95	36	−2.53*
Electrical engineering	Large	3.71	1.16	17	4.22	0.97	176	−2.06*
	Small	3.73	1.35	33	4.06	1.01	53	−1.21
Transportation	Large	3.90	1.60	10	4.41	0.95	174	−1.00
	Small	4.56	0.73	16	4.30	1.06	23	0.84
Rubber/plastic products	Large	4.33	1.20	21	4.45	0.83	291	−0.44
	Small	4.36	1.11	25	4.29	0.94	160	0.32

Use of information provided by managers
Main effect of nation: $F = 62.35$*** (covariates: size $F = 2.06$; industry $F = 1.48$)

		British factories			Japanese factories			t-value
		Average	Standard deviation	N	Average	Standard deviation	N	
All samples		3.66	1.00	199	4.17	0.72	1216	-6.91***
All large factories		3.69	0.93	72	4.19	0.72	858	-4.41***
All small factories		3.64	1.04	127	4.12	0.73	355	-4.81***
All chemicals/pharmaceuticals		3.56	0.94	36	4.15	0.80	184	-3.53***
All machinery		3.59	1.38	41	4.07	0.80	147	-2.61*
All electrical engineering		3.76	0.87	50	4.16	0.74	229	-3.03**
All transportation		3.12	1.14	26	4.31	0.66	201	-5.23***
All rubber/plastic		3.96	1.01	46	4.15	0.67	455	-1.26
Chemicals/pharmaceuticals	Large	3.40	0.91	15	4.07	0.87	103	-2.77**
	Small	3.67	0.97	21	4.25	0.70	81	-2.58*
Machinery	Large	3.56	0.73	10	4.05	0.86	110	-1.70
	Small	3.66	1.07	31	4.14	0.64	36	-2.23*
Electrical engineering	Large	3.82	0.95	17	4.22	0.69	176	-1.66
	Small	3.73	0.84	33	3.98	0.87	53	-1.34
Transportation	Large	3.00	0.82	10	4.31	0.65	177	-6.14***
	Small	3.19	1.33	16	4.33	0.76	24	-3.47***
Rubber/plastic products	Large	4.19	0.81	21	4.19	0.64	292	-0.01
	Small	4.36	1.11	25	4.29	0.94	160	-1.33

Table 6.2 (Cont'd)
Amount of quantitative information
Main effect of nation: $F = 41.44***$ (covariates: size $F = 16.33***$; industry $F = 5.60*$)

		British factories			Japanese factories			t-value
		Average	Standard deviation	N	Average	Standard deviation	N	
All samples		3.88	1.09	199	4.37	0.76	1214	−6.14***
All large factories		4.03	1.16	72	4.43	0.73	857	−2.89**
All small factories		3.79	1.05	126	4.24	0.82	354	−4.37***
All chemicals/pharmaceuticals		3.97	0.88	36	4.24	0.81	184	−1.79
All machinery		3.80	1.23	41	4.24	0.84	147	−2.12*
All electrical engineering		4.06	0.89	50	4.39	0.78	229	−2.67**
All transportation		3.32	1.44	25	4.55	0.68	201	−4.22***
All rubber/plastic		3.98	1.04	46	4.39	0.73	453	−2.59**
Chemicals/pharmaceuticals	Large	4.20	0.94	15	4.28	0.76	103	−0.38
	Small	3.81	0.81	21	4.19	0.87	81	−1.79
Machinery	Large	3.78	1.48	10	4.32	0.81	110	−1.08
	Small	3.81	1.18	31	3.97	0.88	36	−0.63
Electrical engineering	Large	4.29	0.77	17	4.43	0.77	176	−0.68
	Small	3.94	0.93	33	4.28	0.82	53	−1.80
Transportation	Large	3.50	1.72	10	4.58	0.66	177	−1.98
	Small	3.20	1.26	15	4.33	0.82	24	−3.41**
Rubber/plastic products	Large	4.05	1.11	21	4.44	0.69	291	−1.60
	Small	3.92	1.00	25	4.31	0.78	160	−1.85

Amount of qualitative information (reversed scale: adjusted)
Main effect of nation: $F = 430.44$*** (covariates: size $F = 4.31$*; industry $F = 1.56$)

		British factories			Japanese factories			t-value
		Average	Standard deviation	N	Average	Standard deviation	N	
All samples		2.21	1.09	197	3.76	0.88	1213	−19.06***
All large factories		2.00	1.07	72	3.82	0.86	856	−14.00***
All small factories		2.33	1.08	125	3.63	0.91	354	−11.99***
All chemicals/pharmaceuticals		2.17	0.94	36	3.65	0.88	184	−9.16***
All machinery		2.27	1.12	41	3.69	0.96	147	−8.13***
All electrical engineering		2.16	1.09	50	3.75	0.91	229	−10.83***
All transportation		2.42	1.38	24	4.01	0.74	200	−5.54***
All rubber/plastic		2.13	1.02	46	3.73	0.89	453	−11.49***
Chemicals/pharmaceuticals	Large	1.60	0.74	15	3.69	0.86	103	−8.90***
	Small	2.57	0.87	21	3.60	0.90	81	−4.70***
Machinery	Large	2.11	1.27	10	3.75	0.95	110	−4.82***
	Small	2.31	1.09	31	3.56	0.97	36	−4.98***
Electrical engineering	Large	2.24	1.20	17	3.76	0.89	176	−6.50***
	Small	2.12	1.05	33	3.72	0.95	53	−7.27***
Transportation	Large	2.00	1.25	10	4.05	0.71	177	−8.41***
	Small	2.71	1.44	14	3.70	0.88	23	−2.31*
Rubber/plastic products	Large	2.05	1.02	21	3.79	0.87	290	−8.79***
	Small	2.20	1.04	25	3.61	0.91	161	−7.10***

Table 6.2 (Cont'd)
Sharing information with other workers (reversed scale: adjusted)
Main effect of nation: $F = .14$ (covariates: size $F = .15$; industry $F = 13.47***$)

		British factories			Japanese factories			t-value
		Average	Standard deviation	N	Average	Standard deviation	N	
All samples		2.32	0.90	196	2.38	0.88	1213	−0.86
All large factories		2.46	0.90	72	2.38	0.92	855	0.67
All small factories		2.24	0.89	124	2.39	0.92	355	−1.54
All chemicals/pharmaceuticals		2.29	0.79	35	3.87	0.86	184	0.75
All machinery		2.20	0.84	41	2.42	0.92	147	−1.42
All electrical engineering		2.20	0.78	50	2.35	0.99	229	−1.13
All transportation		2.68	1.22	25	2.36	0.93	201	1.55
All rubber/plastic		2.40	0.91	45	2.48	0.90	452	−0.60
Chemicals/pharmaceuticals	Large	2.33	1.05	15	2.09	0.74	103	0.88
	Small	2.25	0.55	20	2.27	0.97	81	−0.13
Machinery	Large	2.33	0.71	10	2.49	0.95	110	−0.49
	Small	2.16	0.88	31	2.25	0.81	36	−0.46
Electrical engineering	Large	2.29	0.77	17	2.35	0.97	176	−0.22
	Small	2.15	0.80	33	2.34	1.04	53	−0.89
Transportation	Large	2.70	1.16	10	2.33	0.91	177	1.24
	Small	2.67	1.29	15	2.63	1.06	24	0.11
Rubber/plastic products	Large	2.62	0.86	21	2.50	0.92	289	0.57
	Small	2.21	0.93	24	2.46	0.86	161	−1.32

Simplified and predetermined jobs

Main effect of nation: $F = 20.93^{***}$ (covariates: size $F = 8.03^{**}$, industry $F = .27$)

		British factories			Japanese factories			t-value
		Average	Standard deviation	N	Average	Standard deviation	N	
All samples		3.42	0.98	198	3.80	0.88	1215	−5.15***
All large factories		3.50	0.96	72	3.85	0.87	857	−2.98**
All small factories		3.38	0.99	126	3.70	0.91	355	−3.25***
All chemicals/pharmaceuticals		3.54	0.98	35	3.87	0.86	184	−2.02*
All machinery		3.49	0.95	41	3.47	0.92	147	0.11
All electrical engineering		3.42	0.91	50	3.82	0.92	229	−2.76**
All transportation		2.81	1.06	26	4.10	0.81	201	−6.00***
All rubber/plastic		3.63	0.93	46	3.75	0.85	454	−0.91
Chemicals/pharmaceuticals	Large	3.40	1.12	15	3.91	0.82	103	−1.71
	Small	3.65	0.88	20	3.81	0.91	81	−0.73
Machinery	Large	3.33	1.00	10	3.47	0.97	110	−0.41
	Small	3.53	0.95	31	3.42	0.73	36	0.56
Electrical engineering	Large	3.52	0.87	17	3.85	0.88	176	−1.45
	Small	3.36	0.93	33	3.70	1.07	53	−1.48
Transportation	Large	3.20	0.92	10	4.14	0.80	177	−3.58***
	Small	2.56	1.09	16	3.79	0.78	24	−4.16***
Rubber/plastic products	Large	3.76	0.94	21	3.79	0.81	291	−0.15
	Small	3.52	0.92	25	3.68	0.91	161	−0.83

Table 6.2 (Cont'd)
Dealing with daily problems of the line (reversed scale: adjusted)
Main effect of nation: $F = 35.20^{***}$ (covariates: size $F = 3.31$; industry $F = .29$)

		British factories			Japanese factories			t-value
		Average	Standard deviation	N	Average	Standard deviation	N	
All samples		3.06	1.12	199	2.52	1.04	1 215	6.72***
All large factories		3.11	1.13	72	2.47	1.03	857	5.00***
All small factories		3.02	1.12	127	2.62	1.05	355	3.62***
All chemicals/pharmaceuticals		2.94	1.07	36	2.59	1.05	184	1.84
All machinery		3.22	1.21	41	2.21	1.37	147	3.66***
All electrical engineering		2.78	0.89	50	2.50	1.06	229	1.96
All transportation		2.96	1.22	26	2.58	1.05	201	1.71
All rubber/plastic		3.35	1.22	46	2.46	1.01	454	4.76***
Chemicals/pharmaceuticals	Large	2.87	1.06	15	2.48	1.07	103	1.33
	Small	3.00	1.10	21	2.74	1.01	81	1.03
Machinery	Large	3.67	1.12	10	2.53	1.06	110	3.10**
	Small	3.09	1.23	31	2.50	1.08	36	2.12*
Electrical engineering	Large	2.88	1.11	17	2.49	1.07	176	1.45
	Small	2.73	0.76	33	2.53	1.03	53	0.96
Transportation	Large	2.90	1.10	10	2.57	1.05	177	0.98
	Small	3.00	1.32	16	2.71	1.04	24	0.78
Rubber/plastic products	Large	3.33	1.20	21	2.39	0.97	291	4.24***
	Small	3.36	1.25	25	2.61	1.08	161	3.17**

Note: 'Large' and 'small' in the second column indicate large factories with 200 or more employees and small factories with less than 200 employees. It is presumed that the higher the average CIU score, the higher the extent of the control-oriented use. *T*-value indicates the result of the *t*-test on average values between British factories and Japanese factories. Significant levels are * $p < .05$, ** $p < .01$ and *** $p < .001$.

true for transportation and chemicals/pharmaceuticals. In terms of rubber/plastic products and electrical engineering, little difference can be observed between British factories and Japanese factories. If we look at 'amount of quantitative information' and 'amount of qualitative information' together, we see that, with regard to the kind of information, Japanese factories actually tend to give workers more quantitative and less qualitative information than British factories. Most subsets show much higher scores in Japanese factories than in British factories in terms of qualitative information, whilst transportation – especially small factories, electrical engineering, rubber/plastic products and machinery – indicate significant differences between British factories and Japanese factories with regard to the amount of quantitative information. It appears that more quantitative information such as production target rates than qualitative information like briefing on company performance is used at work in Japanese factories than in British ones. Regarding information sharing with other workers, no significant differences can be seen between British factories and Japanese factories. As for simplified and predetermined jobs, Japanese factories have much higher scores than British factories – a trend which particularly holds good for transportation. With regard to dealing with the daily problems of the line, however, British factories have acquired higher scores than Japanese factories. The tendency holds good for rubber/plastic products and machinery in particular.

Comparing these data on actual practice with those on managerial preferences, some inconsistencies can be identified. For example, there was almost no difference between British factories and Japanese factories with regard to the preference for a worker's accessibility to strategic information databases, but statistically significant differences can be observed regarding the actual practice on worker's access to the databases. I will discuss this issue later in the chapter.

Japanese factories in Britain

Table 6.3 shows where JFB are situated in terms of each item regarding actual practice at the shop-floor level concerning CIU. The table indicates the descriptive statistics for the JFB. ANOVA was carried out to explore the differences between average scores for each item among JFB, British factories, and Japanese factories. The results of *post hoc* Scheffe's tests are shown in the last two columns. Below the title of each table are shown the results of a two-way ANOVA to look for interaction effects having (i) factory size, and (ii) industry as variables.

The results of a two-way ANOVA show significant differences among nations (that is, British factories, Japanese factories and JFB) in terms of

Table 6.3 Actual practices in CIU in Japanese factories in Britain (JFB) at the shop-floor level
Accessibility to strategic information (reversed scale: adjusted)
(i) Main effect of nation $F = 4.63**$; size $F = .01$; interaction (nation/size) $F = .71$
(ii) Main effect of nation $F = 3.33*$; industry $F = 2.44*$; interaction (nation/industry) $F = 2.70**$

	Japanese factories in Britain (JFB)			British factories' average	Japanese factories' average	F-value	Scheffe's test	
	Average	Standard deviation	N				British factories/ JFB	JFB/Japanese factories
All samples	4.26	0.89	35	4.04	4.30	5.68**	–	–
All large factories	4.25	0.85	24	4.00	4.34	4.10*	–	–
All small factories	4.27	1.01	11	4.06	4.22	0.99	(...)	(...)
All chemicals/ pharmaceuticals	5.00	(...)	1	4.42	4.10	(...)	(...)	(...)
All machinery	3.71	0.76	7	3.59	4.24	(...)	(...)	(...)
All electrical engineering	4.50	0.90	12	3.72	4.18	4.99**	*	–
All transportation	4.50	0.58	4	4.31	4.40	(...)	(...)	(...)
All rubber/plastic products	4.18	0.98	11	4.35	4.39	0.33	–	–

Use of information provided by managers

(i) Main effect of nation $F = 33.25$***; size $F = 2.12$; interaction (nation/size) $F = .41$

(ii) Main effect of nation $F = 45.64$***; industry $F = 1.00$; interaction (nation/industry) $F = 3.82$***

	Japanese factories in Britain (JFB)			British factories' average	Japanese factories' average	F-value	Scheffe's test	
	Average	Standard deviation	N				British factories/ JFB	JFB/Japanese factories
All samples	3.86	0.91	35	3.66	4.17	39.33***	–	–
All large factories	3.96	0.91	24	3.69	4.19	15.65***	–	–
All small factories	3.64	0.92	11	3.64	4.12	16.95***	–	–
All chemicals/ pharmaceuticals	3.00	(...)	1	4.56	4.25	(...)	(...)	(...)
All machinery	4.14	1.07	7	3.63	4.07	(...)	(...)	(...)
All electrical engineering	3.92	0.90	12	3.76	4.16	5.86**	–	–
All transportation	3.75	0.50	4	3.12	4.31	(...)	(...)	(...)
All rubber/plastic products	3.73	1.01	11	3.96	4.15	3.27*	–	*

Table 6.3 (Cont'd)

Amount of quantitative information

(i) Main effect of nation $F = 23.88***$; size $F = 2.44$; interaction (nation/size) $F = 0.14$

(ii) Main effect of nation $F = 36.97***$; industry $F = 0.45$; interaction (nation/industry) $F = 3.15**$

	Japanese factories in Britain (JFB)			British factories' average	Japanese factories' average	F-value	Scheffe's test	
	Average	Standard deviation	N				British factories/ JFB	JFB/Japanese factories
All samples	4.60	0.50	35	3.88	4.37	33.93***	*	–
All large factories	4.63	0.49	24	4.03	4.43	10.19***	*	–
All small factories	4.55	0.52	11	3.79	4.24	13.39***	*	–
All chemicals/ pharmaceuticals	5.00	(...)	1	3.97	4.19	(...)	(...)	(...)
All machinery	4.71	0.49	7	3.80	4.24	(...)	(...)	(...)
All electrical engineering	4.67	0.49	12	4.06	4.39	4.66*	*	–
All transportation	4.75	0.50	4	3.32	4.55	(...)	(...)	(...)
All rubber/plastic products	4.36	0.50	11	3.98	4.39	6.02**	–	–

Amount of qualitative information (reversed scale: adjusted)

(i) Main effect of nation $F = 279.51$***; size $F = 3.06$**; interaction (nation/size) $F = 7.98$***

(ii) Main effect of nation $F = 262.52$***; industry $F = 1.11$; interaction (nation/industry) $F = .91$

	Japanese factories in Britain (JFB)			British factories' average	Japanese factories' average	F-value	Scheffe's test	
	Average	Standard deviation	N				British factories/ JFB	JFB/Japanese factories
All samples	1.66	1.06	35	2.21	3.76	316.51***	*	*
All large factories	1.50	0.83	24	2.00	3.82	214.53***	*	*
All small factories	2.00	1.41	11	2.33	3.63	91.91***	–	*
All chemicals/ pharmaceuticals	1.00	(...)	1	2.17	3.60	(...)	(...)	(...)
All machinery	1.29	0.49	7	2.27	3.69	(...)	(...)	(...)
All electrical engineering	1.50	0.90	12	2.16	3.75	89.93***	*	*
All transportation	1.50	0.50	4	2.42	4.01	(...)	(...)	(...)
All rubber/plastic products	2.18	1.40	11	2.13	3.73	76.94***	–	*

Table 6.3 (Cont'd)
Sharing information with other workers (reversed scale: adjusted)
(i) Main effect of nation *F* = .20; size *F* = .60; interaction (nation/size) *F* = 1.14
(ii) Main effect of nation *F* = .01; industry *F* = .42; interaction (nation/industry) *F* = 1.56

	Japanese factories in Britain (JFB)		N	British factories' average	Japanese factories' average	F-value	Scheffe's test	
	Average	Standard deviation					British factories/ JFB	JFB/Japanese factories
All samples	2.32	0.98	34	2.32	2.38	0.42	(...)	(...)
All large factories	2.35	1.03	23	2.46	2.38	0.25	(...)	(...)
All small factories	2.27	0.90	11	2.24	2.39	1.22	(...)	(...)
All chemicals/ pharmaceuticals	3.00	(...)	1	2.29	2.27	(...)	(...)	(...)
All machinery	2.29	0.95	7	2.20	2.42	(...)	(...)	(...)
All electrical engineering	2.64	1.03	11	2.20	2.35	1.06	(...)	(...)
All transportation	1.50	0.58	4	2.68	2.36	(...)	(...)	(...)
All rubber/plastic products	2.27	1.01	11	2.40	2.48	0.46	(...)	(...)

Simplified and predetermined jobs

(i) Main effect of nation $F = 10.70$***; size $F = 3.71$; interaction (nation/size) $F = .35$

(ii) Main effect of nation $F = 19.13$***; industry $F = 1.47$; interaction (nation/industry) $F = 5.33$***

	Japanese factories in Britain (JFB)			British factories' average	Japanese factories' average	F-value	Scheffe's test	
	Average	Standard deviation	N				British factories/ JFB	JFB/Japanese factories
All samples	3.83	0.89	35	3.42	3.80	15.47***	*	–
All large factories	3.96	0.75	24	3.50	3.85	5.62**	*	–
All small factories	3.55	1.13	11	3.38	3.70	5.27**	–	–
All chemicals/ pharmaceuticals	2.00	(...)	1	3.54	3.81	(...)	(...)	(...)
All machinery	3.86	0.69	7	3.49	3.47	(...)	(...)	(...)
All electrical engineering	4.17	0.94	12	3.42	3.82	5.01**	*	–
All transportation	3.75	0.50	4	2.81	4.10	(...)	(...)	(...)
All rubber/plastic products	3.64	0.92	11	3.63	3.75	0.49	(...)	(...)

Table 6.3 (Cont'd)
Dealing with daily problems of the line (reversed scale: adjusted)
(i) Main effect of nation $F = 22.00***$; size $F = .23$; interaction (nation/size) $F = .98$
(ii) Main effect of nation $F = 22.65***$; industry $F = 1.34$; interaction (nation/industry) $F = 1.45$

	Japanese factories in Britain (JFB)			British factories' average	Japanese factories' average	F-value	Scheffe's test	
	Average	Standard deviation	N				British factories/ JFB	JFB/Japanese factories
All samples	3.09	1.17	35	3.06	2.52	26.23***	–	*
All large factories	3.04	0.91	24	3.11	2.47	15.53***	–	*
All small factories	3.18	1.66	11	3.02	2.62	7.32***	–	–
All chemicals/ pharmaceuticals	4.00	(...)	1	2.94	2.74	(...)	(...)	(...)
All machinery	2.86	1.07	7	3.22	2.51	(...)	(...)	(...)
All electrical engineering	2.83	1.40	12	2.78	2.50	1.92	(...)	(...)
All transportation	3.25	0.50	4	2.96	2.58	(...)	(...)	(...)
All rubber/plastic products	3.36	1.21	11	3.35	2.46	18.50**	–	*

Note: 'Large' and 'small' indicate large factories with 200 or more employees and small factories with less than 200 employees. It is presumed that the higher the average CIU score, the higher the extent of the control-oriented use. The column of 'F-value' shows the results of one-way ANOVA to explore the differences between average scores for each item among JFB, British factories and Japanese factories. Significant levels are $* p < .05$, $** p < .01$ and $*** p < .001$. An asterisk in the last two columns indicates a significant difference ($p < .05$) and '–' indicates no significant differences. '(...)' indicates either no test being conducted or it being impossible to show the value.

all items except 'sharing information with other workers'. With regard to all other items, the values of F show that the main effect of nation is greater than that of factory size and industry. Also, they show significant interactions between size and nation in terms of 'amount of qualitative information' and between industry and nation in terms of 'concentration of important information at the top', 'use of information provided by managers', 'amount of quantitative information' and 'simplified and predetermined job'. This means that the main effect of nation is different depending on factory size or industry in terms of these items.

The results presented in this table shows that in some aspects of CIU, JFB are closer to British factories, and in some other aspects they are closer to Japanese factories. With regard to the accessibility to strategic information, F-values show some significant differences between average scores among the three, but it is difficult to judge where JFB are situated since the results of Scheffe's test show no significance except for electrical engineering in which JFB got the largest score of the three. Regarding the use of information provided by managers, small JFB are somewhat closer to British factories. Regarding the amount of quantitative information, JFB got the highest score of the three groups in most of the subsets. Interestingly, JFB also use qualitative information at the same time, since the score of the amount of qualitative information in JFB – measured by a reversed scale – is the lowest of the three in most of the subsets. With regard to the sharing of information with other workers, little significant differences between the average score can be observed among the three groups. Concerning the simplified and predetermined jobs, JFB are somewhat closer to Japanese factories than to British factories: the tendency holds good particularly with electrical engineering. With regard to dealing with the daily problems of the line, JFB are closer to British factories than to Japanese factories in all subsets: the scores of JFB and British factories are higher than Japanese factories, which means that in JFB and British factories the possibility of workers dealing with daily problems of the line is not as high as in Japanese factories. When all these results are taken into consideration, it is difficult to specify a consistent pattern of IT use that JFB take concerning CIU.

Findings on individual-oriented IT use

General view

The relationship between IIU and the measures of actual practices at the shop-floor level is shown in Table 6.4. The results of reliability tests are

Table 6.4   Measures of actual practices in IIU at the shop-floor level

Pattern of IT use	Actual practices
Individual-oriented IT use (IIU)	• Having an individual password for gaining access to relevant databases • Organised in teams* • Helping each other to finish their work* • Job assignment on an individual basis

Alpha = .18 for British factories; .10 for Japanese factories; and .09 for JFB.
Note: * indicates items measured by a reversed scale.

provided below the table. As the table shows, IIU at the shop-floor level has been presumed to develop in four specific areas: having an individual password for gaining access to relevant databases; organised in teams; helping each others to finish their work; and job assignment on an individual basis. The preference for individual transmission instead of group-oriented transmission of information would make a factory choose a strategy to give each employee their own passwords. Other published work suggests that teamwork may generate conflict among members when a Japanese company, whose value system is based on groupism/collectivism, constructs factories in a Western society in which individualistic values prevail in every part (Oliver and Wilkinson, 1992; Elger and Smith, 1994; Womack, Jones and Roos, 1990). The preference for teamwork would lead a factory to adopt teamwork as the usual way of organising. Also, as suggested in Okubayashi (1995), it is possible to presume that in a highly individualised society each worker would stick to their individual role and thus there would be little need to help each other at work, so there would be few job rotations.

Again, however, statistical tests of the data show that there was poor consistency among the items of the 'composite' measures, and the items cannot be used collectively as a scale. Therefore, again, I present data based on each item individually instead of calculating the overall average scores on actual practices in IIU at the shop-floor level.

Figure 6.2 shows the general trend of each dimension of the actual practices in terms of IIU at the shop-floor level. These illustrations suggest that, concerning two aspects of IIU, there appear to be differences between British factories and Japanese factories: the former tend to use an individual password for gaining access to relevant databases more often than Japanese factories; many more Japanese factories than British factories tend to help one another to finish their work. The other two dimensions of IIU, that is 'organised in teams' and 'job assignment

Having an individual password for gainning access to relevant database(s)

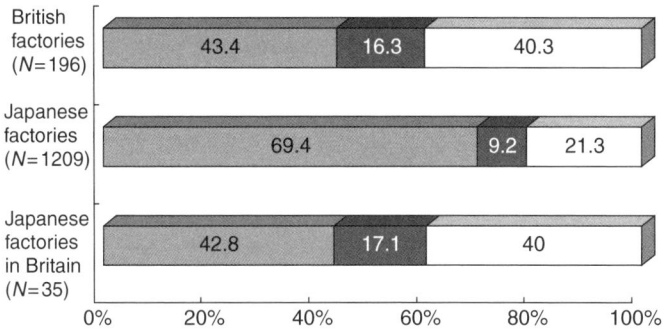

Workers have their own passwords for gaining access to relevant information database(s)

□ False ■ Neither true nor false □ True

Organised in teams

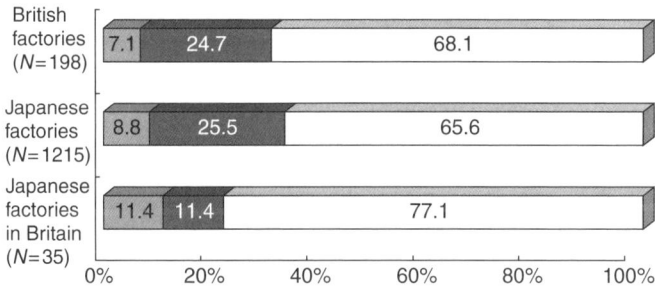

Workers are usually organised in teams

■ False ■ Neither true nor false □ True

Figure 6.2 (Cont'd overleaf)

Helping each other to finish their work

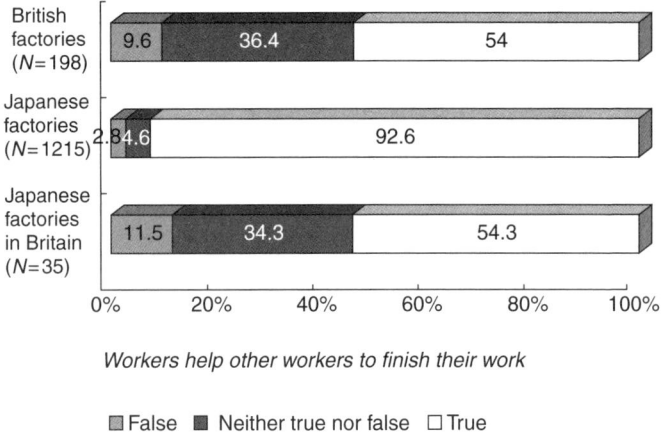

British
factories
(N=198)

| 9.6 | 36.4 | 54 |

Japanese
factories
(N=1215)

| 2.8 | 4.6 | 92.6 |

Japanese
factories
in Britain
(N=35)

| 11.5 | 34.3 | 54.3 |

0%   20%   40%   60%   80%   100%

Workers help other workers to finish their work

☐ False   ■ Neither true nor false   ☐ True

Job assignment on an individual basis

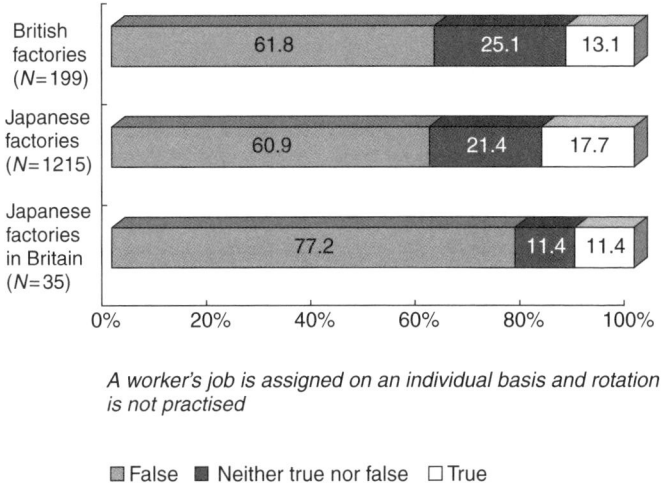

British
factories
(N=199)

| 61.8 | 25.1 | 13.1 |

Japanese
factories
(N=1215)

| 60.9 | 21.4 | 17.7 |

Japanese
factories
in Britain
(N=35)

| 77.2 | 11.4 | 11.4 |

0%   20%   40%   60%   80%   100%

*A worker's job is assigned on an individual basis and rotation
is not practised*

☐ False   ■ Neither true nor false   ☐ True

Figure 6.2   Actual practices in IIU at the shop-floor level – general view

on an individual basis', show more or less similar patterns between British factories and Japanese factories. Concerning every aspect of IIU, JFB appear to have closer tendencies to British factories than to Japanese factories.

Comparison between British factories and Japanese factories

Table 6.5 shows the descriptive statistics for British factories and Japanese factories to examine the general tendencies confirmed in the previous section. Below the title of each table are shown the results of ANOVA to assess whether factory size and/or industry are significant covariates. The ANOVA results show significant differences between nations (that is, British factories and Japanese factories) in terms of 'having an individual password for gaining access to relevant databases', 'organised in teams', and 'helping each other to finish their work'. Factory size is not a significant covariate in terms of all items, but industry sector is a significant covariate in terms of 'having an individual password for gaining access to relevant databases' and 'organised in teams'.

According to this table, in some aspects of IIU British factories have acquired higher average scores than Japanese factories, but in some other aspects they have not. Firstly, with regard to having an individual password for gaining access to relevant information databases, British factories have acquired higher average scores than Japanese factories in general, but with significant differences. This tendency holds good particularly for electrical engineering, small factories in machinery and large factories in rubber/plastic products. Secondly, concerning the adoption of teamwork, it is seen that British factories actually use team organisation at work more often than Japanese factories. This is so in large factories – large electrical engineering in particular. This is not necessarily consistent with the generally admitted fact that teamwork is one of the outstanding characteristics in a Japanese organisation under IT (Currie, 1995; Okubayashi, 1995; Berggren, 1993).[1] Thirdly, with regard to mutually helping each other to finish their work, however, Japanese factories show much lower averages in each subset, which means their workers help each other to finish their work. Finally, in terms of the job assignment on an individual basis, not very significant differences can be observed between British factories and Japanese factories, although significant difference between them were observed in the managerial preference for 'fixed job system' (*cf.* Table 5.5) – I will return to this issue in a later section of this chapter.

Table 6.5 Actual practices in IIU in British factories and Japanese factories at the shop-floor level
Having an individual password for gaining access to relevant databases
Main effect of nation: $F = 36.79***$ (covariates: size $F = .26$; industry $F = 26.45***$)

		British factories			Japanese factories			t-value
		Average	Standard deviation	N	Average	Standard deviation	N	
All samples		2.87	1.60	196	2.15	1.36	1209	5.97***
All large factories		2.90	1.62	72	2.16	1.36	856	3.80***
All small factories		2.85	1.60	124	2.14	1.38	350	4.45***
All chemicals/pharmaceuticals		2.86	1.62	36	2.44	1.53	183	1.49
All machinery		3.10	1.70	41	2.21	1.37	147	3.07**
All electrical engineering		3.22	1.43	50	2.44	1.50	229	3.47***
All transportation		2.21	1.59	24	2.03	1.27	199	0.55
All rubber/plastic		2.65	1.60	45	1.92	1.20	451	2.95**
Chemicals/pharmaceuticals	Large	3.00	1.77	15	2.51	1.50	103	1.14
	Small	2.76	1.55	21	2.35	1.57	80	1.07
Machinery	Large	2.56	1.67	10	2.25	1.40	110	0.63
	Small	3.25	1.70	31	2.08	1.30	36	3.15**
Electrical engineering	Large	3.47	1.33	17	2.45	1.50	176	2.70**
	Small	3.09	1.49	33	2.38	1.53	53	2.12*
Transportation	Large	2.50	1.65	10	2.05	1.29	176	1.07
	Small	2.00	1.57	14	1.87	1.14	23	0.29
Rubber/plastic products	Large	2.71	1.71	21	1.88	1.17	291	2.19*
	Small	2.58	1.53	24	2.00	1.27	158	1.78

Organised in teams (reversed scale: adjusted)
Main effect of nation: $F = 8.90**$ (covariates: size $F = .80$; industry $F = 5.22*$)

		British factories			Japanese factories			t-value
		Average	Standard deviation	N	Average	Standard deviation	N	
All samples		2.06	0.98	198	2.27	0.89	1215	−3.11**
All large factories		1.93	0.96	71	2.27	0.89	857	−3.07**
All small factories		2.13	0.98	127	2.28	0.91	355	−1.62
All chemicals/pharmaceuticals		1.83	0.88	36	1.96	0.81	184	−0.86
All machinery		2.20	1.08	41	2.50	1.00	147	−1.71
All electrical engineering		2.14	1.09	50	2.37	0.84	229	−1.39
All transportation		1.84	0.75	25	2.18	0.89	201	−1.83
All rubber/plastic		2.13	0.93	46	2.32	0.88	454	−1.34
Chemicals/pharmaceuticals	Large	1.53	0.74	15	1.94	0.81	103	−1.83
	Small	2.05	0.92	21	1.99	0.81	81	0.29
Machinery	Large	2.78	1.30	10	2.51	1.03	110	0.73
	Small	2.03	0.97	31	2.50	0.94	36	−2.02
Electrical engineering	Large	1.82	1.01	17	2.32	0.78	176	−2.43*
	Small	2.30	1.10	33	2.53	0.99	53	−0.98
Transportation	Large	1.67	0.71	9	2.16	0.88	177	−1.65
	Small	1.94	0.77	16	2.33	0.96	24	−1.37
Rubber/plastic products	Large	2.05	0.80	21	2.33	0.88	291	−1.41
	Small	2.20	1.04	25	2.29	0.88	161	−0.48

Table 6.5 (Cont'd)

Helping each other to finish their work (reversed scale: adjusted)

Main effect of nation: $F = 112.97^{***}$ (covariates: size $F = .01$; industry $F = 3.27$)

		British factories			Japanese factories			t-value
		Average	Standard deviation	N	Average	Standard deviation	N	
All samples		2.37	0.96	198	1.78	0.67	1215	8.43***
All large factories		2.36	0.95	72	1.78	0.68	857	5.06***
All small factories		2.38	0.96	126	1.77	0.65	355	6.62***
All chemicals/pharmaceuticals		2.31	0.75	36	1.78	0.77	184	3.76***
All machinery		2.38	1.05	40	1.77	0.66	147	3.46***
All electrical engineering		2.28	0.95	50	1.72	0.57	229	4.05***
All transportation		2.19	0.94	26	1.68	0.64	201	2.69**
All rubber/plastic		2.63	1.02	46	2.47	0.97	454	5.06***
Chemicals/pharmaceuticals	Large	2.20	0.56	15	1.73	0.73	103	2.40*
	Small	2.38	0.86	21	1.85	0.81	81	2.64**
Machinery	Large	2.78	1.39	10	1.79	0.71	110	2.10
	Small	2.26	0.93	31	1.69	0.52	36	2.99**
Electrical engineering	Large	2.18	0.81	17	1.74	0.59	176	2.18*
	Small	2.33	1.02	33	1.64	0.52	53	3.61***
Transportation	Large	1.90	0.74	10	1.68	0.66	177	1.03
	Small	2.38	1.02	16	1.70	0.46	24	2.44*
Rubber/plastic products	Large	2.67	1.06	21	1.88	0.71	291	3.32**
	Small	2.60	1.00	25	1.80	0.65	161	3.90***

Job assignment on an individual basis
Main effect of nation: $F = 2.35$ (covariates: size $F = 1.21$; industry $F = 1.34$)

		British factories			Japanese factories			t-value
		Average	Standard deviation	N	Average	Standard deviation	N	
All samples		2.32	1.01	199	2.43	0.97	1215	−1.44
All large factories		2.18	0.94	72	2.42	0.98	857	−2.00
All small factories		2.40	1.04	127	2.45	0.96	355	−0.48
All chemicals/pharmaceuticals		2.28	1.06	36	2.27	0.94	184	0.04
All machinery		2.44	1.03	41	2.61	1.02	147	−0.92
All electrical engineering		2.14	0.83	50	2.43	0.98	229	−2.14*
All transportation		2.54	1.03	26	2.35	0.96	201	0.92
All rubber/plastic		2.33	1.12	46	2.47	0.97	454	−0.96
Chemicals/pharmaceuticals	Large	1.93	0.80	15	2.15	0.90	103	−0.86
	Small	2.52	1.17	21	2.43	0.96	81	0.37
Machinery	Large	2.56	1.01	10	2.65	1.05	110	−0.25
	Small	2.40	1.04	31	2.47	0.97	36	−0.27
Electrical engineering	Large	1.94	0.75	17	2.36	0.94	176	−1.77
	Small	2.24	0.87	33	2.66	1.09	53	−1.97
Transportation	Large	2.40	1.08	10	2.36	0.97	177	0.14
	Small	2.63	1.02	16	2.33	0.92	24	0.94
Rubber/plastic products	Large	2.29	1.06	21	2.51	0.99	291	−0.99
	Small	2.36	1.19	25	2.40	0.92	161	−0.18

Note: 'Large' and 'small' in the second column indicate large factories with 200 or more employees and small factories with less than 200 employees. Reversed scales have been adjusted to indicate that the higher the average IIU score, the higher the extent of the individual-oriented use. T-value indicates the result of the t-test on average values between British factories and Japanese factories. The significant levels of statistical tests are * $p < .05$, ** $p < .01$ and *** $p < .001$.

Japanese factories in Britain

Table 6.6 shows where JFB are situated in terms of each item on actual practices at the shop-floor level concerning IIU. ANOVA was conducted to explore the differences between average scores for each item among JFB, British factories and Japanese factories. Where the overall ANOVA is significant, *post hoc* Scheffe's tests were carried out, the results of which are shown in the last two columns. Below the title of each table are shown the results of a two-way ANOVA to look for interaction effects having (i) factory size, and (ii) industry entered as variables.

The ANOVA results show significant differences among nations (that is, British factories, Japanese factories and JFB) in terms of most items. The value of *F* of the main effect of nation is greater than that of size and industry. Also, the data show significant interactions between size and nation in terms of 'organised in teams' and between industry and nation in terms of 'having an individual password for gaining access to relevant database'.

This table indicates that, in most dimensions of IIU, JFB have closer average scores to British factories than to Japanese factories, since significant differences can be observed between Japanese factories and JFB in most of the dimensions. Also, in each dimension of IIU, it is the large factories that are shown to have quite significant differences between JFB and Japanese factories. With regard to having an individual password for gaining access to information databases, JFB are shown to have closer average scores to British factories than to Japanese factories. With regard to 'organised in teams', JFB get, generally speaking, the lowest scores of the three groups, which means that the degree of the use of teamwork is actually the highest of the three. The tendency holds particularly good in electrical engineering. With regard to helping each other to finish their work, again there are few differences between JFB and British factories, both of which get higher scores than Japanese factories. This suggests that mutual help at work is one of the distinctive characteristics of Japanese factories. Finally, regarding job assignment on an individual basis, JFB get the lowest average scores in general. This suggests that in JFB the extent of the practice of job rotation is actually higher than in the other two groups. Taking all these results into consideration, it is difficult to find JFB's specific patterns of IT use on IIU.

Relationship between managerial preferences and actual practices

In the previous sections, it has been shown how cultural influences on IT use may operate in actual terms at the shop-floor level. It is necessary

Table 6.6 Actual practices in IIU in Japanese factories in Britain (JFB) at the shop-floor level

Having an individual password for gaining access to relevant databases

(i) Main effect of nation $F = 22.53***$; size $F = 1.98$; interaction (nation/size) $F = .91$

(ii) Main effect of nation $F = 15.51***$; industry $F = 3.21*$; interaction (nation/industry) $F = 2.16*$

	Japanese factories in Britain (JFB)			British factories' average	Japanese factories' average	F-value	Scheffe's test	
	Average	Standard deviation	N				British factories/ JFB	JFB/Japanese factories
All samples	2.86	1.56	35	2.87	2.15	25.53***	–	*
All large factories	3.08	1.59	24	2.90	2.16	14.25***	–	*
All small factories	2.36	1.43	11	2.85	2.14	11.36***	–	–
All chemicals/ pharmaceuticals	1.00	(...)	1	2.86	2.44	(...)	(...)	(...)
All machinery	2.71	1.60	7	3.10	2.21	(...)	(...)	(...)
All electrical engineering	3.08	1.38	12	3.22	2.44	6.37**	–	–
All transportation	4.75	0.50	4	2.21	2.03	(...)	(...)	(...)
All rubber/plastic products	2.18	1.47	11	2.64	1.92	6.99***	–	–

Table 6.6 (Cont'd)

Organised in teams (reversed scale: adjusted)

(i) Main effect of nation $F = 6.79$***; size $F = 4.61$*; interaction (nation/size) $F = 1.99$*

(ii) Main effect of nation $F = 6.88$***; industry $F = 1.66$; interaction (nation/industry) $F = .84$

	Japanese factories in Britain (JFB)			British factories' average	Japanese factories' average	F-value	Scheffe's test	
	Average	Standard deviation	N				British factories/ JFB	JFB/Japanese factories
All samples	1.89	1.02	35	2.06	2.27	7.43***	–	*
All large factories	1.71	0.75	24	1.93	2.27	8.94***	–	*
All small factories	2.27	1.42	11	2.13	2.28	1.29	(...)	(...)
All chemicals/ pharmaceuticals	2.00	(...)	1	1.83	1.96	(...)	(...)	(...)
All machinery	1.86	0.90	7	2.20	2.50	(...)	(...)	(...)
All electrical engineering	1.58	0.67	12	2.14	2.37	5.48**	*	*
All transportation	1.50	1.00	4	1.84	2.18	(...)	(...)	(...)
All rubber/plastic products	2.36	1.36	11	2.13	2.32	0.91	(...)	(...)

Helping each other to finish their work (reversed scale: adjusted)

(i) Main effect of nation $F = 58.67***$; size $F = 1.82$; interaction (nation/size) $F = 1.11$
(ii) Main effect of nation $F = 56.70***$; industry $F = 2.32$; interaction (nation/industry) $F = .72$

	Japanese factories in Britain (JFB)			British factories' average	Japanese factories' average	F-value	Scheffe's test	
	Average	Standard deviation	N				British factories/ JFB	JFB/Japanese factories
All samples	2.46	1.12	35	2.37	1.78	67.85***	–	*
All large factories	2.58	1.14	24	2.36	1.78	34.49***	–	*
All small factories	2.18	1.08	11	2.38	1.77	31.18***	–	*
All chemicals/ pharmaceuticals	2.00	(...)	1	2.31	1.78	(...)	(...)	(...)
All machinery	2.14	0.69	7	2.38	1.77	(...)	(...)	(...)
All electrical engineering	2.50	1.45	12	2.28	1.72	18.72***	–	*
All transportation	2.25	0.96	4	2.19	1.68	(...)	(...)	(...)
All rubber/plastic products	2.73	1.10	11	2.63	2.47	29.66***	–	*

Table 6.6 (Cont'd)
Job assignment on an individual basis
(i) Main effect of nation $F = 3.02*$; size $F = 2.09$; interaction (nation/size) $F = .97$
(ii) Main effect of nation $F = 2.41$; industry $F = .66$; interaction (nation/industry) $F = .92$

	Japanese factories in Britain (JFB)			British factories' average	Japanese factories' average	F-value	Scheffé's test	
	Average	Standard deviation	N				British factories/ JFB	JFB/Japanese factories
All samples	2.06	1.11	35	2.32	2.43	3.29*	–	*
All large factories	1.96	0.95	24	2.18	2.42	4.40*	–	*
All small factories	2.27	1.42	11	2.40	2.45	0.26	(...)	(...)
All chemicals/ pharmaceuticals	2.00	(...)	1	2.28	2.27	(...)	(...)	(...)
All machinery	2.00	0.82	7	2.44	2.61	(...)	(...)	(...)
All electrical engineering	2.17	1.33	12	2.14	2.43	2.06	(...)	(...)
All transportation	1.25	0.50	4	2.54	2.35	(...)	(...)	(...)
All rubber/plastic products	2.06	1.11	35	2.32	2.43	3.29*	–	*

Note: 'Large' and 'small' indicate large factories with 200 or more employees and small factories with less than 200 employees. It is presumed that the higher the average IIU score, the higher the extent of the individual-oriented use. The column of 'F-value' shows the results of one-way ANOVA to explore the differences between average scores for each item among JFB, British factories and Japanese factories. The significant levels of statistical tests are $* p < .05$, $** p < .01$ and $*** p < .001$. An asterisk in the last two columns indicates a significant difference ($p < .05$) and '–' indicates no significant differences. '(...)' indicates either no test being conducted or it being impossible to show the value.

to clarify that these cultural influences really reflect managerial preferences. In this section I will develop discussions on the relationship between managerial preferences and actual practices to indicate the degree that the actual practices explained above reflect managerial preferences developed in Chapter 5.

Control-oriented IT use

Table 6.7 shows the results of a partial correlation analysis between managerial preferences and actual practices on IT use in terms of CIU, controlling for nation, industry, factory size, batch size and unionisation.[2] Coefficients of correlation are given in each cell in the table. It is seen that, in general, actual practices on IT use positively correlate with managerial preferences which are proxies for national culture. This means that the greater the managerial preference for CIU, the greater the scores of actual practice of CIU. Although the coefficients are small, the preference for the concentration of important information at the top correlates with accessibility to strategic information, use of information given by managers, and dealing with daily problems of the line.

The preference for top-down information flow correlates with accessibility to strategic information, simplified and predetermined jobs, and dealing with daily problems on a line. The preference for simple job

Table 6.7 The relationship between managerial preferences and actual practices in CIU at the shop-floor level (partial correlation analysis)

	Concentration of important information at the top	Top-down information flow	Simple job design
Use of information given by managers	0.0652**	0.0542	0.1077***
Amount of quantitative information	– 0.0128	0.0123	– 0.0323
Amount of qualitative information (R)	– 0.0297	– 0.0354	0.0399
Sharing information with others (R)	– 0.0100	0.0148	0.0939***
Simplified and predetermined jobs	0.0371	0.0681**	0.1363***

Note: Sample size is $N = 1415$. R indicates items measured with a reversed scale (adjusted). Nation, industry, factory size, batch size and unionisation are controlled for. Two-tailed significant levels are * $p < .05$, ** $p < .01$ and *** $p < .001$.

design correlates with simplified and predetermined jobs, dealing with daily problems of the line, use of information given by managers, and sharing information with others. Generally speaking, the coefficients indicate a positive value, which suggests there is a possibility for managerial preferences to affect actual practices of IT use. In other words, it is confirmed that factories with real CIU can reflect their managerial preference for CIU.

Individual-oriented IT use

Table 6.8 shows the results of a partial correlation analysis between managerial preferences and actual practices on IT use in terms of IIU, controlling for nation, industry, factory size, batch size and unionisation. Again, coefficients of correlation are provided in each cell in the table. As with CIU, positive correlations can be observed between managerial preference for IT use and actual practice of IT use in terms of most of the dimensions in IIU. Again, although some of the coefficients are not big enough, the preference for individual transmission of information correlates with job assignment on an individual basis, organisation in teams, and having an individual password. The preference for teamwork correlates strongly with organisation in teams, and weakly with job assignment on an individual basis and with helping each other to finish work. The preference for fixed job systems correlates strongly with job assignment on an individual basis and with helping each other to finish work. This positive correlation suggests that, in terms of IIU, there is a possibility for managerial preferences for IT use to affect actual practices of IT use.

Table 6.8 The relationship between managerial preferences and actual practices in IIU at the shop-floor level (partial correlation analysis)

	Individual transmission of information	Team-working (R)	Fixed job system
Having an individual password	0.0604*	− 0.0426	− 0.0463
Organisation in teams (R)	0.0764**	0.1562***	0.0143
Helping each other to finish their work (R)	0.0267	0.0609*	0.0976***

Note: Sample size is $N = 1419$. R indicates items measured with a reversed scale (adjusted). Nation, industry, factory size, batch size and unionisation are controlled for. Two-tailed significant levels are * $p < .05$, ** $p < .01$ and ***$p < .001$.

Discussion and implications

The data shown in the previous sections of this chapter have indicated how national cultural influences on IT use actually operate at the shop-floor level in a factory in each country. In this section I will develop some implications of the findings and their theoretical justification. Three major findings have been identified.

Firstly, in terms of CIU, Japanese factories have been identified to be more control-oriented than British factories in general. Among seven dimensions of CIU, Japanese factories have acquired higher average scores than British factories with statistically significant differences in five dimensions: concentration of important information at the top; use of information provided by managers; amount of quantitative information; amount of qualitative information; and simplified and predetermined jobs. The amount of qualitative information in particular has been found to be very different judging from the *t*-value. Regarding the sharing of information with other workers, there are no significant differences between factories in the two countries. With regard to only one dimension among CIU, or dealing with daily problems of the line, British factories have achieved higher averages than Japanese factories. A more or less similar pattern can be identified in each subset divided by factory size and industry, although, as stated in each section, some specific industrial patterns have been identified in some cases. Most of these findings can either be justified theoretically or coincide with the empirical findings of previous studies. Many theoretical and empirical studies (Bratton, 1992; Kumazawa and Yamada, 1989) have shared the presumption that the Japanese work system, coupled with the effects of IT, involves internal mechanisms which intensify and control their work, resulting in Japanese workers' engagement in a relatively higher degree of simplified and standardised jobs. For example, Kumazawa and Yamada (1989) illustrate that Japanese workers typically learn about three dozen tasks, limiting the depth of that learning and entailing transfer for the most part between relatively routine assignments. Although Japanese workers are said to work in standardised and thus predetermined jobs, Koike (1988) suggests significant abilities to deal with 'unusual operations' such as coping with problems of a production line which are so varied that standardisation in the form of a manual is impracticable. This coincides with my empirical result showing Japanese factories' relatively higher degree of ability to deal with daily problems of the line.

Secondly, it has been identified that, in terms of IIU, British factories achieved higher average scores in general regarding 'having an individual password for gaining access to relevant information database' and 'helping each other to finish their work'. This means Japanese factories' lesser tendencies to transmit information on an individual basis and higher tendency to help each other to finish their work. However, regarding job assignment on an individual basis, few differences can be observed between British factories and Japanese factories, or Japanese factories get slightly higher scores than British factories. Surprisingly, British factories actually use teamwork more often than Japanese factories. This result was unexpected, as it has been claimed by many previous studies that teamwork is one of the outstanding features of a Japanese organisation on the shop-floor (Kenny and Florida, 1993; Demes, 1992).

Some of these results – British factories' higher degree of having an individual password and Japanese factories' higher degree of mutual help to finish work – can be theoretically and empirically supported by previous studies. Straub (1994) indicates some empirical evidence for the Japanese having greater cultural preference for using fax instead of email, as compared with US companies which prefer to use email to fax. He suggests the results can reflect cultural differences between the USA and Japan – higher uncertainty avoidance in Japan and structural features of the Japanese written language. Although Straub does not say so, this may also reflect more group-oriented IT use and relatively fewer opportunities for an individual to use email through computers in Japan (Shimada, 1991). Also, some previous studies have clarified that Japanese organisations are based on collectivism/groupism, and that job boundaries are ambiguous and blurred under the introduction of IT, thus the possibility for a worker to help other workers is higher than in a society where individualistic norms prevail (Okubayashi, 1995).

British factories' higher actual use of teamwork cannot be justified by such explanations. A possible explanation might be that teamwork is so natural in the work organisation of a Japanese factory that Japanese respondents are not conscious of their use of teamwork (Tubbs, 1994), whereas in a British factory they cannot help being aware of the use of teamwork as it is not native to the British, having been consciously introduced as an experiment of socio-technical redesign or imported from Japan following its outstanding success there in the 1980s. It seems significant in this context that although in the Japanese sample the use of a 'team' is not necessarily as high as in the British sample, mutual help at work, one of the concrete features of teamwork (Okubayashi, 1995), is indicated as being much higher in Japanese factories than in British factories.

With regard to 'job assignment on an individual basis', not many differences can be observed between British factories and Japanese factories although job rotation has been said to be one of the most out-standing features of Japanese practices at the shop-floor level (Schonberger, 1982). This may suggest again that it is a taken-for-granted practice for the Japanese. Also, considering that Japanese factories showed a stronger *preference* for job rotation than British factories, this may indicate that some influences other than national culture might have been present in the data on the actual practice of job rotation.

Thirdly, with regard to the situation of JFB, specific patterns of IT use in JFB have not necessarily been identified. Some dimensions of CIU and IIU in JFB have been found to be either closer to British factories or Japanese factories, in between the two, or the highest or the lowest. As shown in the above analysis, with regard to 'dealing with daily problems of the line' in CIU and 'having an individual password to gain access to relevant information databases' and 'helping each other to finish their work' in IIU, JFB are rather close to British factories. With regard to 'concentration of important information at the top' and 'simplified and predetermined jobs' in CIU, JFB have a quite similar pattern with Japanese factories. In terms of 'use of information provided by managers' in CIU, JFB can be situated in between British factories and Japanese factories concerning the average scores, and regarding the 'amount of quantitative information' and 'amount of qualitative information' in CIU and 'organised in teams' and 'job assignment on an individual basis' JFB can be situated in an extreme position among the three. However, to simplify the story, JFB can be situated somewhat closer to Japanese factories in terms of CIU, and to British factories in terms of IIU. In other words, JFB actually use IT-based systems in a similar way to Japanese factories with regard to CIU, and to British factories with regard to IIU.

It is difficult to justify these findings theoretically from the literature since few previous studies explicitly mention the patterns of IT use, as discussed in Chapter 2. However, it has been clarified at least that JFB demonstrate a similar pattern of IT use to British factories as well as to Japanese factories. This point cannot have been identified by previous studies on Japanisation, in which JFB's cultural disposition is based on Japanese culture that may become a factor involving cultural conflicts with native British factories' norms (Oliver and Wilkinson, 1992; Bratton, 1992; Womack, Jones and Roos, 1990).

Conclusion

This chapter has depicted the actual practices of IT use at the shop-floor level of organisations. As discussed above, some new empirical findings have been illuminated on CIU and IIU, and I have attempted to standardise British factories/Japanese factories/JFB specific patterns of IT use. It is found to be reasonably difficult to standardise completely each factory's pattern, but generally speaking it can be summarised that Japanese factories take a relatively stronger orientation to CIU, and British factories take a relatively stronger orientation to IIU in actual terms. As described, most of these, both in the dimension of CIU and IIU, have been identified to correlate positively with managerial preferences discussed in the preceding chapter. This suggests a possibility for managerial preferences for IT use in each country to actually operate in the practice of IT use in each country's factory at the shop-floor level. Some implications and theoretical justifications of the findings have been assessed, and in the following chapter my analysis will clarify how cultural effects may operate in actual terms at the line-manager level.

7
How Cultural Influences Operate at the Management Level

Introduction

This chapter describes how managerial preferences examined in Chapter 5 actually operate at the management level in a factory. As discussed in Chapter 3, in the questionnaire, a separate set of questions from the shop-floor level was prepared for data collection as compared to the management level. This was done because different effects of IT had been identified between the shop-floor and management levels from my previous empirical study (Kambayashi, 1996a), and it could be presumed that a different type of IT use would be observed between the two levels. The questions were set to ascertain the use of IT by a line manager in a factory. As with the last chapter, I discuss CIU and IIU in turn in the following sections.

Findings on control-oriented IT use

General view

As I discussed in Chapter 3, CIU at the management level has been presumed to develop in six specific areas, and the relationship between CIU and the measures of actual practices of IT use at the management level is outlined in Table 7.1. The results of reliability tests are indicated below the table. As indicated in the table, managerial preferences for CIU are presumed to appear as these concrete phenomena at the level of management organisation in a factory. Similar to the discussion at the shop-floor level, the managerial preference for the concentration of important information at the top management level would operate as, for instance, limited access for line managers to strategic information

Table 7.1   Measures of actual practices in CIU at the management level

Pattern of IT use	Actual practices
Control-oriented IT use (CIU)	• Accessibility to strategic information* • Rapid access to information databases in a problematic situation • Gaining information from across different functional boundaries* • Liaison as the main job • Communicating instructions as the most important role • The need to report major problems to senior managers

Alpha = .04 for British factories; .12 for Japanese factories; and .14 for JFB.
Note: * shows that the item is measured by a reversed scale.

databases. The managerial preference for top-down information flow may need hierarchical control of information in a factory, which leads to making a line manager's job more like a 'liaison' function, centring on communicating instructions to subordinates. The managerial preference for simple job design, coupled with the preference for top-down information flow, would lead a factory to gain less information from across different functional boundaries, for example. Also it is presumed that a higher control-orientation may well need rapid access to information databases when problems occur on a line, thus requiring a line manager to report the problems to senior manager(s).

Statistical tests of the data, however, show that there was again poor consistency among the items of the 'composite' measures, and the items cannot be used collectively as a scale. Therefore, I present data based on each item individually, instead of calculating the overall average scores on actual practices in CIU at the management level.

Figure 7.1 shows general trends of each dimension of the actual practices in terms of CIU at the management level. As shown, the general tendency of CIU at the management level varies among British factories, Japanese factories and JFB. Regarding accessibility to strategic information, Japanese factories tend to limit line managers' access more than British factories and JFB. More JFB than British factories and Japanese factories have agreed to a line manager accessing strategic information. With regard to rapid access to an information database in an emergency, many more British factories and JFB allow it than Japanese factories. Few differences seem to be observed among British factories, Japanese factories and JFB in terms of 'gaining information from across different

Accessibility to strategic information

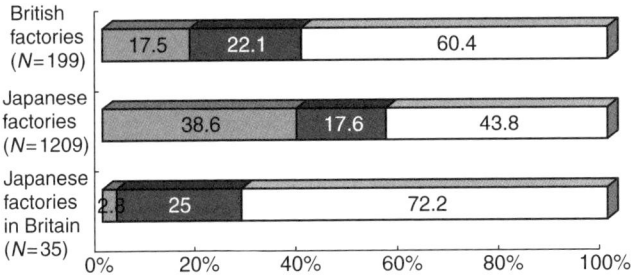

British factories (N=199)	17.5	22.1	60.4
Japanese factories (N=1209)	38.6	17.6	43.8
Japanese factories in Britain (N=35)	2.8	25	72.2

0%   20%   40%   60%   80%   100%

It is possible for line managers to gain strategic information

☐ False ■ Neither false nor true ☐ True

Rapid access to information databases

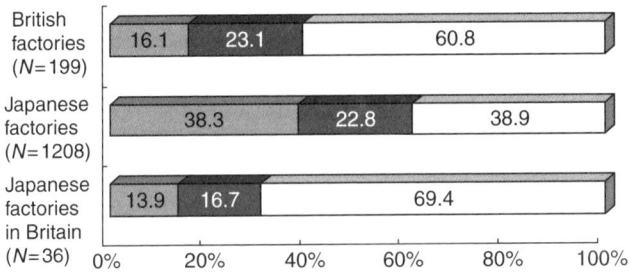

British factories (N=199)	16.1	23.1	60.8
Japanese factories (N=1208)	38.3	22.8	38.9
Japanese factories in Britain (N=36)	13.9	16.7	69.4

0%   20%   40%   60%   80%   100%

Line managers can gain access to relevant database(s) rapidly if any problems occur

☐ False ■ Neither false nor true ☐ True

Figure 7.1   (Cont'd overleaf)

156

Gaining information from across different functional boundaries

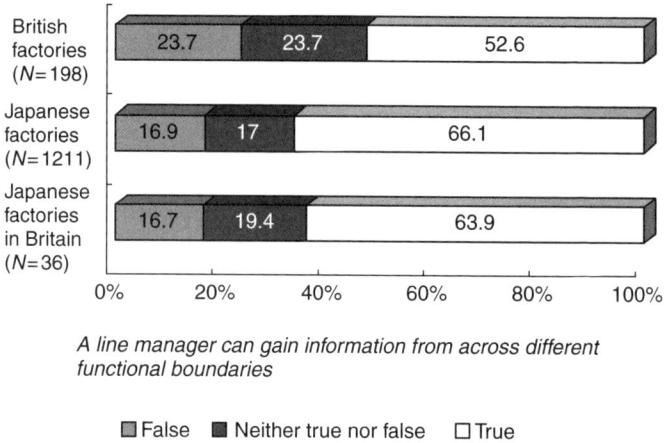

A line manager can gain information from across different functional boundaries

■ False ■ Neither true nor false □ True

Liaison as the main job

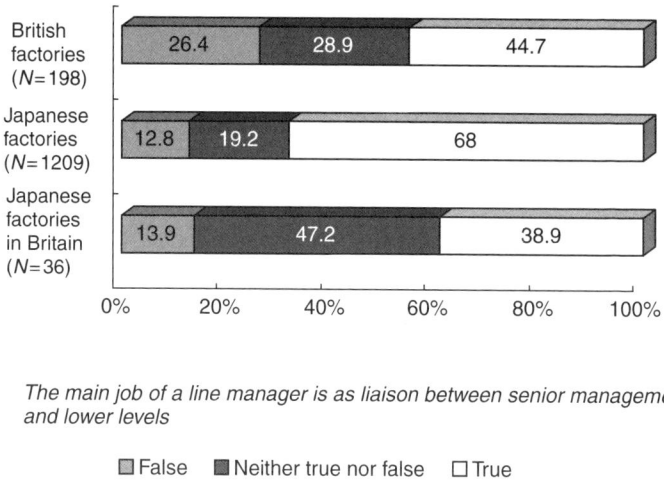

The main job of a line manager is as liaison between senior management and lower levels

■ False ■ Neither true nor false □ True

Figure 7.1

Communicating instructions as the most important role

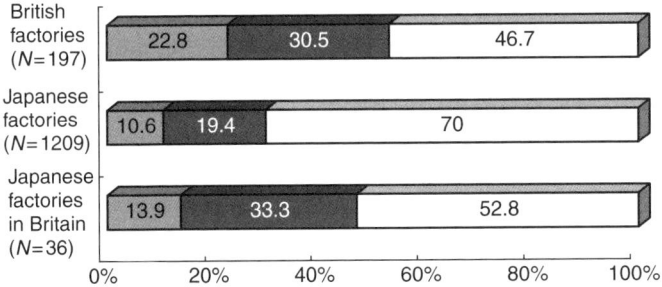

Communicating instructions to subordinates is the most important role

☐ False ■ Neither true nor false ☐ True

The need to report problems to senior managers

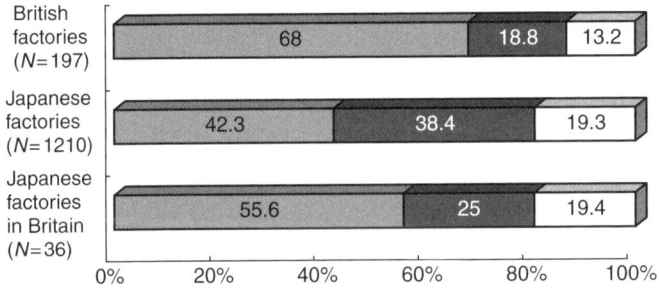

When any major problems occur, line managers have to report to senior managers before taking action

☐ False ■ Neither true nor false ☐ True

Figure 7.1 Actual practices in CIU at the management level – general view

functional boundaries' and 'the need to report major problems to senior managers'. Many more Japanese factories than British factories and JFB agree to the perception of 'liaison as their main job' and 'communicating instructions as the most important job'.

Comparison between British factories and Japanese factories

In order to examine the general outlook statistically, Table 7.2 shows descriptive statistics regarding British factories and Japanese factories and the results of t-tests in terms of the difference between the two average scores in each dimension of CIU. As with analyses in previous chapters, in order to test overall differences controlling for factory size and industry, ANOVA was carried out with factory size and industry as covariates, and the results are shown below the titles of each table.

The ANOVA results show significant differences between nations (that is, British factories and Japanese factories) in terms of all items. Factory size and/or industry are shown to be significant covariates in terms of some items, such as 'accessibility to strategic information', 'gaining information from across different functional boundaries' and 'rapid access to information databases in a problematic situation'. However, the F-value of the main effect of nation is shown to be greater than that of covariates in terms of these items, except for 'gaining information from across different functional boundaries'.

Generally speaking, this table shows higher average scores on CIU in Japanese factories than in British factories, except for 'rapid access to information databases in a problematic situation' and 'gaining information from across different functional boundaries' where British factories are higher than Japanese factories. With regard to 'access to strategic information databases', Japanese factories in general indicate more difficulty for a line manager to gain access to strategic information than British factories. This general tendency holds particularly true in small factories and in all industrial groups except transportation. The average values of large factories and small factories are nearly the same in British factories, whereas the higher values in small factories than in large factories in Japanese factories may suggest greater possibility to access strategic information in small British factories than in small Japanese factories.

With regard to 'rapid access to information databases in a problematic situation', the average values in British factories are much higher than in Japanese factories in all subsets except transportation. In the industrial group of transportation, small factories in particular, no significant differences can be observed between British factories and

Table 7.2 Actual practices in CIU in British factories and Japanese factories at the management level
Accessibility to strategic information (reversed scale: adjusted)
Main effect of nation: $F = 33.21***$ (covariates: size $F = 4.85*$; industry $F = 1.81$)

		British factories			Japanese factories			t-value
		Average	Standard deviation	N	Average	Standard deviation	N	
All samples		2.43	1.17	199	2.97	1.28	1209	−5.94***
All large factories		2.44	1.23	72	2.91	1.27	855	−3.02*
All small factories		2.43	1.14	127	3.11	1.30	352	−5.55***
All chemicals/pharmaceuticals		2.56	1.08	36	3.11	1.36	184	−2.71**
All machinery		2.17	1.07	41	2.93	1.21	147	−3.64***
All electrical engineering		2.14	0.95	50	2.64	1.29	227	−3.14**
All transportation		2.92	1.41	26	3.00	1.31	199	−0.28
All rubber/plastic		2.61	1.29	46	3.08	1.23	452	−2.47*
Chemicals/pharmaceuticals	Large	2.47	1.13	15	3.02	1.32	102	−1.54
	Small	2.62	1.07	21	3.23	1.40	82	−2.18*
Machinery	Large	2.44	1.13	10	2.85	1.26	110	−0.93
	Small	2.09	1.06	31	3.19	1.06	36	−4.27***
Electrical engineering	Large	2.47	1.23	17	2.51	1.22	174	−0.11
	Small	1.97	0.73	33	3.08	1.41	53	−4.77***
Transportation	Large	2.40	1.43	10	3.02	1.30	176	−1.45
	Small	3.25	1.34	16	2.87	1.46	23	0.83
Rubber/plastic products	Large	2.43	1.36	21	3.09	1.23	293	−2.35*
	Small	2.76	1.23	25	3.06	1.24	158	−1.14

Table 7.2 (Cont'd)

Rapid access to information databases in a problematic situation

Main effect of nation: $F = 50.43***$ (covariates: size $F = 10.06**$; industry $F = 1.14$)

		British factories			Japanese factories			t-value
		Average	Standard deviation	N	Average	Standard deviation	N	
All samples		3.63	1.10	199	3.01	1.26	1209	7.32***
All large factories		3.78	0.92	72	3.07	1.23	855	6.07***
All small factories		3.55	1.18	127	2.85	1.32	351	5.59***
All chemicals/pharmaceuticals		3.64	0.90	36	2.89	1.32	184	4.21***
All machinery		3.63	1.07	41	3.09	1.20	147	2.63**
All electrical engineering		3.98	0.96	50	3.20	1.29	227	4.85***
All transportation		3.12	1.28	26	3.01	1.22	199	0.41
All rubber/plastic		3.54	1.21	46	2.93	1.24	451	3.21***
Chemicals/ pharmaceuticals	Large	3.93	0.88	15	3.00	1.33	102	3.54***
	Small	3.43	0.87	21	2.74	1.30	82	2.87**
Machinery	Large	3.44	1.01	10	2.50	1.37	110	0.68
	Small	3.69	1.09	31	2.86	1.20	36	2.96**
Electrical engineering	Large	4.00	0.87	17	3.31	1.22	174	3.00**
	Small	3.97	1.02	33	2.85	1.43	53	4.24***
Transportation	Large	3.60	1.08	10	3.01	1.20	176	1.52
	Small	2.81	1.33	16	3.00	1.45	23	-0.41
Rubber/plastic products	Large	3.71	0.90	21	2.95	1.21	293	2.82**
	Small	3.40	1.41	25	2.87	1.30	157	1.86

Gaining information from across different functional boundaries (reversed scale: adjusted)
Main effect of nation: $F = 3.48*$ (covariates: size $F = 6.93**$ industry $F = 6.78**$)

		British factories			Japanese factories			t-value
		Average	Standard deviation	N	Average	Standard deviation	N	
All samples		2.57	1.25	198	2.37	1.08	1211	2.33*
All large factories		2.57	1.27	72	2.31	1.05	856	1.96*
All small factories		2.56	1.25	126	2.50	1.13	353	0.47
All chemicals/pharmaceuticals		2.83	1.08	36	2.39	1.08	184	2.28*
All machinery		2.32	1.21	41	2.32	1.05	147	-0.01
All electrical engineering		2.30	1.17	50	2.12	0.95	227	1.17
All transportation		3.00	1.26	25	2.28	1.06	201	2.73*
All rubber/plastic		2.63	1.42	46	2.54	1.12	452	0.51
Chemicals/ pharmaceuticals	Large	2.93	1.10	15	2.32	1.05	102	2.10*
	Small	2.76	1.09	21	2.46	1.11	82	1.11
Machinery	Large	2.33	1.41	10	2.21	1.08	110	0.26
	Small	2.31	1.18	31	2.64	0.93	36	-1.26
Electrical engineering	Large	2.12	1.22	17	2.05	0.86	174	0.24
	Small	2.39	1.14	33	2.36	1.18	53	0.14
Transportation	Large	2.80	1.23	10	2.31	1.07	177	1.25
	Small	3.13	1.30	15	2.13	0.99	24	2.57*
Rubber/plastic products	Large	2.67	1.35	21	2.51	1.09	293	0.51
	Small	2.60	1.50	25	2.60	1.18	158	-0.01

Table 7.2 (Cont'd)
Liaison as the main job
Main effect of nation: $F = 34.15^{***}$ (covariates: size $F = 1.98$; industry $F = 2.82$)

		British factories			Japanese factories			t-value
		Average	Standard deviation	N	Average	Standard deviation	N	
All samples		3.30	1.17	197	3.72	0.96	1209	-4.78***
All large factories		3.15	1.23	72	3.70	0.98	855	-3.70***
All small factories		3.38	1.13	125	3.76	0.93	353	-3.35***
All chemicals/pharmaceuticals		3.00	1.29	36	3.78	0.87	184	-3.49***
All machinery		3.41	1.14	41	3.88	0.88	147	-2.41*
All electrical engineering		3.24	1.05	49	3.76	0.99	226	-3.28***
All transportation		3.48	1.01	25	3.68	1.07	202	-0.88
All rubber/plastic		3.39	1.30	46	3.64	0.96	450	-1.27
Chemicals/pharmaceuticals	Large	3.00	1.41	15	3.65	0.93	102	-2.34*
	Small	3.00	1.22	21	3.95	0.77	82	-3.39***
Machinery	Large	3.11	1.05	10	3.94	0.92	110	-2.56*
	Small	3.50	1.16	31	3.69	0.71	36	-0.81
Electrical engineering	Large	3.06	1.14	17	3.79	0.98	174	-2.87**
	Small	3.34	1.00	32	3.67	1.00	52	-1.46
Transportation	Large	3.30	1.06	10	3.64	1.08	177	-0.98
	Small	3.60	0.99	15	3.92	0.95	25	-1.02
Rubber/plastic products	Large	3.29	1.38	21	3.62	0.93	292	-1.09
	Small	3.48	1.26	25	3.86	1.01	158	-0.90

Communicating instructions as the most important role

Main effect of nation: $F = 35.34$*** (covariates: size $F = .66$; industry $F = .06$)

		British factories			Japanese factories			t-value
		Average	Standard deviation	N	Average	Standard deviation	N	
All samples		3.32	1.06	197	3.77	0.90	1209	-5.66***
All large factories		3.19	1.10	72	3.80	0.89	855	-4.53***
All small factories		3.39	1.03	125	3.71	0.92	353	-3.03**
All chemicals/pharmaceuticals		3.14	1.05	36	3.67	0.86	184	-3.26***
All machinery		3.41	1.09	41	3.86	0.88	147	-2.42*
All electrical engineering		3.27	1.06	49	3.86	0.87	227	-3.70***
All transportation		3.40	1.08	25	3.87	0.86	202	-2.08*
All rubber/plastic		3.39	1.31	46	3.64	0.96	450	-2.04*
Chemicals/pharmaceuticals	Large	2.93	1.03	15	3.67	0.94	102	-2.79**
	Small	3.29	1.06	21	3.67	0.75	82	-1.91
Machinery	Large	2.78	0.97	10	3.82	0.92	110	-3.25**
	Small	3.59	1.07	31	4.00	0.76	36	-1.78
Electrical engineering	Large	3.47	1.23	17	3.86	0.84	174	-1.28
	Small	3.16	0.95	32	3.87	1.00	53	-3.23**
Transportation	Large	3.10	0.88	10	3.89	0.85	177	-2.86**
	Small	3.60	1.18	15	3.72	0.94	25	-0.36
Rubber/plastic products	Large	3.38	1.16	21	3.74	0.90	292	-1.37
	Small	3.40	0.96	25	3.61	1.00	157	-0.95

Table 7.2 (Cont'd)
The need to report major problems to senior managers
Main effect of nation: $F = 47.88$*** (covariates: size $F = 1.66$; industry $F = 2.44$)

		British factories			Japanese factories			t-value
		Average	Standard deviation	N	Average	Standard deviation	N	
All samples		2.22	1.04	197	2.71	0.95	1210	−6.67***
All large factories		2.10	1.06	72	2.69	0.95	855	−5.07***
All small factories		2.29	1.03	125	2.75	0.94	354	−4.56***
All chemicals/pharmaceuticals		2.14	1.07	36	2.85	0.94	184	−4.04***
All machinery		2.15	0.88	41	2.66	0.87	147	−3.32***
All electrical engineering		2.27	1.06	49	2.74	0.92	227	−3.21**
All transportation		2.24	0.93	25	2.74	1.03	202	−2.30*
All rubber/plastic		2.28	1.22	46	2.64	0.94	450	−1.93
Chemicals/pharmaceuticals	Large	2.00	1.00	15	2.78	0.97	102	−2.91**
	Small	2.24	1.14	21	2.93	0.90	82	−2.96**
Machinery	Large	2.33	1.00	10	2.71	0.87	110	−1.23
	Small	2.09	0.86	31	2.50	0.88	36	−1.93
Electrical engineering	Large	1.94	0.97	17	2.75	0.92	174	−3.45***
	Small	2.44	1.08	32	2.74	0.96	53	−1.32
Transportation	Large	2.20	0.92	10	2.74	1.02	177	−1.63
	Small	2.27	0.96	15	2.72	1.10	25	−1.32
Rubber/plastic products	Large	2.14	1.31	21	2.60	0.94	292	−1.55
	Small	2.40	1.15	25	2.72	0.93	158	−1.55

Note: 'Large' and 'small' in the second column indicate large factories with 200 or more employees and small factories with less than 200 employees. Reversed scales have been adjusted to indicate that the higher the average CIU score, the higher the extent of the control-oriented use is. *T*-value indicates the result of the *t*-test on average values between British factories and Japanese factories. The significant levels of statistical tests are * $p < .05$, ** $p < .01$ and *** $p < .001$.

Japanese factories with the average score of the group in British factories particularly low as compared with other groups. Regarding 'gaining information from across different functional boundaries', the data show, in general, Japanese factories' relatively higher opportunities to gain information from across different functional boundaries than in British factories. This general tendency fits especially in the large chemicals/pharmaceuticals and small transportation groups in which British factories' average scores are relatively higher than the other groups. With respect to 'liaison as the main job', average scores in Japanese factories are much higher than those in British factories in general terms, which means that line managers in Japanese factories have a stronger tendency to function as a liaison between senior management and lower levels. This general pattern is true particularly of chemicals/pharmaceuticals and electrical engineering. In machinery and electrical engineering, large factories instead of small ones show significant differences between British factories and Japanese factories.

In regard to 'communicating instructions as the most important role', generally speaking, Japanese factories get much higher scores than British factories which implies more detailed instructions to subordinates have been made in Japanese factories than in British ones. This general pattern fits large factories in chemicals/pharmaceuticals, machinery and transportation groups and small factories in electrical engineering. Concerning 'the need to report major problems to senior managers', Japanese factories again get higher average scores than British factories in general, which suggests Japanese factories' higher necessity for a line manager to contact senior management, and thus maybe less delegation in a problematic situation. This general tendency is true for both large and small chemicals/pharmaceuticals, and large electrical engineering in particular.

Japanese factories in Britain

Table 7.3 shows where JFB can be located in terms of each item on actual practices at the management level concerning CIU. The table indicates the descriptive statistics for the JFB. ANOVA was conducted to explore the differences between average scores for each item among JFB, British factories and Japanese factories, and where the overall ANOVA is significant the results of *post hoc* Scheffe's tests are shown to indicate where significant differences can be observed. As with the presentation of the data developed in the previous chapters, below the title of each table are shown the results of a two-way ANOVA to look for interaction effects having (i) factory size, and (ii) industry as variables.

Table 7.3 Actual practices in CIU in Japanese factories in Britain (JFB) at the management level
Accessibility to strategic information (reversed scale: adjusted)
(i) Main effect of nation $F = 24.02***$; size $F = .47$; interaction (nation/size) $F = .54$
(ii) Main effect of nation $F = 14.17***$; industry $F = 2.97*$; interaction (nation/industry) $F = .86$

	Japanese factories in Britain (JFB)			British factories' average	Japanese factories' average	F-value	Scheffe's test	
	Average	Standard deviation	N				British factories/ JFB	JFB/Japanese factories
All samples	1.97	0.94	36	2.43	2.97	25.02***	*	*
All large factories	1.92	0.95	25	2.44	2.91	11.62***	–	*
All small factories	2.09	0.94	11	2.43	3.11	16.07***	–	*
All chemicals/ pharmaceuticals	3.00	(...)	1	2.56	3.11	(...)	(...)	(...)
All machinery	1.29	0.49	7	2.17	2.93	(...)	(...)	(...)
All electrical engineering	1.85	0.90	13	2.14	2.64	5.45**	–	*
All transportation	2.25	0.50	4	2.92	3.00	(...)	(...)	(...)
All rubber/plastic products	2.36	1.12	11	2.61	3.08	4.65**	–	–

Rapid access to information databases in a problematic situation

(i) Main effect of nation $F = 30.69***$; size $F = 2.52$; interaction (nation/size) $F = .02$
(ii) Main effect of nation $F = 18.00***$; industry $F = 1.63$; interaction (nation/industry) $F = 1.22$

	Japanese factories in Britain (JFB)			British factories' average	Japanese factories' average	F-value	Scheffe's test	
	Average	Standard deviation	N				British factories/ JFB	JFB/Japanese factories
All samples	3.86	1.17	36	3.63	3.01	28.79***	–	*
All large factories	3.96	1.02	25	3.78	3.07	17.33***	–	*
All small factories	3.64	1.50	11	3.55	2.85	15.16***	–	–
All chemicals/ pharmaceuticals	2.00	(...)	1	3.64	2.89	(...)	(...)	(...)
All machinery	4.29	0.76	7	3.63	3.09	(...)	(...)	(...)
All electrical engineering	3.85	1.14	13	3.98	3.20	9.20***	–	–
All transportation	4.50	0.58	4	3.12	3.01	(...)	(...)	(...)
All rubber/plastic products	3.55	1.44	11	3.54	2.93	6.22**	–	–

Table 7.3 (Cont'd)
Gaining information from across different functional boundaries (reversed scale: adjusted)
(i) Main effect of nation $F = 2.46$; size $F = .01$; interaction (nation/size) $F = .91$
(ii) Main effect of nation $F = 5.53$**; industry $F = 1.48$; interaction (nation/industry) $F = 1.48$

	Japanese factories in Britain (JFB)			British factories' average	Japanese factories' average	F-value	Scheffe's test	
	Average	Standard deviation	N				British factories/ JFB	JFB/Japanese factories
All samples	2.19	1.17	36	2.57	2.37	3.30*	–	–
All large factories	2.24	1.09	25	2.57	2.31	2.00	(...)	(...)
All small factories	2.09	1.38	11	2.56	2.50	0.85	(...)	(...)
All chemicals/ pharmaceuticals	4.00	(...)	1	2.83	2.39	(...)	(...)	(...)
All machinery	2.14	1.22	7	2.32	2.32	(...)	(...)	(...)
All electrical engineering	2.23	1.09	13	2.30	2.12	0.72	(...)	(...)
All transportation	2.00	0.82	4	3.00	2.28	(...)	(...)	(...)
All rubber/plastic products	2.09	1.38	11	2.63	2.54	0.97	(...)	(...)

Liaison as the main job

(i) Main effect of nation $F = 20.09$***; size $F = .35$; interaction (nation/size) $F = .66$

(ii) Main effect of nation $F = 17.47$***; industry $F = .41$; interaction (nation/industry) $F = 1.12$

	Japanese factories in Britain (JFB)			British factories' average	Japanese factories' average	F-value	Scheffe's test	
	Average	Standard deviation	N				British factories/ JFB	JFB/Japanese factories
All samples	3.22	0.76	36	3.30	3.72	18.81***	–	*
All large factories	3.24	0.83	25	3.15	3.70	12.36***	–	*
All small factories	3.18	0.60	11	3.38	3.76	8.16***	–	*
All chemicals/ pharmaceuticals	3.00	(...)	1	3.00	3.78	(...)	(...)	(...)
All machinery	3.00	1.15	7	3.41	3.88	(...)	(...)	(...)
All electrical engineering	3.23	0.60	13	3.24	3.76	6.76***	–	*
All transportation	3.75	0.50	4	3.48	3.68	(...)	(...)	(...)
All rubber/plastic products	3.18	0.75	11	3.39	3.64	2.39	(...)	(...)

Table 7.3 (Cont'd)

Communicating instructions as the most important role

(i) Main effect of nation $F = 19.85$***; size $F = .35$; interaction (nation/size) $F = 1.95$

(ii) Main effect of nation $F = 21.84$***; industry $F = .22$; interaction (nation/industry) $F = .42$

	Japanese factories in Britain (JFB)			British factories' average	Japanese factories' average	F-value	Scheffe's test	
	Average	Standard deviation	N				British factories/ JFB	JFB/Japanese factories
All samples	3.47	0.84	36	3.32	3.77	21.47***	–	*
All large factories	3.44	0.87	25	3.19	3.80	16.15***	–	*
All small factories	3.55	0.82	11	3.39	3.71	5.14**	(...)	–
All chemicals/ pharmaceuticals	3.00	(...)	1	3.14	3.67	(...)	(...)	(...)
All machinery	3.43	0.79	7	3.41	3.86	(...)	(...)	(...)
All electrical engineering	3.54	0.88	13	3.27	3.86	9.11***	–	–
All transportation	3.25	0.50	4	3.40	3.87	(...)	(...)	(...)
All rubber/plastic products	3.55	1.04	11	3.39	3.64	2.15	(...)	(...)

The need to report major problems to senior managers

(i) Main effect of nation $F = 23.28***$; size $F = 1.58$; interaction (nation/size) $F = .48$

(ii) Main effect of nation $F = 22.16***$; industry $F = .38$; interaction (nation/industry) $F = .71$

	Japanese factories in Britain (JFB)			British factories' average	Japanese factories' average	F-value	Scheffe's test	
	Average	Standard deviation	N				British factories/ JFB	JFB/Japanese factories
All samples	2.47	1.23	36	2.22	2.71	22.41***	–	–
All large factories	2.40	1.22	25	2.10	2.69	13.44***	–	–
All small factories	2.64	1.29	11	2.29	2.75	10.40***	–	–
All chemicals/ pharmaceuticals	3.00	(...)	1	2.14	2.85	(...)	(...)	(...)
All machinery	2.86	1.57	7	2.15	2.66	(...)	(...)	(...)
All electrical engineering	2.31	1.38	13	2.27	2.74	5.73**	–	–
All transportation	2.00	0.82	4	2.24	2.74	(...)	(...)	(...)
All rubber/plastic products	2.55	1.04	11	2.28	2.64	2.86	(...)	(...)

Note: 'Large' and 'small' indicate large factories with 200 or more employees and small factories with less than 200 employees. It is presumed that the higher the average CIU score, the higher the extent of the control-oriented use. The column of '*F*-value' shows the results of one-way ANOVA to explore the differences between average scores for each item among JFB, British factories and Japanese factories. The significant levels of statistical tests are $* p < .05$, $** p < .01$ and $*** p < .001$. An asterisk in the last two columns indicates a significant difference ($p < .05$) and '–' indicates no significant differences. '(...)' indicates either no test being conducted or it being impossible to show the value.

The results of the two-way ANOVA show significant differences among nations (that is, British factories, Japanese factories and JFB) in terms of all items except 'gaining information from across different functional boundaries', and show no significant interaction both between size and nation and between industry and nation.

According to this table, JFB can be located closer to British factories than to Japanese factories in general concerning each dimension of CIU. With regard to the 'accessibility to strategic information', JFB have acquired either the least average scores of the three sets of factories, or somewhat closer scores to British factories than to Japanese factories in each subset. This means that there is a higher possibility for a line manager to access strategic information in JFB than in Japanese factories in general terms. Regarding 'rapid access to information databases in a problematic situation', JFB have acquired, generally speaking, either the highest average scores of the three or quite close to those of British factories. This suggests that it is possible for a line manager in JFB to access more rapidly relevant information databases in a problematic situation than in Japanese factories. Concerning 'gaining information from across different functional boundaries', little difference can be observed both between JFB and British factories and between JFB and Japanese factories in general and in each subset. Regarding 'liaison as the main job', JFB's average scores in general are closer to those of British factories than to those of Japanese factories. This implies that JFB's line managers do not play a liaison role between senior management and lower levels as much as Japanese factories' counterparts. With respect to 'communicating instructions as the most important role', the results of Scheffe's tests show that JFB in general can be located somewhat closer to British factories than to Japanese factories again. With regard to 'the need to report major problems to senior managers', JFB can be located in between British factories and Japanese factories, judging from the results of Scheffe's tests. When all these results are taken into consideration, JFB at the management level have a pattern of IT use closer to British factories than to Japanese factories concerning CIU.

Findings on individual-oriented IT use

General view

As discussed in Chapter 3, IIU at the management level has been presumed to develop in four specific areas, and the relationship between IIU and the measures of actual practices at the management level is shown in Table 7.4. The results of reliability tests are also given below the table. As shown in the table, IIU at the management level has been presumed to develop in four specific areas: having an individual password for gaining access to relevant information databases; sharing of information to attain group consensus; use of group decision support system (GDSS); and being stuck to a particular section. Similar to the discussions at the shop-floor level, the preference for individual transmission of information enable a factory to provide individual managers with their own passwords for gaining access to information databases. The managerial preference for teamwork may lead a factory to use a group-oriented work system such as GDSS particularly in the context of IT use (Briggs, Nunamaker and Sprague, 1998). In the use of GDSS, information sharing within the group may be achieved through regular/ irregular exchanges of information among members on-line. Finally, the managerial preference for a fixed job system may well bring about a line manager remaining in a particular section and frequent job rotations may well be not practised. In this case, group consensus through information sharing may not be highly prioritised thus the score may remain lower.

The results of the reliability test, however, indicate that there was very poor consistency among items of the 'composite' measures, and the items cannot be used collectively as a scale. Therefore, again, I present data based on each item individually instead of calculating the overall average scores on actual practices in IIU at the management level.

Figure 7.2 shows the general trend of each dimension of the actual practices in terms of IIU at the management level. These graphs seem to show Japanese factories' different tendencies on IIU compared to British factories and JFB. Regarding 'having an individual password for gaining access to relevant information databases', there appear to be little

Table 7.4   Measures of actual practices in IIU at the management level

Pattern of IT use	Actual practices
Individual-oriented IT use	• Having an individual password for gaining access to relevant databases • Sharing of information to attain group consensus* • Use of GDSS* • Being stuck to a particular section

Reliability test Alpha = – .01 for British factories; .05 for Japanese factories; and 0.21 for JFB.
Note: * indicates items measured by a reversed scale.

174

Having an individual password

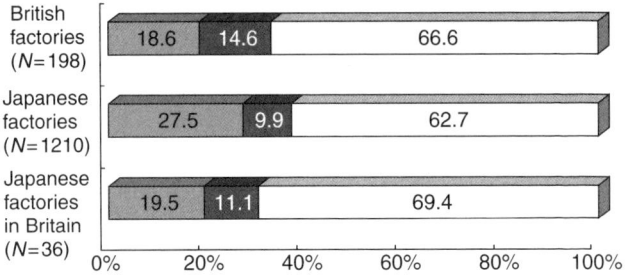

British factories (N=198): 18.6 | 14.6 | 66.6
Japanese factories (N=1210): 27.5 | 9.9 | 62.7
Japanese factories in Britain (N=36): 19.5 | 11.1 | 69.4

Line managers have their own passwords for gaining access to relevant information database(s)

☐ False ■ Neither true nor false ☐ True

Sharing of information to attain group consensus

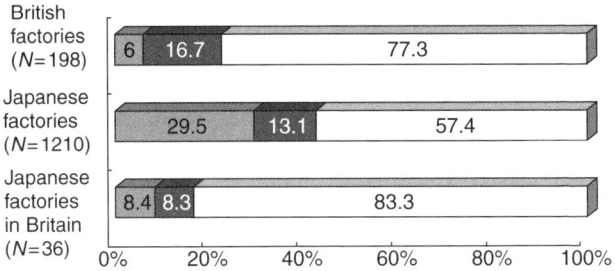

British factories (N=198): 6 | 16.7 | 77.3
Japanese factories (N=1210): 29.5 | 13.1 | 57.4
Japanese factories in Britain (N=36): 8.4 | 8.3 | 83.3

Information sharing with other line managers is important for achieving group consensus

☐ False ■ Neither true nor false ☐ True

Figure 7.2

Use of GDSS

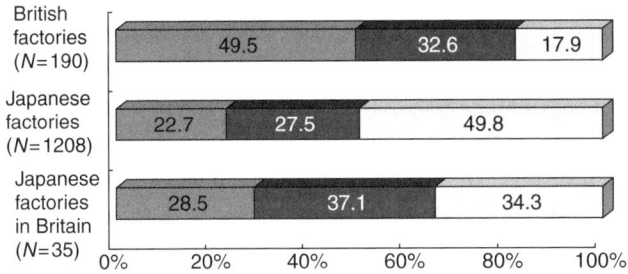

Group decision support system (GDSS) is adopted in enhancing a group's decision outcome

■False ■ Neither true nor false □True

Being stuck to a particular section

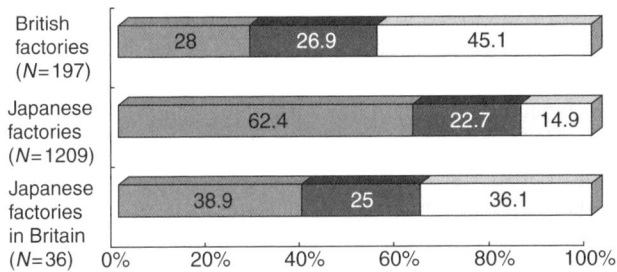

A line manager sticks to a particular section and rotation is not practised

■False ■ Neither true nor false □True

Figure 7.2   Actual practices in IIU at the management level – general view

differences among the three kinds of factories except for a little more agreement observed in Japanese factories. With respect to 'sharing of information to attain group consensus', many more Japanese factories have disagreed than the other two kinds of factories. With regard to the 'use of GDSS', more Japanese factories have shown agreement whilst more British factories have indicated disagreement. With regard to 'being stuck to a particular section', many more Japanese factories have shown disagreement than British factories and JFB.

Comparison between British factories and Japanese factories

Table 7.5 shows the descriptive statistics for British factories and Japanese factories to examine the general tendencies confirmed in the previous section. Again, below the title of each table are shown the results of ANOVA to assess whether factory size and/or industry are significant covariates. The ANOVA results show significant differences between nations (that is, British factories and Japanese factories) in terms of all items. They also show that factory size is a significant covariate in all items, and industry as well as for 'having an individual password for gaining access to relevant databases'. For the latter item, the F-value of size and industry is greater than that of nation. The main effect of nation is shown to be greater than the covariates for other items.

According to these tables, three out of the four dimensions of IIU at the management level indicate higher average scores in British factories than in Japanese factories, which means a more or less higher tendency in British factories than in Japanese factories to use IT in an individualistic way. With regard to 'having an individual password for gaining access to relevant information databases', British factories show relatively higher average scores than Japanese factories. This general tendency particularly fits small factories, as small factories in Japan especially have shown lower scores. Regarding 'use of GDSS', the data shows much higher average scores in British factories than in Japanese factories. The general pattern can be observed in nearly all subsets with statistically significant differences. This shows Japanese factories' higher degree of use of GDSS. With regard to 'being stuck to a particular section', again British factories' average scores have been generally shown to be much higher than those of Japanese factories – so are small chemicals/pharmaceuticals, small machinery, large electrical engineering, small transportation, and large rubber/plastic products. This suggests that job rotations at the management level are practised more often in Japanese factories than in British factories. Regarding 'sharing of information to attain group consensus', however, the average scores have been shown

Table 7.5 Actual practices in IIU in British factories and Japanese factories at the management level
Having an individual password for gaining access to relevant databases
Main effect of nation: $F = 8.50$** (covariates: size $F = 36.81$***; industry $F = 12.09$***)

		British factories			Japanese factories			t-value
		Average	Standard deviation	N	Average	Standard deviation	N	
All samples		3.77	1.41	198	3.57	1.48	1210	1.86
All large factories		3.99	1.35	72	3.72	1.43	856	1.53
All small factories		3.64	1.43	126	3.19	1.55	352	2.98**
All chemicals/pharmaceuticals		3.81	1.39	36	3.52	1.59	184	1.09
All machinery		4.10	1.18	41	3.69	1.35	147	1.77
All electrical engineering		3.96	1.26	50	3.92	1.38	227	0.21
All transportation		3.12	1.59	25	3.70	1.06	201	-1.86
All rubber/plastic		3.59	1.57	46	3.31	1.50	452	1.20
Chemicals/pharmaceuticals	Large	4.33	1.18	15	3.79	1.52	102	1.32
	Small	3.43	1.43	21	3.18	1.62	82	0.63
Machinery	Large	4.11	1.36	10	3.85	1.30	110	0.59
	Small	4.09	1.15	31	3.17	1.38	36	2.99**
Electrical engineering	Large	3.94	1.25	17	4.13	1.22	174	-0.61
	Small	3.97	1.29	33	3.21	1.63	53	2.40*
Transportation	Large	3.30	1.49	10	3.75	1.42	177	-0.98
	Small	3.00	1.69	15	3.30	1.71	23	-0.54
Rubber/plastic products	Large	4.05	1.47	21	3.38	1.50	293	1.98*
	Small	3.20	1.58	25	3.18	1.51	158	0.07

Table 7.5 (Cont'd)

Sharing of information to attain group consensus (reversed scale: adjusted)

Main effect of nation: $F = 56.61$*** (covariates: size $F = 37.34$***; industry $F = 2.72$)

		British factories			Japanese factories			t-value
		Average	Standard deviation	N	Average	Standard deviation	N	
All samples		1.92	1.00	198	2.60	1.44	1210	−8.13***
All large factories		1.79	0.90	72	2.44	1.38	856	−5.57***
All small factories		2.00	1.06	126	2.97	1.50	352	−7.86***
All chemicals/pharmaceuticals		1.92	1.00	36	2.76	1.50	184	−4.20***
All machinery		1.93	1.08	41	2.67	1.41	147	−3.64***
All electrical engineering		1.72	0.73	50	2.05	1.27	227	−2.50**
All transportation		2.32	1.22	25	2.60	1.41	200	−1.07
All rubber/plastic		1.93	1.06	46	2.78	1.45	452	−4.94***
Chemicals/pharmaceuticals	Large	1.73	0.70	15	2.67	1.50	102	−3.98***
	Small	2.05	1.16	21	2.87	1.51	82	−2.70***
Machinery	Large	1.78	1.09	10	2.50	1.37	110	−1.54
	Small	1.97	1.09	31	3.22	1.42	36	−4.11***
Electrical engineering	Large	1.76	0.83	17	1.83	1.07	174	−0.26
	Small	1.70	0.68	33	2.77	1.59	53	−4.33***
Transportation	Large	2.00	1.25	10	2.55	1.38	177	−1.24
	Small	2.53	1.19	15	2.96	1.66	23	−0.91
Rubber/plastic products	Large	1.76	0.89	21	2.63	1.42	293	−4.12***
	Small	2.08	1.19	25	3.04	1.46	158	−3.62***

Use of GDSS (reversed scale: adjusted)

Main effect of nation: $F = 88.58^{***}$ (covariates: size $F = 11.30^{***}$; industry $F = .48$)

		British factories			Japanese factories			t-value
		Average	Standard deviation	N	Average	Standard deviation	N	
All samples		3.54	1.13	190	2.69	1.02	1 208	9.72***
All large factories		3.51	1.21	69	2.63	0.99	854	5.90***
All small factories		3.56	1.09	121	2.85	1.06	353	6.29***
All chemicals/pharmaceuticals		3.71	1.30	35	2.69	0.97	183	4.42***
All machinery		3.67	1.20	39	2.68	0.97	147	4.74***
All electrical engineering		3.29	0.97	48	2.66	1.06	227	3.81***
All transportation		3.67	1.01	24	2.55	1.03	202	5.03***
All rubber/plastic		3.50	1.17	44	2.78	1.02	449	4.43***
Chemicals/pharmaceuticals	Large	3.64	1.50	14	2.62	0.97	102	2.49*
	Small	3.76	1.18	21	2.79	0.98	81	3.87***
Machinery	Large	4.00	1.41	10	2.64	1.00	110	2.68*
	Small	3.58	1.15	31	2.81	0.89	36	3.11**
Electrical engineering	Large	3.31	0.95	16	2.56	0.98	174	2.95**
	Small	3.28	0.99	32	3.00	1.22	53	1.10
Transportation	Large	3.90	0.88	10	2.53	1.01	177	4.23***
	Small	3.50	1.09	14	2.76	1.16	25	1.95
Rubber/plastic products	Large	3.19	1.21	21	2.73	1.00	291	2.02*
	Small	3.78	1.09	23	2.86	1.07	158	3.86***

180

Table 7.5 (Cont'd)
Being stuck to a particular section
Main effect of nation: $F = 94.38{***}$ (covariates: size $F = 34.74{***}$; industry $F = .16$)

		British factories			Japanese factories			t-value
		Average	Standard deviation	N	Average	Standard deviation	N	
All samples		3.26	1.25	197	2.33	1.02	1209	9.86***
All large factories		3.08	1.22	72	2.22	0.98	855	5.83***
All small factories		3.36	1.27	125	2.59	1.07	353	6.04***
All chemicals/pharmaceuticals		2.92	1.27	36	2.34	1.06	183	2.86**
All machinery		3.32	1.19	41	2.50	0.99	147	4.48***
All electrical engineering		3.22	1.21	49	2.34	1.01	227	5.35***
All transportation		3.16	1.18	25	2.11	0.92	202	5.22***
All rubber/plastic		3.57	1.34	46	2.37	1.05	450	5.86***
Chemicals/pharmaceuticals	Large	2.33	0.98	15	2.25	1.06	102	0.31
	Small	3.33	1.32	21	2.47	1.06	81	3.16**
Machinery	Large	2.89	1.17	10	2.43	0.97	110	1.35
	Small	3.44	1.19	31	2.69	1.04	36	2.75**
Electrical engineering	Large	3.41	1.12	17	2.24	0.98	174	4.67***
	Small	3.13	1.26	32	2.70	1.03	53	1.70
Transportation	Large	2.40	0.84	10	2.09	0.92	177	1.04
	Small	3.67	1.11	15	2.24	0.93	25	4.37***
Rubber/plastic products	Large	3.76	1.22	21	2.21	0.98	292	6.89***
	Small	3.40	1.44	25	2.66	1.11	158	2.46*

Note: 'Large' and 'small' in the second column indicate large factories with 200 or more employees and small factories with less than 200 employees. Reversed scales have been adjusted to indicate that the higher the average IIU score, the higher the extent of the individual-oriented use. T-value indicates the result of the t-test on average values between British factories and Japanese factories. The significant levels of statistical tests are $* p < .05$, $** p < .01$ and $*** p < .001$.

to be much higher in British factories than in Japanese factories in general. This means that information-sharing for group consensus has been perceived to be much more important in British factories than in Japanese factories. The general tendency is coherent in all subsets except transportation.

Japanese factories in Britain

Table 7.6 shows where JFB can be located in terms of each item on actual practices at the management level concerning IIU. The table indicates the descriptive statistics for JFB. ANOVA was carried out to explore the differences between average scores for each item among JFB, British factories and Japanese factories, and the results of *post hoc* Scheffe's tests are shown in the last two columns where the overall ANOVA is significant. Below the title of each table are shown the results of a two-way ANOVA to look for interaction effects having (i) factory size, and (ii) industry as variables.

The ANOVA results show significant differences among nations (that is, British factories, Japanese factories and JFB) in terms of all items. No significant interactions are observed, except between industry and nation in terms of 'use of GDSS'. The table shows that the general average scores in JFB are closer to British factories than Japanese factories, except for 'use of GDSS'. Regarding 'having an individual password for gaining access to relevant information databases', little difference can be seen among the three kinds of factories concerning the average scores. With regard to 'sharing of information to attain group consensus', the data show that the average scores in JFB are again closer to British factories than to Japanese factories in general. This suggests that, generally speaking, information-sharing has been perceived as more important in JFB and in British factories than in Japanese factories. With regard to 'being stuck to a particular section', the average scores in general have been shown to be a little closer to British factories than to Japanese factories again. This general pattern is consistent especially in large factories. In small factories and in each industrial group, little difference can be observed among the three sets of factories concerning the average scores. However, in regard to 'use of GDSS', it is difficult to see a specific pattern. The data indicate much variety among industrial group – note that the interaction between industry and nation is statistically significant. In all samples, the average score has been shown to be closer to Japanese factories than to British factories, which shows the opposite result to the other dimensions of IIU. The results of Scheffe's tests suggest a higher use of GDSS in large JFB than in large British factories.

Table 7.6 Actual practices in IIU in Japanese factories in Britain (JFB) at the management level

Having an individual password for gaining access to relevant databases

(i) Main effect of nation $F = 4.84^{**}$; size $F = 7.67^{**}$; interaction (nation/size) $F = .40$

(ii) Main effect of nation $F = 4.50^{*}$; industry $F = 2.59^{*}$; interaction (nation/industry) $F = .19$

	Japanese factories in Britain (JFB)			British factories' average	Japanese factories' average	F-value	Scheffe's test	
	Average	Standard deviation	N				British factories/ JFB	JFB/Japanese factories
All samples	3.78	1.48	36	3.77	3.57	1.88	(...)	(...)
All large factories	4.00	1.22	25	3.99	3.72	1.59	(...)	(...)
All small factories	3.27	1.90	11	3.64	3.19	4.07*	–	–
All chemicals/ pharmaceuticals	5.00	(...)	1	3.81	3.52	(...)	(...)	(...)
All machinery	4.00	1.41	7	4.10	3.69	(...)	(...)	(...)
All electrical engineering	3.92	1.04	13	3.96	3.92	0.02	(...)	(...)
All transportation	4.75	0.50	4	3.12	3.70	(...)	(...)	(...)
All rubber/plastic products	3.00	1.95	11	3.59	3.31	0.97	(...)	(...)

Sharing of information to attain group consensus (reversed scale: adjusted)
(i) Main effect of nation $F = 32.04$***; size $F = 2.96$; interaction (nation/size) $F = 1.26$
(ii) Main effect of nation $F = 16.06$***; industry $F = 2.18$; interaction (nation/industry) $F = 1.73$

	Japanese factories in Britain (JFB)		N	British factories' average	Japanese factories' average	F-value	Scheffe's test	
	Average	Standard deviation					British factories/ JFB	JFB/Japanese factories
All samples	1.78	1.10	36	1.92	2.60	25.01***	–	*
All large factories	1.72	1.06	25	1.79	2.44	10.71***	–	*
All small factories	1.91	1.22	11	2.00	2.97	24.33***	–	*
All chemicals/ pharmaceuticals	5.00	(...)	1	1.92	2.76	(...)	(...)	(...)
All machinery	1.43	0.53	7	1.93	2.67	(...)	(...)	(...)
All electrical engineering	1.85	0.99	13	1.72	2.05	1.71	(...)	(...)
All transportation	1.25	0.50	4	2.32	2.60	(...)	(...)	(...)
All rubber/plastic products	1.82	1.25	11	1.93	2.78	9.49***	–	*

Table 7.6 (Cont'd)

Use of GDSS (reversed scale: adjusted)

(i) Main effect of nation $F = 45.25***$; size $F = 3.11$; interaction (nation/size) $F = .72$
(ii) Main effect of nation $F = 61.18***$; industry $F = 3.68**$; interaction (nation/industry) $F = 2.59**$

	Japanese factories in Britain (JFB)			British factories' average	Japanese factories' average	F-value	Scheffe's test	
	Average	Standard deviation	N				British factories/ JFB	JFB/Japanese factories
All samples	3.06	1.16	35	3.54	2.69	55.95***	*	–
All large factories	2.92	1.06	24	3.51	2.63	24.75***	*	–
All small factories	3.36	1.36	11	3.56	2.85	20.06***	–	–
All chemicals/ pharmaceuticals	5.00	(...)	1	3.71	2.69	(...)	(...)	(...)
All machinery	2.14	0.90	7	3.67	2.68	(...)	(...)	(...)
All electrical engineering	2.85	0.69	13	3.29	2.66	7.46***	–	–
All transportation	4.25	0.96	4	3.67	2.55	(...)	(...)	(...)
All rubber/plastic products	3.30	1.34	10	3.50	2.78	10.65***	–	–

Being stuck to a particular section

(i) Main effect of nation $F = 49.85$***; size $F = 7.30$**; interaction (nation/size) $F = .20$

(ii) Main effect of nation $F = 58.56$***; industry $F = 1.66$; interaction (nation/industry) $F = 1.02$

	Japanese factories in Britain (JFB)			British factories' average	Japanese factories' average	F-value	Scheffe's test	
	Average	Standard deviation	N				British factories/ JFB	JFB/Japanese factories
All samples	2.94	1.24	36	3.26	2.33	68.36***	–	*
All large factories	2.80	1.15	25	3.08	2.22	27.58***	–	*
All small factories	3.27	1.42	11	3.36	2.59	22.07***	–	–
All chemicals/ pharmaceuticals	2.00	(...)	1	2.92	2.34	(...)	(...)	(...)
All machinery	3.29	1.38	7	3.32	2.50	(...)	(...)	(...)
All electrical engineering	2.85	1.28	13	3.22	2.34	14.67***	–	–
All transportation	2.50	0.58	4	3.16	2.11	(...)	(...)	(...)
All rubber/plastic products	3.09	1.38	11	3.57	2.37	27.09***	(...)	–

Note: 'Large' and 'small' indicate large factories with 200 or more employees and small factories with less than 200 employees. It is presumed that the higher the average IIU score, the higher the extent of individual-oriented use. The column of '*F*-value' shows the results of one-way ANOVA to explore the differences between average scores for each item among JFB, British factories and Japanese factories. The significant levels of statistical tests are * $p < .05$, ** $p < .01$ and *** $p < .001$. An asterisk in the last two columns indicates a significant difference ($p < .05$) and '–' indicates no significant differences. '(...)' indicates either no test being conducted or it being impossible to show the value.

Taking all these results into consideration, it is possible to assert that, generally speaking, IIU scores of JFB are closer to British factories than to Japanese factories except for the use of GDSS.

Relationship between managerial preferences and actual practices

In the sections above I have shown how cultural influences on IT use may operate in actual terms at the management level. As at the shop-floor level developed in the preceding chapter, I examine the relationship between managerial preferences and actual practices to show the degree to which the actual practices really reflect managerial preferences.

Control-oriented IT use

Table 7.7 shows the results of a partial correlation analysis between managerial preferences and actual practices in IT use in terms of CIU, controlling for nation, industry, factory size, batch size and unionisation.[1] Coefficients of correlation are provided in each cell in the table.

Table 7.7   The relationship between managerial preferences and actual practices in CIU at the management level (partial correlation analysis)

	Concentration of important information at the top	Top-down information flow	Simple job design
Accessibility to strategic information (R)	0.0716**	– 0.0162	0.0434
Rapid access to information databases in a problematic situation	– 0.0043	0.0271	0.0151
Gaining information from across different functional boundaries (R)	0.0383	0.0239	0.0703**
Liaison as the main job	0.1302***	0.1453***	0.0872***
Communicating instructions as the most important role	0.1262***	0.1318***	0.1270***
The need to report of major problems to senior managers	0.1624***	0.1419***	0.1326***

Note: Sample size is $N = 1417$. R is indicating items measured with a reversed scale (adjusted). Nation, industry, factory size, batch size, and unionisation are controlled for. Two-tailed significant level is * $p < .05$, ** $p < .01$ and *** $p < .001$.

As with the results at the shop-floor level (*cf.* Table 6.7), this table shows that the actual practices in IT use in the aspect of CIU at the management level, generally speaking, positively correlate with managerial preferences of CIU. This means that there is a relationship between managerial practices and actual practices in which the greater the managerial preferences, the greater the degree of actual practice in CIU becomes. Although some coefficients have shown small values, the managerial preference for 'the concentration of important information at the top' correlates with 'the need to report major problems to senior managers', with 'liaison as the main job', and with 'communicating instructions as the most important role'. The preference also positively correlates with 'accessibility to strategic information', but the coefficient is a little lower than the above-mentioned three dimensions.

The managerial preference for 'top-down information flow' has shown positive correlation again with 'liaison as the main job', with 'the need to report major problems to senior managers', and with 'communicating instructions as the most important role'. The managerial preference for 'simple job design' has shown positive correlation with 'the need to report major problems to senior managers', 'communicating instructions as the most important role', and 'liaison as the main job' and with 'gaining information from across different functional boundaries'.

These positive coefficients may represent real appearances of the managerial preferences on actual practices in the dimension of CIU. As examined above, all managerial preferences for CIU are highly correlated with the following three dimensions of actual practices in CIU: 'liaison as the main job', 'communicating instructions as the most important role' and 'the need to report major problems to senior managers'.

Individual-oriented IT use

Table 7.8 shows the results of a partial correlation analysis between managerial preferences and actual practices in IT use in terms of IIU, controlling for nation, industry, factory size, batch size and unionisation. Coefficients of correlation are given in each cell in the table. As with CIU, some of the coefficients show positive correlation, but others show little correlation or even negative correlation. The managerial preference for 'individual transmission of information' positively correlates with 'having an individual password' with strong statistical significance, and negatively correlates with 'sharing of information to attain group consensus'. The managerial preference for teamwork shows positive correlation with the 'use of GDSS'. The managerial preference for the

Table 7.8 The relationship between managerial preferences and actual practices in IIU at the management level (partial correlation analysis)

	Individual transmission of information	Team-working (R)	Fixed job system
Having an individual password	0.0845**	–0.0221	–0.0759**
Sharing of information to attain group consensus (R)	–0.0818**	0.0260	0.0457
Use of GDSS (R)	–0.0056	0.0802**	0.0300
Being stuck to a particular section	–0.0022	–0.0405	0.1659***

Note: Sample size is $N = 1412$. R is indicating items measured with a reversed scale (adjusted). Nation, industry, factory size, batch size, and unionisation are controlled for. Two-tailed significant level is ** $p < .01$ and *** $p < .001$.

'fixed job system' shows high positive correlation with 'being stuck to a particular section'.

Although not as significant a positive relationship between managerial preferences and actual practices as in CIU, the positive coefficients shown above may represent real appearances of the preferences in actual practices. However, comparing with CIU (*cf.* Table 7.7), a less significant positive relationship between managerial preferences and actual practices than in CIU can be observed in IIU in general.

Discussion and implications

The data presented in this chapter have indicated how cultural influences on IT use actually operate at the management level in each set of factories in each country. In this section I develop some implications of the findings and their theoretical justification.

Three major findings have been identified. In the first place, in respect of CIU four out of the total of six dimensions of CIU in Japanese factories have shown relatively higher average scores than in British factories: 'the accessibility to strategic information', 'liaison as the main job', 'communicating instructions as the most important role' and 'the need to report major problems to senior managers'. These four are dimensions all associated with hierarchical control in an organisation. Such results which indicate a high control-orientation in Japanese factories are consistent with those of my own previous study of Japanese manufacturing firms (Kambayashi, 1998; see also Okubayashi *et al.*, 1994). In the previous study, cultural influences were not consciously measured, but some results suggested a strong orientation towards hierarchical control in Japan: Japanese factories maintaining hierarchical control through a rank hierarchy even under the use of IT; very limited accessibility for a manager to information databases especially regarding strategic and business planning information, and so on.

Some other previous studies have also suggested Japanese factories' orientation towards strong hierarchical control at the management level. For instance, Lincoln (1989) identified, in his comparative study between Japanese and American companies, that the Japanese had more hierarchical levels. Hofstede (1980) revealed that strong 'uncertainty avoidance' and a high 'power-distance' culture prevailed in Japanese offices, which may explain the results shown above. Also, Mead (1998) suggested that, in Japanese cultural contexts, 'top management in large Japanese companies provide top-down strategic guidance, which gives a framework within which policy details are formulated' (p. 177), and that middle-level managers and below contribute 'bottom-up' enthusiasm such as quality circles suggesting process modifications, which are reviewed by top management. She admits that this does not mean that formal authority is delegated downwards, but rather that strategic decision-making processes are centralised and strategic decisions are taken by management in Japanese offices.

At first glance, the higher tendency towards hierarchical control in Japanese factories appears to contradict the results of Japanese factories' relatively lower average scores than British factories concerning the other two dimensions of CIU, that is 'rapid access to information databases in a problematic situation' and 'gaining information from across different functional boundaries', because it can be inferred that the higher tendency towards hierarchical control leads to the necessity of more rapid access to information databases in a problematic situation and less opportunities to gain information from across different functional boundaries at the horizontal level in an organisation. However, some previous studies can support this seemingly contradictory result, especially about Japanese factory managers' high opportunities to gain information from across other functional boundaries. For example, Currie (1995) suggested that Japanese managers in the IT/IS area frequently exchange information with other managers through regular/irregular meetings, and thus lateral communication has been achieved in Japanese offices. Mead (1998) also identified that Japanese managers have many chances to negotiate informally both with other managers and with workers after working hours while eating and drinking to make a consensus. Also, Mair (1994) observed, in his case study of Honda, horizontal as well as vertical communication flows among managers, which he sees as associated with Japan and with Japanese firms abroad. Abrahamsson (1993) also suggested that the Japanese office had flexibility at the horizontal level in the form of job rotation, even while maintaining a quite rigid hierarchical ladder. Lower scores in 'rapid access to information database in a problematic situation' in Japanese factories than in British factories are difficult to justify by previous studies, but this may be concerned with relatively lower diffusion of IT in Japanese factories than in British factories. Taking into account all these results, however, CIU in general has been shown to be greater in Japanese factories than British factories – a finding similar to that at the shop-floor level.

Secondly, in terms of IIU, three out of the four IIU dimensions have shown higher scores in British factories than in Japanese factories: 'having an individual password for gaining access to information database', 'use of GDSS' and 'being stuck to a particular section'. Some previous studies help explain this finding of a relative higher tendency to use GDSS in Japanese factories: for example, Mejias *et al.* (1997) suggested that in the study of comparison between American and Mexican groups, Mexican groups, because of their highly collectivistic propensities, felt more impelled to seek and generate higher levels of group agreement in the use of GDSS. Considering that Japan has a more collectivist cultural root than Britain (for example Hofstede, 1980), the higher tendency to use GDSS in Japanese factories than in British factories may reflect Japanese collectivistic propensities. Similar experimental evidence has been identified to varying effects for GDSS technology in different national cultures (Watson, Ho and Raman, 1994). Ramen and Watson (1994) have shown that the Executive Information Systems (EIS) which provide information to individual managers, instead of GDSS which provide information to groups of managers, is widely used in organisations in the so-called *low-context* societies such as America and many other Anglo-Saxon countries (Hall, 1976), but they are not used as much in *high-context* cultures such as Japan and many other Asian countries, as 'managers in high-context cultures believe that while a computer can capture the low-context, explicit information relating to a situation, it cannot satisfactorily reflect the full context' (Raman and Watson, 1994, p. 507). According to them, for a manager in a high-context society, EIS is a poor substitute for the meaning that comes from high context communication. This result is quite consistent with the study here. My data show that 62.0 per cent of British factories use MIS which provide information to individual managers, like EIS, whilst only 29.6 per cent of British factories use Lotus Notes and/or GDSS where information is provided to groups of managers. On the other hand, 31.6 per cent of Japanese factories adopt EIS and 68.4 per cent adopt Lotus Notes and/or GDSS (see Q4 in the Appendix).

Japanese factories' lower average scores than British factories on 'being stuck to a particular section' can also be confirmed by previous studies. Bensaou and Earl (1998) have suggested that many Japanese managers spend a few years in an IT department as part of job-rotation schemes. The postings help them develop knowledge that will prove useful in their subsequent jobs – not only technological know-how but also knowledge about how to get things done in IT and about who can help with what. According to Bensaou and Earl, the rotations can be seen as 'an institutionalised version of Western companies' creation of hybrid managers' (p. 125). Koike (1988) discussed the issue along the same lines. He points out that Japanese line managers have not only experienced a variety of sections during their career promotions, becoming experts, but are also engaged in a range of sections *at the same time* so that they absorb much knowledge at work and have the perspectives to make appropriate decisions. This greater tendency towards job rotation might lead us to expect a result of Japanese factories' higher average scores concerning the 'sharing of information to attain group consensus', but this is not the case. A tentative explanation is that Japanese factories have already achieved high group consensus (Schonberger, 1982), so that it is not perceived as important as in British factories. In other words, British factories may perceive that the level of group consensus should be enhanced.

Regarding lower average scores concerning 'having an individual password for gaining access to information databases', it is possible to consider the result as reflecting a managerial preference for individual transmission of information, but it may be again because of relatively less diffusion of IT at the management level. Comparing these results with those at the shop-floor level, it is possible to judge the difference between British factories and Japanese factories on IIU as being greater at the management level than at the shop-floor level.

Thirdly, in terms of the situation of JFB, JFB can be located closer to British factories than to Japanese factories both in respect of CIU and IIU, which is not as clear-cut at the shop-floor level. Except for the 'use of GDSS', all dimensions of CIU and IIU suggest JFB's relatively closer average scores to British factories than to Japanese factories. It is difficult to justify these results on JFB, because, as far as I know, no other studies have looked at IT use in overseas Japanese factories at the line-management level. Many previous studies have presumed that JFB have rather strong Japanese cultural roots which can cause cultural conflicts with indigenous British factories (Oliver and Wilkinson, 1992; Bratton, 1992), but my data suggest that JFB take a rather similar position with British factories as far as IT use is concerned.

Conclusion

This chapter has described the actual practices in IT use at the management level of factory organisations. As discussed above, some new empirical findings have been clarified on CIU and IIU, and I have attempted to standardise British factories/Japanese factories/JFB specific patterns of IT use. On the whole, it can be summarised that, similar to the shop-floor level, Japanese factories actually take a relatively stronger orientation towards CIU and less orientation towards IIU. British factories actually exhibit a relatively lower orientation towards CIU and a stronger orientation towards IIU. JFB have been found to exhibit a closer pattern of IT use to British factories than Japanese factories both in terms of CIU and IIU, except the dimension of 'use of GDSS' in IIU. As examined earlier, some dimensions, in CIU in particular, have been identified to correlate positively with managerial preferences discussed in Chapter 5. This suggests, as was shown at the shop-floor level, a possibility for managerial preferences for IT use in each country to actually operate in practice on IT use in each country's factory at the level of line management.

8
Conclusions

Summary of the research: lessons to be learned

It was noted in Chapter 1 that more research into cross-national comparisons on IT use in organisations was required. Based on the recent rapid development of IT since the 1980s, much research has been conducted on the relationship between IT and organisational structure in order to clarify whether technology determines organisation structure, or if there is space for an organisational designer to develop an organisational structure of their choice in an organisation. Some studies have attempted to focus on the theme at an international level, and some have drawn useful implications about national cultural influences on organisational structure – Sorge *et al.* (1983), Sorge and Warner (1986), Clark (1987), Clark and Staunton (1989), Sorge (1995), Lam (1997) and Bensaou and Earl (1998) for instance. However, few studies have tried to illuminate the specific relationship between national culture and organisational IT use in a factory. In other words, a cross-national comparison has been needed to illuminate whether or not national culture can affect organisational IT use, and if so how such influences operate in real terms. In view of this, the overall objective of the study has been to explore the question of national cultural influences and investigate organisational mechanisms through which national culture may influence IT use in a factory, employing empirical data collected from British and Japanese factories.

To examine the extent previous studies have clarified the theme, a review of these previous studies was undertaken in Chapter 2: the general relationship between technology and organisation; national cultural influences on IT use; and specific British/Japanese cultural influences on IT use. Firstly, through the review of studies on the relationship between technology and organisational structure it has been revealed that 'the emergent perspective' holds better for the IT era than the other two perspectives, namely technological determinism and organisational determinism. Given such dispositions of IT as involving 'stochastic and continuous processing' (Weick, 1990, p. 9), it is important to acknowledge that the relationship between technology and organisation is an interactive one and not a question of linear causality which technological/organisational determinism would suggest. The emergent perspective seems to be useful in indicating some of the mechanisms through which national culture may influence IT use and, if so, what implications the influences have for its use. However, it also raises the question of whether it is possible to isolate and disentangle technological effects from other influences on organisational IT use.

Secondly, through the review of national cultural influences on organisational IT use, few studies appear to have considered cultural effects despite international comparisons: most studies have neglected cultural influences to focus on institutional influences. Clark and Staunton's (1989) and Sorge's (1995) study had some important suggestions to make on how cultural influences could be analysed, but still did not clarify what national cultural influences might specifically operate in the organisational use of IT. Recent developments on the effects of national culture on MIS and GDSS technologies have some implications on IT use, but these studies have been mainly based upon Hofstede's (1980) work on national cultural dimensions with little consideration of the justification of the model. Weick's (1990) development of Giddens' (1979) notion of 'structuration' has been shown to be important to confirm whether or not national culture plays important roles in the emergent process shaping organisational IT use in a factory.

Thirdly, through the review of specific British/Japanese cultural influences on organisational IT use, it has been revealed that national culture has been neglected, or has been dealt with as a residual factor, in international comparisons between the two countries. This is partly because more institutional and/or economic factors have been the focus of the previous studies, as they have had an interest in the transferability of Japanese 'successful' systems. The discussion on 'Japanisation' of British industries, though, has some important implications for the theme in this study. Admitting cultural uniqueness, the discussion has disclosed that the Japanisation process such as the introduction of JIT systems sometimes does involve cultural conflicts with existing Western values. Also, Lam's (1997) study has shown how the dominant form of knowledge exists in organisations, and that the ways in which it is structured, utilised and transmitted vary considerably between firms in Britain and Japan, based on their different value/cultural systems. Furthermore, Bensaou and Earl (1998) have suggested that there are some differences in the way Western and Japanese managers frame IT management, given the different national contexts. However, these studies have still not specified what effects national *cultural* values have on the use of IT.

The review of those previous studies indicated the necessity for an analytical framework in which to explore the cultural effects on the use of IT in an organisational setting. In other words, an analytical model is required to assess those differences between patterns of IT use that might reflect national cultural values rather than other differences such as economic, political and institutional issues.

Chapter 3 developed the analytical model and research methodologies. First of all, I looked for the relevance of a survey-based approach to the theme. Since national culture is a diffuse phenomenon, a large sample size is required to enable serious discussion, for which the survey approach is best suited. Then the levels of analysis of organisational IT use were set. Two hierarchical levels in a factory – shop-floor and line management – were targeted. Both managerial preferences for, and actual practices of, IT use were set for the analysis in order to differentiate cultural effects from other possible effects on organisational IT use. How to operationalise national culture was examined by referring to previous studies on national cultural dimensions, resulting in two hypothesised patterns of IT use likely to display cultural influences: control-oriented IT use (CIU) and individual-oriented IT use (IIU). The analytical model employing these newly developed concepts is one of the most distinctive methodological features of the present study, as most previous empirical investigations on national culture are based only on Hofstede's (1980) dimensions to construct and test hypotheses. Methodological details, such as sampling procedures and the structure of the samples, were also provided in this chapter.

In an analysis of organisational IT use under the influences of national culture, some contextual factors should be controlled for such as type of IT/systems, type of industry, organisational size, unionisation, batch size and organisational sub-cultures. The analysis of the data collected on these contextual factors was described in Chapter 4. I have shown that the type of IT/systems at the shop-floor level can be controlled for by analysing data under a division of each industry separately, as it has been observed that more or less similar IT-based systems have been introduced within an industry. My analysis has also indicated that there is less need to control for the technologies/systems at the management level, as the technological basis is more or less similar as compared to at the shop-floor level. Furthermore, the batch size of a factory is found to be represented by industrial group quite well. Organisational size must be controlled for, as my data have indicated that most of the British factories that responded are smaller in terms of number of employees than the Japanese sample. Unionisation has been identified to be well-represented by organisational size, or the number of full-time employees. The control for the effects of an individual organisation's sub-culture involves more difficulties, but it is expected that its effects may well be reduced to the extent that large samples can be gathered. The large sample size is expected to make more distinctive what the substantial differences are between Britain and Japan, rather than differences among individual organisations. As a result, the analysis of the context showed that the data analysis should be conducted on the basis of controlling for the two main contextual factors, that is industry and size of a factory, in order to isolate cultural effects.

In the subsequent three chapters, the empirical data collected in the survey have been presented. Some evidence for the cultural influences on organisational IT use has been presented in Chapter 5, and some evidence about how such influences operate in actual terms at the shop-floor level in Chapter 6 and at the management level in Chapter 7. The main findings are summarised in Table 8.1. As shown in the table, some significant differences between British factories and Japanese factories have been identified. In terms of managerial preferences, compared with British factories, Japanese factories have shown a higher preference for top-down information flow and simpler design of jobs in the dimension of CIU, and more preference for individual transmission of information and less preference for teamwork and for fixed job system in the dimension of IIU. Therefore, in general, Japanese factories have shown higher average scores on CIU and IIU than British factories.

In terms of actual practices of IT use at the shop-floor level, concerning CIU, Japanese factories have been identified to put more limits on workers' accessibility to strategic information; greater use of information provided by managers; greater use of quantitative instead of qualitative information; and more opportunities for a worker to deal with daily problems of the line in a factory. With regard to IIU, Japanese factories actually adopt less teamwork; fewer give an individual password for gaining access to relevant databases; and much more mutual help is conducted. To simplify the story, it can be summarised that Japanese factories take a relatively stronger orientation to CIU, and British factories

Table 8.1 Summary of the findings

	Japanese factories' distinctive features in comparison with British factories		The approximate situation of Japanese factories in Britain (JFB)		Notes on size, industry, etc.	
Managerial preferences for IT use	CIU	Higher preference for top-down information flow and simple job design	CIU	Closer to British factories regarding simple job design	CIU	concerning simple job design, Japanese factories show much higher preference particularly in transportation
	IIU	More preference for individual transmission of information; less preference for teamwork and fixed job system	IIU	Closer to British factories regarding individual transmission of information; in between British factories/Japanese factories regarding fixed job system	IIU	concerning teamwork, British factories show much higher preference particularly in electrical engineering and rubber/plastic products
Actual practices at the shop-floor level	CIU	More limited worker accessibility to strategic information; more use of information given by managers; more use of quantitative information; less use of qualitative information; higher ability of workers to deal with daily problems of the line	CIU	Closer to Japanese factories regarding the amount of quantitative information and simplified and predetermined jobs; closer to British factories regarding dealing with daily problems of the line	CIU	Japanese factories show much higher scores than British factories in transportation in particular, regarding especially amount of information given by managers, amount of quantitative information, and simplified and predetermined jobs
	IIU	Less organisation in teams; less given an individual password to databases; more mutual help	IIU	Closer to British factories regarding having an individual password to access databases, organised in teams, help each other, and job assignment on an individual basis	IIU	Team is organised in large factories in British factories whereas in Japanese factories it is organised both in large and small factories

Table 8.1 (Cont'd)

	Japanese factories' distinctive features in comparison with British factories	The approximate situation of Japanese factories in Britain (JFB)	Notes on size, industry, etc.
Actual practices at the management level	CIU More limited line-manager accessibility to strategic information; higher regard for liaison role and communicating instructions as important; more need to report major problems of the line to senior managers; lower need of rapid access to information databases in a problematic situation; higher opportunities to get information from across different functional boundaries IIU More use of GDSS; less stuck to a particular section; lower importance of information-sharing	CIU Rather closer to British factories, especially regarding rapid access to databases, importance of liaison role, importance of communicating instructions; the highest opportunity for a manager to gain access to strategic information IIU Rather closer to British factories regarding importance of information sharing; being stuck to a particular section	CIU in Japanese factories, small factories in particular, accessibility to important information databases is limited, whereas the score is more or less the same in spite of size in British factories IIU in Japanese factories, small factories in particular, an individual password to access databases is given less than in British factories, especially machinery and electrical engineering

take a relatively stronger orientation to IIU in actual terms at the shop-floor level. Taking into account the fact that a significant correlation, controlling for contextual factors, has been observed between managerial preferences and actual practices, both on CIU and on IIU, it can be inferred that such managerial preferences actually operate at the shop-floor level in a factory.

On the other hand, at the management level, concerning CIU, Japanese factories actually put more limits on line managers' accessibility to strategic information; more regard the liaison role and communicating instructions to subordinates as important; put greater emphasis on the need to report major problems of the line to senior managers; need less rapid access to information databases in a problematic situation; and provide greater opportunities to get information from across different functional boundaries. With regard to IIU at the management level, Japanese factories actually make more use of GDSS; are less likely to stick to a particular section over time; and regard information sharing as less important. On the whole, it can be summarised that Japanese factories actually take a relatively stronger orientation towards CIU, and British factories take a relatively stronger orientation towards IIU at the management level. Again, the managerial preferences and the actual practices at the management level have been identified to be positively correlated controlling for contextual factors. This tendency holds good in the dimension of CIU in particular. This suggests that such managerial preferences operate in real terms in CIU at the management level as well as at the shop-floor level.

The summary of relationships between managerial preferences and actual practices in British factories and Japanese factories discussed above is given in Table 8.2. As shown, there is a consistent relationship between managerial preferences and actual practices – both at the shop-floor and

Table 8.2 Summary of relationships between managerial preferences and actual practices

	Dimension of CIU	Dimension of IIU
Managerial preferences for IT use	Japanese factories > British factories	Japanese factories > British factories
Actual practices in IT use		
Shop-floor	Japanese factories > British factories	Japanese factories < British factories
Management	Japanese factories > British factories	Japanese factories < British factories

management level – in the dimension of CIU; that is, Japanese factories have relatively higher average scores in general both in managerial preferences and actual practices. However, the actual practices in the dimensions of IIU show an inconsistent pattern with managerial preference. That is, although Japanese factories have higher scores in managerial preferences for IIU than British factories, British factories have higher scores than Japanese factories in terms of actual practices in IIU.

It is difficult to explain the inconsistent result concerning IIU, but since preferences may relate to future intentions as well as current practice, a possible interpretation is that the result indicates Japanese factories' *future* preferences for IIU. As Kokuryo (1997) has discussed, Japanese firms have been successful in building a 'context' and thereby stimulating creative activities within the organisation. Following the globalisation of Japanese firms, however, such an approach has recently been criticised by Western firms as a 'closed system', and thus some Japanese firms have begun to prepare for an 'open-network environment'. The high managerial preference for IIU in Japanese factories may reflect this new movement of Japanese firms. The process of accumulating a context based on collectivistic/group-oriented relations has encouraged the relation of a closed society in which localised and proprietary protocols (for example vocabulary, grammar, procedure and norm) have developed. Much of the knowledge created has been tacit and is difficult to share with or be transmitted to the outside world. Therefore, the inconsistent relationship may suggest that actual practices in IIU may become more individual-oriented in future. Allowing for this significant caveat, the finding of a higher score on IIU in terms of the *actual practices* of British factories versus Japanese factories is again broadly consistent with expectations regarding national cultural influences.

However, it should be noted that the discussion above still involves some limitations. In particular, the fact that present managerial preferences may not be translated into actual patterns of IT use suggests that it depends on the national culture and the extent to which the managers whose managerial preferences are being elicited are able to influence the types of IT/systems that are implemented in a factory. It is also possible that managerial preferences regarding IT use are, to some extent, formed by the types of IT/systems that they are currently exposed to. The anomalous finding on relatively lower Japanese managerial preferences for group-oriented IT use is not only an important signpost for future research in this area, but it may also represent an initial indication of the extent to which the deeply rooted cultural contexts for IT use are themselves changing under the global economic pressures that have driven the diffusion and design of IT-based systems (Kambayashi and Scarbrough, 2001).

With regard to the situation of JFB, on the managerial preferences for CIU they have been shown to be closer to British factories regarding simple job design. On the dimension of IIU, they are again closer to British factories regarding the preference for the individual transmission of information and that for teamwork, and in between Japanese factories and British factories regarding the fixed job system. In terms of actual practices of CIU at the shop-floor level, JFB have closer scores to Japanese factories concerning the amount of quantitative information flow, and simplified and predetermined jobs, whereas they are closer to British factories with regard to dealing with daily problems of the line. With respect to actual practices of IIU at the shop-floor level, JFB have been found to be closer to British factories in having an individual password to gain access to relevant databases; organised in teams; mutual help among workers; and job assignments on an individual basis. Concerning actual practices of CIU at the management level, JFB have indicated somewhat closer scores to British factories, especially regarding rapid access to relevant information databases; the importance of liaison roles; the importance of communicating instructions; and the highest opportunities are given for a manager to gain access to strategic information. Concerning actual practices of IIU at the management level, JFB have indicated closer scores to British factories again regarding the importance of information sharing and being stuck to a particular section. As far as the JFB are concerned, it seems difficult to identify a consistent pattern of IT use, except that the JFB have a tendency to appear closer to British factories than to Japanese factories in actual terms at the management level.[1]

Taking all these empirical findings into consideration, it is possible to draw the following two conclusions. Firstly, national culture is playing an important role in the emergent process shaping organisational IT use. As shown in Chapter 2, national culture has been a less fully examined concept in previous studies on IT use, but my empirical findings suggest that the concept should not be neglected as the influences of national culture on IT use may not be negligible. It has been shown that national cultural attributes may influence managerial preferences – for instance, top-down information flow, simple job design – which actually operate in a factory in such forms as the use of information given by managers and the use of quantitative information at the shop floor level, and as regards liaison and communicating instructions to subordinates as an important role at the management level. My analysis

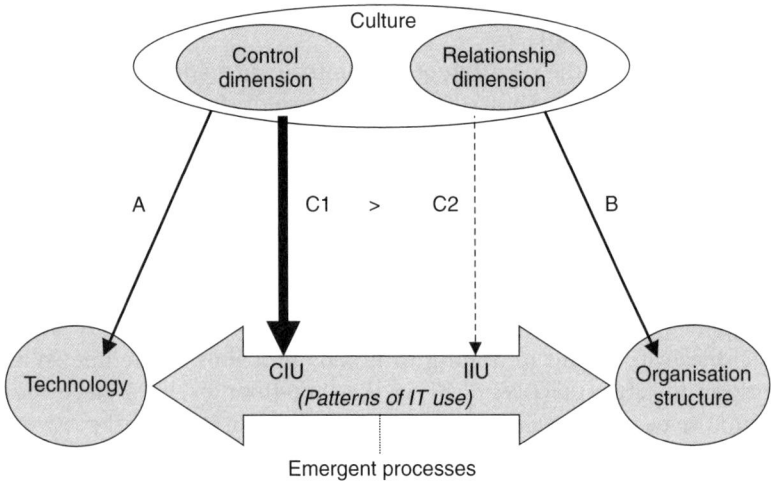

Figure 8.1   Technology, organisation and national culture

has shown that in terms of most items measured in the questionnaire, the main effect of national culture is greater than that of factory size and/or industry, which means the differences on IT use are found at a mainly national level – rather than individual organisational and sectoral levels. These findings are illustrated in Figure 8.1.

My analysis has illuminated the channels of influence of national culture on organisational IT use, that is, the arrows C1 and C2 in the middle of the figure. The figure also illustrates that the cultural dimension of CIU is likely to have greater and more explicit influences than that of IIU on organisational IT use. Some previous studies have focused on what arrows A and B suggest. Such notions as 'social construction' and/or 'social shaping' of technology (Bloomfield, Coombs and Owen, 1994; Howells, 1995; Williams and Edge, 1996) may be seen as being related to arrow A, which are controlled for in my study by trying to analyse within an industry that has a similar technological basis. A number of previous studies on a cross-cultural comparison of organisation and/or management (Hofstede, 1980; Tayeb, 1988; Trompenaars, 1993) are suggested by arrow B in the figure. Clearly, my analysis has not investigated the workings of these organisational mechanisms themselves through which the wider culture influences IT use, but has investigated what such mechanisms are and outlined the ways in which cultural factors feed into the use of IT.

Secondly, judging from Tables 8.1 and 8.2, the influences of national culture are likely to be displayed in actual practices more clearly in CIU than in IIU. As shown in Chapter 3, CIU and IIU were conceptualised from the previous studies on national culture, but the empirical results suggest that national culture has a relatively lower effect on individual/ group-oriented IT use – not as a significant positive relationship between managerial preferences and actual practices in CIU observed in IIU at the management level in particular. This suggests that IIU may reflect factors other than national culture and possibly technology. Also, it should be noted that the findings on IIU are somewhat contradictory with the cultural attributes which Britain and Japan are generally claimed to possess. A number of previous studies (Hofstede, 1980; Whitehill, 1991; Trompenaars, 1993; Peterson, 1993) suggest that Britain has a more individualistic culture, whereas Japanese culture is rather group-oriented or collectivist as shown in Chapter 3. Of course my study does not aim to test whether or not these cultural attributes or dimensions as such are correct, but the inconsistent finding on IIU suggests there is a possibility that some elements other than national culture might have been investigated. Another possible interpretation is that Japanese factories are currently in the process of changing from group-oriented into individualistically-oriented IT use, possibly under the pressure of industrialisation and globalisation, as I discussed earlier in this chapter. Some studies indicate such changes in traditional Japanese culture; for instance Whitehill (1991) claims that there is a clear trend among the younger generation in Japan to want more freedom and individuality, particularly in the case of non-work-related activities.

Taking all these findings into consideration, it can be concluded that national culture is affecting organisational IT use in Britain and Japan, in the shape of CIU in particular. My conclusion is, therefore, that national cultural influences appear to be important elements in the emergent processes shaping IT use in a sample of British and Japanese factories, and that such influences are likely to operate through some organisational mechanisms in a complex interactive process.

Implications for further research

The findings appear to have some implications for both information systems research and organisation theory. In the discipline of information systems research, discussions have been developed quite separately between the level of blue-collar factory workers and the level of white-collar managers – the term 'new technology' rather than IT has been used at the former level. The discussion on the impacts of new technology on shop-floor workers has been developed by labour process theorists and by socio-technical systems researchers; the discussion on effective design and use of information systems has been an emergent theme and has been recently pursued by MIS researchers. In this study, the integration of the two analytical levels has been attempted through the concept of organisational IT use. When we are to view such a diffuse phenomenon as national cultural influence on organisational IT use, and when we take into consideration the fact that even factory workers are quite familiar with IT-equipped machines, it appears to be important for the study to bring the two levels of discussion together.

In addition, the present study has indicated that a manager's day-to-day use of IT, as well as strategic use of IT, should be analysed in detail. Most work in the discipline of information systems research has focused on the *strategic* use rather than daily use of IT in management (Earl, 1996; Galliers, 1998). As I have mentioned before, national cultural influences on strategic use of IT have been empirically investigated in some studies (Watson *et al.*, 1997) employing Hofstede's (1980) cultural dimensions. My data in Chapter 7, however, suggest that national culture influences not only strategic use of IT but also a manager's day-to-day activities using IT. A manager as well as a shop-floor worker is an employee of a company, therefore not only occasional activities such as the formulation and implementation of a company strategy but also his/her organisational behaviour and tasks in an everyday sense should also be examined. In fact, my data have produced evidence that some daily activities of a manager using IT, such as communicating instructions and job rotation, are subject to national cultural influences.

There is a view amongst some organisation theorists (for example Donaldson, 1996) that efficient ideas travel from one society to another since they share the same economic system, with the same culture-free technological influences which act as the main influence on the shape of organisation structure. The research findings of the present study have revealed that this deterministic thinking needs to be revised. More societal factors like national culture, and sometimes even tradition and history of a nation, can have influences upon the organisational IT use in a factory. The limitations of the deterministic perspectives, technological and organisational determinism, have been discussed at the organisational level in previous studies – especially in the emergent school – but the present research has indicated its limitation at the societal/international level as well.

As a direction for future research, recognised limitations mentioned in the last section of this chapter will have to be overcome. Of particular need for further investigation are reasons why present managerial preferences may not be translated into actual patterns of IT use. As suggested in the last section, it may involve the extent to which managers whose preferences are being elicited are able to affect the types of IT that are implemented in a factory. Also, managerial preferences regarding IT use may be formed by the types of IT/systems that they are exposed to. The investigation of these issues will further clarify the present research's findings on the mechanisms of cultural influences on IT use.

Certainly, this study has established that there are influences of national culture on organisational IT use. However, the scope and the extent of the influences still remains to be clarified and will require further research. For example, relationships between national culture and organisational sub-cultures could not be fully clarified in this study. Although national culture is viewed by some researchers as the 'dominant force' in shaping organisational behaviour, for example in MIS professionals (Raman and Watson, 1994), other sub-cultures such as corporate culture and MIS culture may well also act in shaping it. For instance, Mair (1994) discovered that Honda is a company in which traditional Japanese ideas such as lifetime employment and seniority waged systems are developed within a distinctive new philosophy with their unique leadership style. It is conceivable that the dominant Japanese culture is challenged in factories with their own strong organisational sub-cultures.

Also, the research is on relationships between organisational IT use and national culture, but the *process* of how national culture influences organisational IT use has not been fully developed in this study, although some of the organisational mechanisms and their channels through which wider culture may influence IT use have been suggested. The research findings show that it is possible for national culture to have an influence on the emergent processes between IT and organisational structure through such organisational mechanisms, but more work needs to be done on how and through what concrete processes national culture influences IT use. This will require more intensive case studies and a focus on the role of IT professionals in the processes. A case-study approach appears to be of relevance, as the approach can further analyse and explain the phenomena in more detail. As I discussed in Chapter 3, it is necessary to take up some of the organisational phenomena which have been shown in the study to be under the influence of national culture (for example top-down information flow; simple job design), and to focus on and interpretively examine how a manager relates to his/her subordinates in the use of IT through a new case study.

The significance of the research

One of this research's key contributions is that the present study is based on a large original sample (more than 1400) obtained from British and Japanese factories, producing systematic evidence that national culture actually influences organisational IT use. National culture has been treated as an unimportant and thus negligible factor in international comparisons in some literature (Donaldson, 1996; Whitley, 1992; Dore, 1973), while some other works have important suggestions that cultural influences are important in the use of IT (Bensaou and Earl, 1998; Sorge, 1995; Clark and Staunton, 1989). For instance, Oliver and Wilkinson (1992) have disclosed that, admitting cultural uniqueness, the introduction of a JIT system sometimes does involve cultural conflicts with existing Western values. However, even in these studies, *systematic data* on national cultural influences are missing – they have simply speculated that national culture may be one of the important factors.

As well as the originality of the data, the multidisciplinarity of what I have done in this research is another key contribution to our understanding. As discussed in the previous section, discussions have been developed quite separately between the level of blue-collar factory workers and the level of white-collar managers in the discipline of information systems research. Discussions on the impacts of IT on shop-floor workers have been mainly developed by researchers in the fields of organisational behaviour and production management (such as Francis, 1986), whereas the effective design and strategic use of information have been pursued by MIS researchers (for example Earl, 1996). The integration of the two analytical levels has been attempted through the concept of organisational IT use in this research.

Another contribution is developing an original model in which cultural effects can be differentiated from other possible factors to affect IT use: two patterns of IT use, CIU and IIU, have been conceptualised for the purpose. My data are broadly in line with an hypothesis that national culture influences IT use in the dimension of CIU – CIU in Japanese factories is found to be higher than that in British factories due to the difference of national culture between Britain and Japan. As discussed in the previous section, further research – qualitative and case-study-based – needs to be undertaken to complement our discussions. However, my data at least suggest the necessity of a more detailed examination of the concept of national culture in a cross-national comparison.

According to Galliers (1995), there is a tendency in information systems research to 'pay lip service only to the reference, or cognate, disciplines of, for example, organisational behaviour, strategic management, cognitive psychology and computer science', which leads to 'the likelihood of information management researchers being overly introspective and narrow in their treatment of their chosen topic' (p. S50). Furthermore, he suggests that there is a tendency to assume that British and American ideas, as well as their technology, should be taken on board lock, stock and barrel even when international work is undertaken. Thus he claims that interdisciplinary work should be encouraged and that more international and cross-cultural studies of information management should be undertaken to test out their ideas in other countries and to learn both from this experience and from the research being undertaken by overseas researchers. I hope that the present research is a step forward in the right direction.

Appendix: The Questionnaire

THE DESIGN AND USE OF IT IN MANUFACTURING INDUSTRY: A COMPARATIVE SURVEY OF BRITAIN AND JAPAN

Questionnaire

The following questionnaire should take no more than 10 minutes to complete. Please complete the questions as far as possible. If you cannot answer some specific questions for any reasons, please leave them blank and proceed to the next question. We need a sufficient number of responses in order to analyse the general characteristics of British firms and of Japanese firms in the UK, so all returns are valuable even if not complete. Confidentiality will be protected and the responses of any individual company will not be disclosed in any external report.

Please note following points:

1. 'The design and use of IT' in the survey refers to the job design of the employees and information flows in your factory, in the context of the use of IT-based system.
2. If you are unable to complete, please pass this on to a person with knowledge of shop-floor production processes and of management information processing (eg the Production, Operations, or Logistics Manager) to complete.
3. If there are any queries on the content of the questionnaire, please feel free to contact: Norio Kambayashi, Warwick Business School Research Bureau, University of Warwick (tel: 01203-522802; fax: 01203-524965; e-mail: wbsrbnk@ razor.wbs.warwick.ac.uk). After completing the questionnaire, please return in the enclosed prepaid envelope (no stamp is needed) **before 30 May.** Thank you in advance for your co-operation.

Your name (please print): _____

Your position (*e.g. Operations Director*): _____

Company name: _____

The company address to which a summary report should be mailed:

_____

_____

_____ Post code _____

Q1. What kind of production method is used in your factory? Please tick one box. If several methods are used, please indicate *the most important*.

❏ Custom (or made-to-order) process
❏ Small batch process
❏ Large batch process
❏ Mass production process
❏ Continuous process

Q2. Which of these manufacturing technologies/systems are used in your factory? Please tick box(es).

❏ NC (numerical control)
❏ MC (machining centre)
❏ FMS (flexible manufacturing system)
❏ GPT (group technology)
❏ CAM (computer-aided manufacturing)
❏ CAE (computer assisted engineering)
❏ MRP (materials requirements planning)
❏ JIT (just in time or *kanban*)
❏ CNC (computerised numerical control)
❏ Other(s): *please specify*: _____

❏ DNC (direct numerical control)
❏ Cellular Manufacturing System
❏ CAD (computer-aided design)
❏ CAD/CAM
❏ CIM (computer integrated manufacturing)
❏ MRP2 (manufacturing resource planning)

Q3. What is the scope of the *Management Information System* (MIS) in your factory? Please tick one box.

❏ No integrated MIS
❏ PC-based distributed processing – no central processing (information is processed separately in each functional area)
❏ Networked PCs
❏ Company-wide integrated MIS
❏ Other(s): *please specify*: _____

Q4. What is the focus of the MIS in your factory? Please tick one box.

❏ Provides information to individual managers (for example, Executive Information System)
❏ Provides information to groups of managers (for example, Lotus Notes and/or Group Decision Support System)
❏ Other(s): *please specify*: _____

Q5. To what extent do the following statements describe *preferences* for using IT-based systems in your factory? Please circle one number for each.

	strongly disagree		neither agree nor disagree		strongly agree
a) Top management should have exclusive access to the most important kinds of information.	1	2	3	4	5
b) Information flow should always reflect the management hierarchy in any situation.	1	2	3	4	5
c) Lower-graded employees should have the simplest jobs.	1	2	3	4	5
d) Information should be communicated individually to each employee rather than to teams or groups.	1	2	3	4	5
e) Team working and/or GDSS are generally the best way for achieving company goals.	1	2	3	4	5
f) Each employee should stick to their assigned role.	1	2	3	4	5

Q6. To what extent do the following statements reflect the use of IT-based systems among <u>shop-floor workers</u> in your factory? Please circle one number for each.

	not at all true		somewhat true		very true
a) It is possible for workers to gain access to strategic information (eg sales forecasts).	1	2	3	4	5
b) Workers usually use information provided by managers.	1	2	3	4	5
c) Workers are usually given quantitative information (eg production target rates).	1	2	3	4	5
d) Workers are usually given qualitative information (eg briefing on company performance).	1	2	3	4	5
e) Workers usually share information with other workers.	1	2	3	4	5
f) Workers have their own passwords for gaining access to relevant information database(s).	1	2	3	4	5

Q7. To what extent do the following statements reflect the jobs of <u>shop-floor workers</u>? Please circle one number for each.

	not at all true		somewhat true		very true
a) Workers are usually organised in teams.	1	2	3	4	5
b) Workers help other workers to finish their work.	1	2	3	4	5
c) Workers' jobs are simplified and predetermined as much as possible.	1	2	3	4	5
d) Workers can deal with daily problems (eg machine breakdowns) by themselves without reporting to superiors.	1	2	3	4	5
e) A worker's job is assigned on an individual basis and rotation is not practised.	1	2	3	4	5

Q8. How important is it that your <u>shop-floor workers</u> have the following skills in the jobs they do? Please circle one number for each.

	not at all important	somewhat important		very important
a) Operation of machinery	1	2	3	4	5
b) Set-up, preparation, planning	1	2	3	4	5
c) Observation of machinery	1	2	3	4	5
d) Trouble-shooting	1	2	3	4	5
e) Improvements/repairs of surrounding equipment/tools	1	2	3	4	5
f) Development/revision of software programmes	1	2	3	4	5
g) Teaching/instruction to other workers	1	2	3	4	5
h) Quality management	1	2	3	4	5

Q9. To what extent do the following statements reflect the use of IT-based systems among <u>line managers</u> in your factory? Please circle one number for each.

	not at all true	somewhat true		very true
a) It is possible for line managers to gain strategic information.	1	2	3	4	5
b) Line managers can gain access to relevant database(s) rapidly if any problems occur.	1	2	3	4	5
c) A line manager can gain information from across different functional boundaries.	1	2	3	4	5
d) Line managers have their own passwords for gaining access to relevant information database(s).	1	2	3	4	5
e) Information sharing with other line managers is important for achieving group consensus.	1	2	3	4	5

Q10. To what extent do the following statements reflect the jobs of <u>line managers</u>? Please circle one number for each.

	not at all true	somewhat true		very true
a) The main job of a line manager is as liaison between senior management and lower levels.	1	2	3	4	5
b) Communicating instructions to subordinates is the most important role.	1	2	3	4	5
c) When any major problems occur, line managers have to report to senior managers before taking actions.	1	2	3	4	5
d) A line manager is sometimes engaged in a team/group project.	1	2	3	4	5
e) A line manager sticks to a particular section and rotation is not practised.	1	2	3	4	5

Q11. How important are the following abilities for <u>shop-floor workers</u>? Please circle one number for each.

	not at all important	somewhat important			very important
a) Ability to gather necessary information	1	2	3	4	5
b) Ability to analyse data/information	1	2	3	4	5
c) Ability to judge by oneself what ought to be done	1	2	3	4	5
d) Ability to reorganise whole work processes	1	2	3	4	5

Q12. How important are the following abilities for <u>line managers</u>? Please circle one number for each.

	not at all important	somewhat important			very important
a) Ability to gather necessary information	1	2	3	4	5
b) Ability to analyse data/information	1	2	3	4	5
c) Ability to judge by oneself what ought to be done	1	2	3	4	5
d) Ability to reorganise whole work processes	1	2	3	4	5

Q13. Over the last 5 years, how has IT changed the following aspects of your factory? Please tick one box for each.

a) The number of levels in the management structure:
❏ Has increased ❏ No changes ❏ Has decreased ❏ Changes not linked to IT

b) The speed of decision-making:
❏ Has become faster ❏ No changes ❏ Has decreased ❏ Changes not linked to IT

c) The amount of information flow between your factory and the head office if appropriate:
❏ Has increased ❏ No changes ❏ Has decreased ❏ Changes not linked to IT

d) The span of control:
❏ Has increased ❏ No changes ❏ Has decreased ❏ Changes not linked to IT

e) The total number of full-time employees:
❏ Has increased ❏ No changes ❏ Has decreased ❏ Changes not linked to IT

f) The number of part-timers:
❏ Has increased ❏ No changes ❏ Has decreased ❏ Changes not linked to IT

g) QC (quality control) activity:
❏ Has increased ❏ No changes ❏ Has decreased ❏ Changes not linked to IT

h) The number of grades in the wage system:
❏ Has increased ❏ No changes ❏ Has decreased ❏ Changes not linked to IT

i) Working hours for shop-floor workers:
❏ Have become ❏ No changes ❏ Have become longer ❏ Changes not
shorter linked to IT

j) Working hours for line managers:
❏ Have become ❏ No changes ❏ Have become longer ❏ Changes not
shorter linked to IT

k) Skill levels of shop-floor workers on average:
❏ Have been ❏ No changes ❏ Have been downgraded ❏ Changes not
upgraded linked to IT

l) Task-related abilities of line managers on average:
❏ Have been improved ❏ No changes ❏ Have dropped ❏ Changes not
linked to IT

m) The degree of concentration of information:
❏ Information is provided on a more 'need to know' basis
❏ No changes
❏ Information is provided more widely throughout the organisation
❏ Changes not linked to IT

Q14. Please answer following questions about your firm/workplace.

a) What is the type of industry that your firm is engaged in?

❏ Food and beverages ❏ Tobacco products
❏ Textiles ❏ Leather and leather products
❏ Wood and wood products ❏ Pulp and paper
❏ Printing and publishing ❏ Petroleum products
❏ Chemicals ❏ Rubber and plastic products
❏ Non-metal mineral products ❏ Metal production
❏ Metal products ❏ Machinery and equipment
❏ Office machinery and computers ❏ Electrical machinery and apparatus
❏ Communication and recording ❏ Medical and precision instruments
equipment ❏ Transport equipment other than
❏ Motor vehicles and parts motor vehicles
❏ Furniture
❏ Other manufacturing: *please specify*: _____

b) How many full-time employees do you have in your factory?
❏ Less than 200 ❏ 200~499
❏ 500~999 ❏ 1,000~1,499
❏ 1,500~1,999 ❏ Greater than 2,000

-----Is it a part of a wider corporation?
❏ Yes   ❏ No

-----If yes, how many full-time employees of the wider corporation?
❏ Less than 1,000   ❏ 1,000~1,999
❏ 2,000~4,999   ❏ 5,000~9,999
❏ 10,000~24,499   ❏ Greater than 25,000

c) When was your factory established?
❏ Before 1960   ❏ 1960–1969
❏ 1970~1979   ❏ 1980~ 1989
❏ After 1990

d) Is your workforce unionised?
❏ Yes   ❏ No

Thank you very much for your thoughtful co-operation! Please post the completed questionnaire in the enclosed prepaid envelope as soon as convenient. If you have any comments, please write in the following space:

Notes

Chapter 1

1 Such a systemic view is particularly useful for the emergent perspective on the basis of which my analysis is being conducted. I will discuss this issue in Chapter 2. However, my analysis attempts to isolate different technological effects by controlling for each technology. I will return to this issue in Chapter 4.

2 Dore admitted that on reflection too much emphasis had been placed on institutional aspects and the role of cultural tradition should have been examined in more detail. Refer to Preface in the Japanese translated version of Dore (1973), published in 1990.

Chapter 2

1 Empirical studies on technology–structure relationships under this perspective are summarised in Fry (1982).

2 It should be noted, however, that the emergent perspective raises the question of whether it is possible to isolate technological effects from other influences on organisational IT use, since it is viewed that IT and organisations dynamically develop each other. I will return to this methodological issue in Chapter 3.

3 A more detailed review and examination of the concept 'national culture' will be given in Chapter 3.

4 I will return to this issue in Chapter 4 to show factors to be controlled for in the study.

5 A more detailed explanation of Hofstede's (1980) way of operationalisation of national culture is given in the next chapter.

6 According to Bensaou and Earl (1998), 'Western managers' are defined as a group of senior executives in the United States or Europe.

Chapter 3

1 The four major journals on information systems research are the following: *Communications of the ACM, The MIS Quarterly, Proceedings of ICIS*, and *Management Science*.

2 Of course, not only the nature of the research topic and the aim of this study stated above, but also the interests and abilities of the researcher may affect the decision on which research approach is taken. However, the discussion developed in this section has revealed that the survey approach, rather than the case study approach, is relevant for the theme and purpose of the study here.

3 Using Hall's concept of 'high-context cultures', Kokuryo (1997) has outlined some differences on the accumulation and transmission of organisational knowledge between Western and Japanese firms, which suggests Japanese firms have adopted different IT strategies (i.e., 'closed networks') from other Western firms. According to Kokuryo, Japanese firms have been successful in

building context and thereby stimulating creative activities within firms. Refer to discussion in Chapter 8.

4 In his later work, Hofstede (1991) identified another cultural dimension called 'long-term orientation index', originally named 'Confucian dynamism'. This is a measure for the degree of long-term orientation in a country's culture, based on the Chinese Value Survey research project among student samples. Long-term orientation is claimed to stand for 'the fostering of virtues oriented towards future rewards, in particular perseverance and thrift' (p. 261).

5 More than 80% of studies that I reviewed on national culture and organisations used the dimensions developed by Hofstede (1980).

6 The study is preceded by that of Laurent (1983), in which data were collected from nine European countries and the United States.

7 For example, Gannon (1994) suggests shortcomings of dimensional approaches to national culture, and a more symbolic and metaphorical way of description of cultural attributes in each country (e.g., 'symphony' in Germany; 'opera' in Italy) is useful to grasp the broad image of national culture. However, such an approach is not relevant to the present study because it is not as analytical as the dimensional approach.

8 The analysis of data on these contextual factors will be presented in the next chapter.

9 The pilot study in Britain was conducted on 16 April 1997; that in Japan was conducted on 10 September 1997.

10 As explained later in this chapter, the Japanese survey was conducted after finishing collecting data from British factories.

11 In rare cases in which number of employees was not available, other information (e.g., profit as per cent of turnover) was used to specify the largest factory in each firm.

12 My collaborators were Professor Koji Okubayashi, Professor Tadao Kagono and Professor Masayuki Munakata, all of whom belong to Kobe University. In Japan, sending from a group consisting of several famous names among business practitioners, instead of a single name, is a key factor in obtaining higher response rates in surveys. My three collaborators were experienced in the business world and well-known among business practitioners in the country.

13 In fact, this was one of the comments obtained from the Japanese pilot study.

14 The large differences in response rates are perhaps indicative of national cultural differences (Smith and Bond, 1993).

15 Regarding names of respondents in JFB, only two were Japanese.

Chapter 4

1 Another important problem which occurs in a national comparative survey is the language differences used in the focused countries. This is reasonably difficult to be controlled for, but I attempted to minimise the effects as described in Chapter 3.

2 The chi-square test excludes the sample of JFB, as the sample size is too small.

3 In fact, judging from the results of chi-square test, the scope and focus of MIS do not vary systematically across five industries: the values of chi-square are 19.72 ($p < .11$) in the scope of MIS, and 10.35 ($p < .15$) in the focus of MIS.

4 For example, Bensaou and Earl (1998) investigate senior executives' use of IT in 20 leading Japanese companies, which include Seven-Eleven Japan (retailer) and Toyota (car manufacturer), to find some similarities in the usage of IT as compared to American counterparts. This suggests that the use of IT at the management level is more or less similar across different sectors.

5 The result of Pearson's chi-square test (25.747, $p < .000$, degree of freedom 4) for the independence of these sectors and nations with the exclusion of the group of JFB indicates the necessity to control for the industry's effects. Again, the JFB group is excluded as it does not have a sufficient sample size to execute a chi-square test.

6 Some financial data, such as turnover and capital, are sometimes used as an index for organisational size, but the number of employees is more relevant as a surrogate for size here, as I am to focus on organisational behaviour on the patterns of IT use rather than financial aspects of the organisation. Therefore, I try to control for the organisational size by the number of employees.

7 210.95 ($p < .001$) in the wider corporation and 116.47 ($p < .001$) in factories, both excluding the JFB column.

8 Judging from the result of chi-square test carried out in each industrial group with the exclusion of JFB, the batch size does not vary systematically across nations (i.e., BF and JF).

Chapter 5

1 As explained in the last chapter, factory size has been measured by the number of factory employees, and a 'large factory' is defined as having 200 or more employees and a 'small factory' as having less than 200 employees.

2 Statistical tests are not relevant to some sub-samples classified by industry, as the sample size is too small to carry out the tests. Also, sub-samples classified by factory size *and* industry are not shown, as the sample size is too small.

3 The 2-way ANOVA was carried out as follows: (i) dependent variable = item in question, two independent variables = nation, factory size; (ii) dependent variable = item in question, two independent variables = nation, industry.

Chapter 6

1 The reason for the inconsistency will be discussed later in this chapter.

2 These factors to be controlled for derive from the analysis on data developed in Chapter 4.

Chapter 7

1 These factors to be controlled for derive from the analysis on data developed in Chapter 4.

Chapter 8

1 Despite these empirical findings, however, some statistical limitations need to be recognised. For instance, I must acknowledge that analyses on JFB include some weaknesses and thus the conclusions are tentative, as the sample size of JFB is not big enough to conduct some statistical tests.

Bibliography

Abegglen, J. (1958) *The Japanese Factory: Aspects of its Social Organisation* (Glencoe, IL: The Free Press).

Abegglen, J. and Stalk, G. (1985) *Kaisha: The Japanese Corporation* (New York: Basic Books).

Abrahamsson, B. (1993) *Why Organisations? How and Why People Organise* (London: Sage).

Adler, N. J., Campbell, N. C. and Laurent, A. (1989) 'In Search of Appropriate Methodology: From Outside the People's Republic of China Looking', *Journal of International Business Studies*, vol. 20(1), pp. 61–74.

Albach, H. (1994) *Culture and Technical Innovation: A Cross-cultural Analysis and Policy Recommendations*, The Academy of Sciences and Technology in Berlin, Research Report vol. 9 (Berlin: Walter de Gruyter).

Alsène, È. and Lessard, J. (1995) 'The Influence of Technology on the Organisation: From Impact to Specific Effects and Design Space', *International Journal of Human Factors in Manufacturing*, vol. 5(4), pp. 377–400.

Applegate, L. M., Cash, J. I. and Quinn-Mills, D. (1988) 'Information Technology and Tomorrow's Manager', *Harvard Business Review*, vol. 66, pp. 128–36.

Badham, R. J. (1994) 'International Perspectives on Computer-Integrated Manufacturing', in W. Karwowski and G. Salvendy (eds), *Organisation and Management of Advanced Manufacturing* (New York: John Wiley).

Barley, S. R. (1986) 'Technology as an Occasion for Structuring: Evidence from Observations of CT Scanners and the Social Order of Radiology Departments', *Administrative Science Quarterly*, vol. 31, pp. 78–108.

Barley, S. R. (1990) 'The Alignment of Technology and Structure through Roles and Networks', *Administrative Science Quarterly*, vol. 35, pp. 61–103.

Barley, S. R. (1996) 'Technicians in the Workplace: Ethnographic Evidence for Bringing Work into Organisation Studies', *Administrative Science Quarterly*, vol. 41, pp. 403–41.

Beirne, M. and Ramsay, H. (1992) 'Manna or Monstrous Regiment?' in M. Beirne and H. Ramsay (eds), *Information Technology and Workplace Democracy* (London: Routledge).

Bell, D. (1973) *The Coming of Post-industrial Society: A Venture in Social Forecasting* (New York: Basic Books).

Bensaou, M. and Earl, M. (1998) 'The Right Mind-set for Managing Information Technology', *Harvard Business Review*, vol. 76(5), pp. 118–28.

Berggren, C. (1993) *The Volvo Experience* (London: Macmillan – now Palgrave Macmillan).

Bessant, J. (1993) 'Towards Factory 2000: Designing Organisation for Computer-Integrated Technologies', in J. Clark (ed.), *Human Resource Management and Technical Change* (London: Sage).

Bessant, J. and Grunt, M. (1985) *Management and Manufacturing Innovation in the UK and West Germany* (London: Gower).

Blauner, R. (1964) *Alienation and Freedom: The Factory Worker and His Industry* (London: The University of Chicago Press).

Bloomfield, B. P., Coombs, R. and Owen, J. (1994) 'The Social Construction of Information Systems: The Implications for Management Control', in R. Mansell (ed.), *The Management of Information and Communication Technologies: Emerging Patterns of Control* (London: The Association for Information Management).

Bratton, J. (1992) *Japanisation at Work: Managerial Studies for the 1990s* (London: Macmillan – now Palgrave Macmillan).

Braverman, H. (1974) *Labour and Monopoly Capital: The Degradation of Work in the Twentieth Century* (New York: Monthly Review Press).

Briggs, R. O., Nunamaker, J. and Sprague, R. (1998) '1001 Unanswered Research Questions in GSS', *Journal of Management Information Systems*, vol. 14(3), pp. 3–22.

Bryman, A. (1989) *Research Methods and Organisation Studies* (London: Routledge).

Buchanan, D. A. and Boddy, D. (1983) *Organisations in the Computer Age* (Aldershot: Gower).

Buchanan, D. A. and Huczynski, A. A. (1991) *Organisational Behaviour: An Introductory Text*, 2nd edn (London: Prentice-Hall).

Burn, J. M. (1995) 'The New Cultural Revolution: The Impact of EDI on Asia', *Journal of Global Information Management*, vol. 3(4), pp. 16–23.

Calori, R. (1994) *Common Characteristics of European Management* (London: Prentice-Hall).

Carter, N. M. (1984) 'Computerisation as a Predominance Technology: Its Influence on the Structure of Newspaper Organisations', *Academy of Management Journal*, vol. 27(2), pp. 247–70.

Child, J. (1972) 'Organisation Structure, Environment and Performance: The Role of Strategic Choice', *Sociology*, vol. 6, pp. 1–22.

Child, J. (1981) 'Culture, Contingency and Capitalism in the Cross-National Study of Organisation', in L. L. Cummings and B. W. Staw (eds), *Research in Organisational Behaviour*, vol. 3 (Greenwich, CT: JAI Press).

Child, J. (1987) 'Organisational Design for Advanced Manufacturing Technology', in T. Wall *et al.* (eds), *The Human Side of Advanced Manufacturing Technology* (London: John Wiley).

Chow, C. W., Kato, Y. and Shields, M. D. (1994) 'National Culture and the Preference for Management Control', *Accounting, Organisations & Society*, vol. 19(4/5), pp. 381–400.

Chow, C. W., Shields, M. D. and Chan, Y. K. (1991) 'The Effects of Management Controls and National Culture on Manufacturing Performance: An Experimental Investigation', *Accounting, Organisations & Society*, vol. 16(3), pp. 209–26.

Ciborra, C. U. (1996) 'Introduction: What does Groupware mean for the Organisations Hosting it?' in C. U. Ciborra (ed.), *Groupware and Teamwork: Invisible Aid or Technical Hindrance?* (Chichester: John Wiley).

Clark, P. A. (1987) *Anglo-American Innovation* (New York: Walter de Gruyter).

Clark, P. A. and Newell, S. (1993) 'Societal Embedding of Production and Inventory Control System: American and Japanese Influences on Adaptive Implementation in Britain', *International Journal of Human Factors in Manufacturing*, vol. 3, pp. 69–81.

Clark, P. A. and Staunton, N. (1989) *Innovation in Technology and Organisation* (London: Routledge).

Clark, T. (1996) 'HRM: A Unified Understanding or Multiplicity of Meanings?' in T. Clark (ed.), *European Human Resource Management: An Introduction to Comparative Theory and Practice* (Oxford: Blackwell).

Cooper, R. B. (1994) 'The Inertial Impact of Culture on IT Implementation', *Information & Management*, vol. 27, pp. 17–31.

Cressey, P. (1992) 'Trade Unions and New Technology: European Experience and Strategic Questions', in M. Beirne and H. Ramsay (eds), *Information Technology and Workplace Democracy* (London: Routledge).

Currie, W. (1995) *Management Strategy for IT: An International Perspective* (London: Pitman).

Daft, R. L. and Macintosh, N. B. (1981) 'A Tentative Exploration into the Amount and Equivocality of Information Processing in Organisational Work Units', *Administrative Science Quarterly*, vol. 26, pp. 207–24.

Davis, G. B. (1992) 'An Individual Group Strategy for Research in Information Systems', in R. D. Galliers (ed.), *Information Systems Research: Issues, Methods and Practical Guidelines* (Oxford: Blackwell Scientific).

Davis, L. E. and Wacker, G. J. (1987) 'Job Design', in G. Salvendy (ed.), *Handbook of Human Factors* (New York: John Wiley).

Deans, P. C. and Ricks, D. A. (1991) 'MIS Research: A Model for Incorporating the International Dimension', *The Journal of High Technology Management Research*, vol. 2(1), pp. 57–81.

Demes, H. (1992) 'The Japanese Production Mode as a Model for the 21st Century?' in S. Tokunaga, N. Altmann and H. Demes (eds), *New Impacts of Industrial Relations: Internationalisation and Changing Production Strategies* (Berlin: German Institute for Japanese Studies, Monograph 3).

Despres, C. (1996) 'Information, Technology and Culture', *Technovation*, vol. 16(1), pp. 1–20.

Donaldson, L. (1996) *For Positivist Organisation Theory: Proving the Hard Core* (London: Sage).

Dore, R. (1973) *British Factory – Japanese Factory: The Origins of National Diversity in Industrial Relations* (London: Allen & Unwin), Translated into Japanese by Y. Yamanouchi and K. Nagayasu (1990) *Igirisu no Koujou – Nihon no Koujou* (Tokyo: Chikuma Shobou).

Dore, R. (1986) *Flexible Rigidities: Industrial Policy and Structural Adjustment in the Japanese Economy 1970–80* (London: Allen & Unwin).

Drucker, P. F. (1989) *The New Realities* (New York: Harper & Row).

Earl, M. J. (1996) 'An Organisational Approach to IS Strategy-Making', in M. J. Earl (ed.), *Information Management: The Organisational Dimension* (Oxford: Oxford University Press).

Edwards, P. K. (1987) *Managing the Factory: A Survey of General Managers* (Oxford: Basil Blackwell).

Ein-Dor, P., Segev, E. and Orgad, M. (1993) 'The Effect of National Culture on IS: Implications for International Information Systems', *Journal of Global Information Management*, vol. 1(1), pp. 33–44.

Elger, T. and Smith, C. (1994) 'Global Japanisation? Convergence and Competition in the Organisation of the Labour Process', in T. Elger and C. Smith (eds), *Global Japanisation? The Transnational Transformation of the Labour Process* (London: Routledge).

Ellul, J. (1974) *The Technological Society* (New York: Vintage Books).

Ford, J. B. and Honeycutt, E. D. (1992) 'Japanese National Culture as a Basis for Understanding Japanese Business Practices', *Business Horizons*, vol. 35(6), pp. 27–34.

Francis, A. (1986) *New Technology at Work* (Oxford: Clarendon Press).

Francis, A. and Southern, G. (1995) 'Epochs and Institutions: Contextualising Business Process Re-engineering', *New Technology, Work and Employment*, vol. 10(2), pp. 110–19.

Franke, R. H., Hofstede, G. and Bond, M. H. (1991) 'Cultural Roots of Economic Performance: A Research Note', *Strategic Management Journal*, vol. 12, pp. 165–73.

Fry, L. W. (1982) 'Technology – Structure Research: Three Critical Issues', *Academy of Management Journal*, vol. 25, pp. 532–52.

Galbraith, J. R. (1973) *Designing Complex Organisations* (Reading, Mass.: Addison-Wesley).

Galliers, R. D. (1992) 'Choosing Information Systems Research Approaches', in R. D. Galliers (ed.), *Information Systems Research: Issues, Methods and Practical Guidelines* (Oxford: Blackwell Scientific).

Galliers, R. D. (1995) 'A Manifesto for Information Management Research', *British Journal of Management*, vol. 6 (special issue), pp. S45–52.

Galliers, R. D. (1998) 'Reflections on BPR, IT and Organisational Change', in R. D. Galliers and W. R. J. Baets (eds), *Information Technology and Organisational Transformation: Innovation for the 21st Century Organisation* (Chichester: John Wiley).

Gannon, M. J. (1994) *Understanding Global Cultures: Metaphoric Journeys Through 17 Countries* (Thousand Oaks, CA: Sage).

Gibson, C. B. (1994) 'The Implications of National Culture for Organisation Structure: An Investigation of Three Perspectives', *Advances in International Comparative Management*, vol. 9, pp. 3–38.

Giddens, A. (1979) *Central Problems in Social Theory: Action, Structure and Contradiction in Social Analysis* (Berkeley: University of California Press).

Glastonbury, B. and MacKean, J. (1991) 'Survey Methods', in G. Allan and C. Skinner (eds), *Handbook for Research Students in the Social Science* (London: The Falmer Press).

Gordon, D. D. (1988) *Japanese Management in America and Britain: Revelation or Requiem for Western Industrial Democracy?* (Aldershot: Avebury).

Goyder, J. (1988) *The Silent Minority: Non-respondents on Social Surveys* (Oxford: Polity Press).

Griffith, T. L. (1996) 'Cross-Cultural and Cognitive Issues in the Implementation of New Technology: Focus on Group Support Systems in Bulgaria', Working paper, Washington University, St Louis.

Grootings, P. (1989) 'New Forms of Work Organisation in Europe: East–West Comparisons', in P. Grootings, B. Gustavsen and L. Hèthy (eds), *New Forms of Work Organisation in Europe* (Oxford: Transaction Publishers).

Guerrieri, P. and Tylecote, A. (1998) 'Cultural and Institutional Determinants of National Technological Advantage', in R. Coombs, K. Green, A. Richards and V. Walsh (eds), *Technological Change and Organisation* (Cheltenham: Edward Elgar).

Hall, E. T. (1976) *Beyond Culture* (Doubleday: Anchor Press).

Hamilton, G. G. and Biggart, N. W. (1988) 'Market, Culture, and Authority: A Comparative Analysis of Management and Organisation in the Far East', *American Journal of Sociology*, vol. 94, Supplement, pp. 52–94.

Hamilton, S. and Ives, B. (1982) 'MIS Research Strategies', *Information and Management*, vol. 5, pp. 339–47.

Harrison, G. L., McKinnon, J. L., Panchapakesan, S. and Leung, M. (1994) 'The Influence of Culture on Organisational Design and Planning and Control in Australia and the United States Compared with Singapore and Hong Kong', *Journal of International Financial Management & Accounting*, vol. 5(3), pp. 242–61.

Hayes, J. and Allinson, C. W. (1988) 'Cultural Differences in the Learning Styles of Managers', *Management International Review*, vol. 28(3), pp. 75–80.

Hickson, D. J., Hinings, C. R., McMillan, C. J. and Schwitter, J. P. (1974) 'The Culture-Free Context of Organisation Structure: A Tri-National Comparison', *Sociology*, vol. 8, pp. 59–80.

Hildebrandt, E. (1989) 'The Social Constitution of the Firm', Paper Presented to CAPIRN Workshop, Santa Cruz, November.

Hitt, M. A., Ireland, R. D. and Stadter, G. (1982) 'Functional Importance and Company Performance: Moderating Effects of Grand Strategy and Industry Type', *Strategic Management Journal*, vol. 3(4), pp. 315–30.

Hodgetts, R. (1993) 'A Conversation with Greet Hofstede', *Organisational Dynamics*, vol. 21(4), pp. 53–61.

Hofstede, G. (1980) *Culture's Consequences: International Differences in Work-related Values* (Beverly Hills CA: Sage).

Hofstede, G. (1984) *Culture's Consequences: International Differences in Work-related Values*, abridged edition (Beverly Hills CA: Sage).

Hofstede, G. (1991) *Cultures and Organisations: International Co-operation and its Importance for Survival: Software of the Mind* (London: McGraw Hill).

Hofstede, G. (1996) 'Cultural Constraints in Management Theories', in R. Patson, G. Clark, G. Jones, J. Lewis and P. Quintas (eds), *The New Management Reader* (London: Open University Press).

Hoos, I. (1960) 'When the Computer Takes Over the Office', *Harvard Business Review*, vol. 38(4), pp. 102–12.

Hoppe, M. H. (1993) 'The Effects of National Culture on the Theory and Practice of Managing R&D Professionals Abroad', *R&D Management*, vol. 23(4), pp. 313–25.

Hortum, M. and Muller, L. H. (1989) 'Management and Culture', *Supervision*, vol. 50(1), pp. 14–17.

Howells, J. (1995) 'The Social Constitution of Technical Expertise', *Technology Analysis & Strategic Management*, vol. 7(2), pp. 249–65.

Hyman, R. (1988) 'Flexible Specialisation: Miracle or Myth?' in R. Hyman and W. Streeck (eds), *New Technology and Industrial Relations* (Oxford: Blackwell).

Jackofsky, E. F., Slocum, J. W. Jr and Mcquaid, S. J. (1988) 'Cultural Values and the CEO: Alluring Comparisons?' *Academy of Management Executive*, vol. 2(1), pp. 39–49.

Jaeger, A. M. (1986) 'Organisation Development and National Culture: Where's the Fit?' *Academy of Management Review*, vol. 11(1), pp. 178–90.

Kaisha Shikihou [*The Annual Book of Japanese Companies*], Toyou Keizai Shimpou Sya, April 1998 (in Japanese).

Kambayashi, N. (1995) 'Changes in Organisational Structure and New Development in Personnel Management', *Journal of Japanese Economic Studies*, vol. 23(5), pp. 74–96.

Kambayashi, N. (1996a) 'Organisational Structure and Employee's Job Content: From Job Design to Organisation Design', *The Annals of the School of Business Administration*, Kobe University, vol. 40, pp. 18–41.

Kambayashi, N. (1996b) 'New Forms of Management Organisation Under New Technology: Empirical Evidence from Japanese Manufacturing Companies', Paper Presented to the Third International Federation of Scholarly Association of Management (IFSAM) Conference, Paris, July 1996. Published in *Management*, vol. 3(1), pp. 17–27.

Kambayashi, N. (1998) 'The Job Content and Management Structure of Blue-Collar Workers under the Influence of Information Technology: Empirical Evidence from Japanese Manufacturing Companies', *The Annals of the School of Business Administration*, Kobe University, vol. 42, pp. 1–22.

Kambayashi, N. and Scarbrough, H. (2001) 'Cultural Influences on IT Use Amongst Factory Managers: A UK–Japanese Comparison' *Journal of Information Technology*, vol. 16(4), pp. 221–36.

Katz, J. P. and Townsend, J. B. (1998) 'National Culture and Organisational Structure: Information Technology Implications for International Human Resource Management', Paper Presented to Sixth Conference on International Human Resource Management, Paderborn, Germany, January 1998.

Kavrakoğlu, I. (1992) 'The MS Connection in IS', *International Journal of Technology Management*, vol. 7(6/7/8), pp. 444–54.

Kedia, B. L. and Bhagat, R. S. (1988) 'Cultural Constraints on Transfer of Technology Across Nations: Implications for Research in International and Comparative Management', *Academy of Management Review*, vol. 13(4), pp. 559–71.

Kenny, M. and Florida, R. (1993) *Beyond Mass Production: The Japanese System and its Transfer to the US* (Oxford: Oxford University Press).

Kerr, C., Dunlop, T., Harbison, F. H. and Myers, C. A. (1960) *Industrialism and Industrial Man* (Boston, Mass.: Harvard University Press).

Kimble, C. and McLoughlin, K. (1994) 'Changes to the Organisation and the Work of Managers Following the Introduction of an Integrated Information System', in R. Mansell (ed.), *The Management of Information and Communication Technologies: Emerging Patterns of Control* (London: The Association for Information Management).

Klatsky, S. R. (1970) 'Automation, Size, and the Locus of Decision Making: The Cascade Effect', *Journal of Business*, vol. 43(2), pp. 141–51.

Kluckhohn, F. R. and Strodtbeck, F. L. (1961) *Variations in Value Orientations* (New York: Peterson).

Knights, D. and Willmott, H. (eds) (1988) *New Technology and the Labour Process* (London: Macmillan – now Palgrave Macmillan).

Kogut, B. and Singh, H. (1988) 'The Effect of National Culture on the Choice of Entry Mode', *Journal of International Business Studies*, vol. 19(3), pp. 411–32.

Koike, K. (1988) *Understanding Industrial Relations in Modern Japan* (London: Macmillan – now Palgrave Macmillan).

Kokuryo, J. (1997) 'Information Technologies and the Transformation of Japanese Industry', Paper Presented to Pacific-Asia Conference on Information Systems, Brisbane, Australia 1997.

Kono, T. and Clegg, S. (2001) *Trends in Japanese Management: Continuing Strength, Current Problems and Changing Priorities* (Basingstoke: Palgrave Macmillan).

Kumazawa, M. and Yamada, J. (1989) 'Jobs and Skills under the Lifelong Employment Practice', in S. Wood (ed.), *The Transformation of Work?* (London: Unwin Hyman).

Lam, A. (1994) 'The Utilisation of Human Resources: A Comparative Study of British and Japanese Engineers in Electronics Industries', *Human Resource Management Journal*, vol. 4(3), pp. 22–40.

Lam, A. (1996) 'Engineers, Management and Work Organisations: A Comparative Analysis of Engineers' Work Roles in British and Japanese Electronics Firms', *Journal of Management Studies*, vol. 33(2), pp. 183–212.

Lam, A. (1997) 'Embedded Firms, Embedded Knowledge: Problems of Collaboration and Knowledge Transfer in Global Co-operative Ventures', *Organisation Studies*, vol. 18(6), pp. 973–96.

Land, F. (1992) 'The Information Systems Domain', in R. D. Galliers (ed.), *Information Systems Research: Issues, Methods and Practical Guidelines* (Oxford: Blackwell Scientific).

Laurent, A. (1983) 'The Cultural Diversity of Western Conceptions of Management', *International Studies of Management and Organisation*, vol. 13(1/2), pp. 75–96.

Laurent, A. (1986) 'The Cross-Cultural Puzzle of International Human Resource Management', *Human Resource Management*, vol. 25(1), pp. 91–102.

Leavitt, H. J. and Whisler, T. L. (1958) 'Management in the 1980's', *Harvard Business Review*, vol. 36, pp. 41–8.

Leifer, R. (1986) 'Matching Computer-Based Information Systems with Organisational Structures', *MIS Quarterly*, vol. 12(1), pp. 63–73.

Leifer, R. and McDonough, E. F. (1985) 'Computerisation as a Predominant Technology Affecting the Work Unit Structure', *Proceedings of the Sixth International Conference on Information Systems*, pp. 238–48.

Lincoln, J. R. (1989) 'Employee Work Attitudes and Management Practices in the US and Japan: Evidence from a Large Comparative Survey', *California Management Review*, vol. 32(3), pp. 89–106.

Lincoln, J. R. and Kalleberg, A. (1990) *Culture Control and Commitment: A Study of Work Organisation and Work Attitudes in the United States and Japan* (Cambridge: Cambridge University Press).

Lynn, L. H. (1990) 'Technology and Organisations: A Cross-National Analysis', in P. S. Goodman, L. S. Sproull and Associates, *Technology and Organisations* (Oxford: Jossey-Bass).

Mabey, C. and Iles, P. (1996) 'Human Resource Management in the UK: A Case of Fundamental Change, Facelift or Façade?' in T. Clark (ed.), *European Human Resource Management: An Introduction to Comparative Theory and Practice* (Oxford: Blackwell).

Maher, T. E. and Wong, Y. Y. (1994) 'The Impact of Cultural Differences on the Growing Tensions Between Japan and the United States', *SAM Advanced Management Journal*, vol. 59(1), pp. 40–6.

Mair, A. (1994) *Honda's Global Local Corporation* (London: Macmillan – now Palgrave Macmillan).

Markus, M. L. and Robey, D. (1988) 'Information Technology and Organisational Change: Causing Structure in Theory and Research', *Management Science*, vol. 34(5), pp. 583–98.

Marx, K. (1847) *The Poverty of Philosophy* (Moscow: Progress Publishers), new edn (1975).

Bibliography 225

Maurice, M., Sorge, A. and Warner, M. (1980) 'Societal Differences in Organising Manufacturing Units: A Comparison of France, West Germany and Great Britain', *Organisation Studies*, vol. 1, pp. 59–86.

Mead, R. (1998) *International Management: Cross-cultural Dimensions*, 2nd edn (Oxford: Blackwell).

Mejias, R. J., Shepherd, M. M., Vogel, D. R. and Lazaneo, L. (1997) 'Consensus and Perceived Satisfaction Levels: A Cross-Cultural Comparison of GSS and Non-GSS Outcomes within and between the United States and Mexico', *Journal of Management Information Systems*, vol. 13(3), pp. 137–61.

Nath, R. (1988) 'Regional Culture, Entrepreneurship, and High Technology Development in India', in J. W. Weiss, *Regional Cultures, Management Behaviour, and Entrepreneurship* (New York: Quorum).

Nonaka, I. (1994) 'A Dynamic Theory of Organisational Knowledge Creation', *Organisation Science*, vol. 5, pp. 14–37.

Nunamaker, J. F., Briggs, R. O., Mitleman, D. D., Vogel, D. R. and Balthazard, P. A. (1997) 'Lessons from a Dozen Years of Group Support Systems Research: A Discussion of Lab and Field Findings', *Journal of Management Information Systems*, vol. 13(3), pp. 163–207.

Okubayashi, K. (1995) 'Japanese Effects of New Technology on Organisation and Work', *Zfb–Erganzungsheft*, vol. 4, pp. 35–51.

Okubayashi, K., Shomura, H., Takebayashi, H., Morita, M. and Kambayashi, N. (1994) *Jukozo Soshiki Paradaimu Josetsu: Shinsedai no Nihonteki Keiei [The Paradigm of Loosely-coupled Organisation: Japanese Management System in the New Generation]* (Tokyo: Bunshindo, in Japanese).

Olie, R. (1995) 'The "Culture" Factor in Personnel and Organisation Policies', in A. Harzing and J. V. Ruysseveldt (eds), *International Human Resource Management: An Integrated Approach* (London: Sage).

Oliver, N. and Wilkinson, B. (1992) *The Japanisation of British Industry: New Developments in the 1990s*, 2nd edn (Oxford: Blackwell).

Orlikowski, W. J. (1992) 'The Duality of Technology: Rethinking the Concept of Technology in Organizations', *Organisation Science*, vol. 3(3), pp. 398–427.

Orlikowski, W. J. and Baroudi, J. J. (1991) 'Studying Information Technology in Organisations: Research Approaches and Assumptions', *Information Systems Research*, vol. 2(1), pp. 1–28.

Orlikowski, W. J. and Robey, D. (1991) 'Information Technology and the Structuring of Organisations', *Information Systems Research*, vol. 2(2), pp. 143–69.

Osterman, P. (1991) 'The Impact of IT on Jobs and Skills', in M. S. Scott Morton (ed.), *The Corporation of the 1990s: Information Technology and Organisational Transformation* (New York: Oxford University Press).

Palvia, P. C. and Palvia, S. C. (1996) 'Understanding the Global Information Technology Environment: Representative World Issues', in P. C. Palvia, S. C. Palvia and E. M. Roche (eds), *Global Information Technology and Systems Management: Key Issues and Trends* (Westford, MA.: Ivy League Publishing).

Panteli, A. V. (1995) 'Computer-Based Informated Environments: Emergent Forms of Work Organisation', Unpublished Thesis submitted for the Degree of Doctor of Philosophy at University of Warwick.

Park, S. H. and Ungson, G. R. (1997) 'The Effects of National Culture, Organisational Complementarity, and Economic Motivation on Joint Venture Dissolution', *Academy of Management Journal*, vol. 40(2), pp. 279–307.

Perterson, R. B. (ed.) (1993) *Managers and National Culture: A Global Perspective* (London: Quorum Books).

Pfeffer, J. (1982) *Organisations and Organisation Theory* (Marshfield, MA: Pitman).

Pfeffer, J. and Leblebici, H. (1977) 'Information Technology and Organisational Structure', *Pacific Sociological Review*, vol. 20(2), pp. 241–61.

Polanyi, M. (1966) *The Tacit Dimension* (New York: Anchor Day Books).

Pugh, D. S. and Hickson, D. J. (1976) *Organisation Structure in its Context: The Aston Programme 1* (Aldershot: Saxon House).

Ralston, D. A., Holt, D. H., Terpstra, R. H. and Kai-Cheng, Y. (1997) 'The Impact of Culture and Ideology on Managerial Work Values: A Study of the United States, Russia, Japan, and China', *Journal of International Business Studies*, vol. 28(1), pp. 177–207.

Raman, K. S. and Watson, R. T. (1994) 'National Culture, IS, and Organisational Implications', in P. C. Deans and K. R. Karwan (eds), *Global Information Systems and Technology: Focus on the Organisation and its Functional Areas* (Harrisburg, PA: Idea Group).

Rose, M. (1985) 'Universalism, Culturalism and the Aix Group', *European Sociological Review*, vol. 1, pp. 65–83.

Rowlinson, M. (1997) *Organisations and Institutions: Perspectives in Economics and Sociology* (London: Macmillan – now Palgrave Macmillan).

Sampler, J. L. (1996) 'Exploring the Relationship Between Information Technology and Organisational Structure', in M. J. Earl (ed.), *Information Management: The Organisational Dimension* (Oxford: Oxford University Press).

Scarbrough, H. (1998) 'BPR and the Knowledge-Based View of the Firm', *Knowledge and Process Management*, vol. 5(3), pp. 192–200.

Scarbrough, H. and Corbett, J. M. (1992) *Technology and Organisation: Power, Meaning and Design* (London: Routledge).

Scarbrough, H. and Terry, M. (1998) 'Forget Japan: The Very British Response to Lean Production', *Employee Relations*, vol. 20(3), pp. 224–36.

Schein, E. H. (1996) 'Culture: the Missing Concept in Organisation Studies', *Administrative Science Quarterly*, vol. 41, pp. 229–40.

Schneider, S. C. (1989) 'Strategy Formulation: The Impact of National Culture', *Organisation Studies*, vol. 10(2), pp. 149–68.

Schneider, S. C. and De Meyer, A. (1991) 'Interpreting and Responding to Strategic Issues: The Impact of National Culture', *Strategic Management Journal*, vol. 12(4), pp. 307–20.

Schonberger, R. (1982) *Japanese Manufacturing Techniques: Nine Hidden Lessons in Simplicity* (New York: Free Press).

Scott Morton, M. S. (1991) *The Corporation of the 1990s: Information Technology and Organisational Transformation* (New York: Oxford University Press).

Scott, W. R. (1990) 'Technology and Structure: An Organisational-Level Perspective', in P. S. Goodman, L. S. Sproull and Associates, *Technology and Organisations* (Oxford: Jossey-Bass).

Senker, P. (1989) 'Technology, Work Organisation and Training: Some Issues Relating to the Role of Market Forces', *New Technology, Work and Employment*, vol. 4(1), pp. 46–53.

Shane, S. (1994) 'Cultural Values and the Championing Process', *Entrepreneurship: Theory & Practice*, vol. 18(4), pp. 25–41.

Shane, S., Venkataraman, S. and MacMillan, I. (1995) 'Cultural Differences in Innovation Championing Strategies', *Journal of Management*, vol. 21(5), pp. 931–52.

Shimada, T. (1991) *Jouhou Gijutsu to Keiei Soshiki [Information Technology and
Business Organisation]* (Tokyo: Nikka-giren, in Japanese).

Shore, B. (1996a) 'Using Information Technology to Co-ordinate Transnational
Service Operations', *Journal of Global Information Management*, vol. 4(2),
pp. 5–14.

Shore, B. (1996b) 'A Conceptual Framework to Assess Gaps in Information Sys-
tems Cultures Between Headquarters and Foreign Subsidiaries', in P. C. Palvia,
S. C. Palvia and E. M. Roche (eds), *Global Information Technology and Systems
Management: Key Issues and Trends* (Westford, MA.: Ivy League Publishing).

Shore, B. and Venkatachalam, A. R. (1995) 'The Role of National Culture in
Systems Analysis and Design', *Journal of Global Information Management*,
vol. 3(3), pp. 5–14.

Smith, P. B. (1992) 'Organisational Behaviour and National Cultures', *British
Journal of Management*, vol. 3(1), pp. 39–51.

Smith, P. B. (1994) 'National Cultures and the Values of Organisational Employees:
Time for Another Look', Workshop of the European Institute for the Advanced
Study of Management, Henley Management College, pp. 1–15.

Smith, P. B. and Bond, M. H. (1993) *Social Psychology Across Cultures: Analysis and
Perspectives* (New York: Harvester Wheatsheaf).

Sorge, A. (1982) 'Cultured Organisation', *International Studies of Management and
Organisation*, vol. 12(4), pp. 106–38.

Sorge, A. (1991) 'Strategic Fit and the Societal Effect: Interpreting Cross-National
Comparisons of Technology, Organisation and Human Resources', *Organisation
Studies*, vol. 12(2), pp. 161–90.

Sorge, A. (1995) 'Cross-National Differences in Personnel and Organisation', in
A. Harzing and J. V. Ruysseveldt (eds), *International Human Resource Management:
An Integrated Approach* (London: Sage).

Sorge, A., Hartmann, G., Warner, M. and Nicholas, I. (1983) *Microelectronics and
Manpower in Manufacturing: Applications of Computer Numerical Control in Great
Britain and West Germany* (Aldershot: Gower).

Sorge, A. and Streeck, W. (1988) 'Industrial Relations and Technical Change: The
Case for an Extended Perspective', in R. Hyman and W. Streeck (eds), *New
Technology and Industrial Relations* (Oxford: Blackwell).

Sorge, A. and Warner, M. (1986) *Comparative Factory Organisation: An Anglo-German
Comparison of Management and Manpower in Manufacturing* (Aldershot: Gower).

Sproull, L. S. and Goodman, P. S. (1990) 'Technology and Organisations: Integration and Opportunities', in P. S. Goodman, L. S. Sproull and Associates, *Technology and Organisations* (Oxford: Jossey-Bass).

Stebbins, M. W. and Shani, A. B. (1995) 'Information Technology and Organisation Design', *Journal of Information Technology*, vol. 10, pp. 101–13.

Straub, D. W. (1994) 'The Effect of Culture on IT Diffusion: E-mail and Fax in
Japan and the US', *Information Systems Research*, vol. 5(1), pp. 23–47.

Susman, G. I. (1990) 'Work Groups: Autonomy, Technology, and Choice', in
P. S. Goodman, L. S. Sproull and Associates, *Technology and Organisations*
(Oxford: Jossey-Bass).

Suutari, V. H. T. (1995) 'Dimensions Differentiating National Cultures', *International Journal of Management*, vol. 12(2), pp. 162–72.

Tan, B. C. Y., Watson, R. T. and Wei, K. K. (1995) 'National Culture and Group Support System: Filtering Communication to Dampen Power Differentials', *European Journal of Information Systems*, vol. 4(2), pp. 82–92.

Tata, J. and Prasad, S. (1992) 'Optimum Production Process, National Culture, and Organisation Design', *European Business Review*, vol. 92(1), pp. vi-xii.

Tayeb, M. (1988) *Organisations and National Culture* (London: Sage).

Tayeb, M. (1994) 'Organisations and National Culture: Methodology Considered', *Organisation Studies*, vol. 15(3), pp. 429–46.

Taylor, M. S. (1991) 'American Managers in Japanese Subsidiaries: How Cultural Differences are Affecting the Work Place', *Human Resource Planning*, vol. 14(1), pp. 43–9.

Thomas, R. J. (1994) *What Machines Can't Do: Politics and Technology in the Industrial Enterprise* (New York: University of California Press).

Tidd, J., Bessant, J. and Pavitt, K. (1997) *Managing Innovation: Integrating Technological, Market and Organisational Change* (Chichester: John Wiley).

Triandis, H. C., Bontempo, R., Bond, M., Leung, K., Brenes, A., Georgas, J., Hui, C. H., Marin, G., Setiadi, B., Sinta, J., Verma, J., Spangenberg, J. and de Montmollin, H. T. G. (1986) 'The Measurement of the Ethic Aspects of Individualism and Collectivism Across Cultures', *Australian Journal of Psychology*, vol. 38(3), pp. 257–67.

Tricker, R. I. (1988) 'Information Resource Management: A Cross-Cultural Perspective', *Information and Management*, vol. 15, pp. 37–46.

Trist, E. L., Higgin, G. W., Murray, H. and Pollock, A. B. (1963) *Organisational Choice: Capabilities of Groups at the Coal Face under Changing Technologies: The Loss, Rediscovery and Transformation of a Work Tradition* (London: Tavistock).

Trompenaars, F. (1993) *Riding the Waves of Culture: Understanding Cultural Diversity in Business* (London: Nicholas Brealey).

Tubbs, S. L. (1994) 'The Historical Roots of Self-Managing Work Teams in the Twentieth Century: An Annotated Bibliography', in M. Beyerlein and D. Johnson (eds), *Advances in Interdisciplinary Studies of Work Teams* (Greenwich, Connecticut: JAI Press).

Turner, J. A. (1998) 'The Role of Information Technology in Organisational Transformation', in R. D. Galliers and W. R. J. Baets (eds), *Information Technology and Organisational Transformation: Innovation for the 21st Century Organisation* (Chichester: John Wiley).

Ueno, S. and Wu, F. H. (1993) 'The Comparative Influence of Culture on Budget Control Practices in the United States and Japan', *The International Journal of Accounting*, vol. 28, pp. 17–39.

Vitalari, N. P. (1985) 'The Need for Longitudinal Designs in the Study of Computing Environments', in E. Mumford, R. A. Hirschheim, G. Fitzgerald and A. T. Wood-Harper (eds), *Research Methods in Information Systems*, Proceedings of the IFIPWG 8.2 Colloquium, 1–3 September 1984, Manchester Business School, Amsterdam: Elsevier.

Wainwright, J. and Francis, A. (1984) *Office Automation, Organisation and the Nature of Work* (Aldershot: Gower).

Warner, M. (1994) 'Japanese Culture, Western Management: Taylorism and Human Resources in Japan', *Organisation Studies*, vol. 15(4), pp. 509–33.

Watson, R. T. and Brancheau, J. C. (1992) 'Key Issues in Information Systems Management: An International Perspective', in R. D. Galliers (ed.), *Information*

Systems Research: Issues, Methods and Practical Guidelines (Oxford: Blackwell Scientific).
Watson, R. T., Ho, T. H. and Raman, K. (1994) 'Culture: A Fourth Dimension of Group Support Systems', *Communications of the ACM*, vol. 37(10), pp. 45–55.
Watson, R. T., Kelly, G. G., Galliers, R. D. and Brancheau, J. C. (1997) 'Key Issues in Information Systems Management: An International Perspective', *Journal of Management Information Systems*, vol. 13(4), pp. 91–115.
Weber, W., Kabst, R. and Gramley, C. (1998) 'Human Resource Policies in European Organisations: Country vs. Company-Specific Antecedents', Paper Presented to Sixth Conference on International Human Resource Management, Paderborn, Germany, January 1998.
Weick, K. E. (1990) 'Technology as Equivoque: Sensemaking in New Technologies', in P. S. Goodman, L. S. Sproull and Associates, *Technology and Organisations* (Oxford: Jossey-Bass).
Wensley, A. K. P. (1989) 'Research Directions in Expert System', in G. Dukidis, F. Land and G. Miller (eds), *Knowledge-based Management Support Systems* (London: Ellis Horwood).
Wensley, A. K. P. (1998) 'Editorial', *Knowledge and Process Management*, vol. 5(3), pp. 141–42.
Whisler, T. L. (1970) *Information Technology and Organisational Change* (Belmont, California: Wadsworth).
Whitehill, A. M. (1991) *Japanese Management: Tradition and Transition* (London: Routledge).
Whitley, R. (1992) *Business Systems in East Asia: Firms, Markets and Societies* (London: Sage).
Whittaker, D. H. (1990) *Managing Innovation: A Study of British and Japanese Factories* (Cambridge: Cambridge University Press).
Wilkinson, B. (1983) *The Shopfloor Politics of New Technology* (London: Heinemann).
Williams, R. and Edge, D. (1996) 'The Social Shaping of Technology', *Research Policy*, vol. 25, pp. 865–99.
Winner, L. (1986) *The Whale and the Reactor* (Chicago: University of Chicago Press).
Woldu, H. G. (1998) 'Measuring How Cultural Perspectives Differ Across Countries: The Impact of Cultural Differences on Management Styles', Paper Presented to Sixth Conference on International Human Resource Management, Paderborn, Germany, January 1998.
Womack, J. P., Jones, D. T. and Roos, D. (1990) *The Machine that Changed the World* (New York: Rawson Associates).
Woodward, J. (1965) *Industrial Organisation: Theory and Practice* (London: Oxford University Press).
Yeh, R. and Lawrence, J. J. (1995) 'Hofstede's Cultural Root to Economic Growth', *Journal of International Business Studies*, vol. 26(3), pp. 655–69.
Yin, R. K. (1984) *Case Study Research: Design and Methods* (London: Sage).
Zuboff, S. (1985) 'Technologies that Informate: Implications for Human Resource Management in the Computerised Industrial Workplace', in R. E. Walton and P. R. Lawrence (eds), *Human Resource Management: Trends and Challenges* (Boston: Harvard Business School Press).
Zuboff, S. (1988) *In the Age of the Smart Machine: The Future of Work and Power* (New York: Basic Books).

Index